COMMON CENTS ESTATE PLANNING

You may check out Craig's profile at
SuperLawyers.com®, a lawyer rating service.

**http://www.superlawyers.com/florida/lawyer/C
raig-R-Hersch/bde9646a-e83d-4300-8c4c-
66770a137b0d.html**

He is also rated as an *AV-Preeminent Lawyer* by
Martindale Hubbell®—the highest rating possible
by this national independent rating service.

**http://www.martindale.com/Results.aspx?ft=1&f
rm=freesearch&afs=Craig%20R.%20Hersch**

Common Cents Estate Planning

Craig R. Hersch

THE FAMILY ESTATE & LEGACY SERIES™

Family Estate & Legacy Publishing House

ISBN-13: 978-1502757142
ISBN-10: 1502757141

Book editing and interior design by Jean Boles
http://jeanboles.elance.com

Dedication

This book is dedicated to my wife Patti and all of the good times we've had in over 25 years of marriage! Only good things for our next 25!

Acknowledgements

While I like to call myself a "self-made" man, I also realize that I've had a lot of love, help, coaching and mentoring along the way.

I simply could not do what I do without the love and support of my wife, Patti and daughters, Gabrielle, Courtney and Madison. Over the years they've had to share me with my law practice as well as my outside pursuits (my daughters jokingly refer to me as "Mr. Triathlon"). Nothing I do would be worth it without them.

My parents, Joel and Phyllis Hersch, helped guide me during my childhood and adolescence, instilling a work ethic and a can-do attitude while also stressing the importance of enjoying the small moments in life. I was mortified when they decided to move all of us from our hometown of Indianapolis, Indiana just before my junior year in high school, but their gutsy decision paid off for me, for which I am grateful.

I've had hard-working teachers and professors—too numerous to name—who helped me to form an intellectual curiosity and a solid base, allowing me to do what I do. This book is therefore devoted to all of my teachers—from Greenbriar, Frank H. Hammond and Spring Mill Elementary schools; Northview Junior High, North Central High, Countryside High; The University of Florida Fisher School of Accounting and The University of Florida Levin College of Law.

In my law practice I've had an important mentor in John W. Sheppard, as well as my long-time law partner Jay A. Brett, who taught me all of the most important things that they simply don't teach you in law school. Michael Hill has been invaluable as we've built our Family Estate & Legacy Solution™ estate planning process. My other law partners, including Hugh Kinsey and now retired John Stewart, deserve special kudos for putting up with me every workday.

This book wouldn't have happened without Lorin Arundel and Ken Rasi, publishers of *The Island Sun* weekly, who gave me the opportunity to write a column on a dry topic such as estate planning and have stuck with me all of these years. Jean Boles did a yeoman's job in categorizing a bunch of unrelated columns, editing them and putting them in some semblance of an order. Her knowledge of Amazon and CreateSpace made things super easy for me to publish as well.

Dan Sullivan's Strategic Coach program showed me how to develop my intellectual capital and abilities into unique processes that my clients and colleagues adore. I can't mention this program without acknowledging my good buddy Dan Taylor, (who passed away in 2009), Marilyn Waller, Jan Mohammed, Stephanie Song and others in their Chicago and Toronto offices who continue to help me unlock a greater future for myself and for those around me.

Mark Merenda and his crew at SmartMarketing did a great job with the graphics as they have done throughout the years, and my public relations guru Gail Dolan got the word out to the media.

There are others. A big shout-out to my sister, Valerie and my brothers-and-sisters-in-law (Stuart, Ellen, Steve, Ira, Tina), mother-and-father in-laws (I have the best mother-in-law— Rhoda Morris!), uncles, aunts and cousins, as well as to my wife's extended family. Rosh Hashanas, Passovers and Chanukahs have always been memorable. My "Bubby" Frieda

Kaplan, who showed me what unqualified and undying love looks like until her passing in 1976, as well as my wife's grandmother, Mollie Leber, who treated me as her own grandson until her passing in 2012.

I've had the best friends over the years who have helped keep me laughing, fit and sane—not so easy if you know me well. I'd mention you all but it would take too many pages. A special mention goes to Richard Glasser (1960-2012).

Whew! Maybe I'm not so self-made after all.

Contents

Preface

I understand that when you speak to a professional, whether a doctor, CPA, architect or an estate planning attorney like me, you oftentimes feel that although the words sound like the English language, everything the professional says is otherwise incomprehensible.

Per stirpes?! Grantor?! Attorney-in-Fact?! Generation-skipping tax exemption?! Estate planning certainly has its own vocabulary. Not only do these phrases come at you fast and furiously during a consultation, but your lawyer acts as if you fully understand them and how his ramblings apply to your situation. You may even feel awkward asking your attorney to slow down and explain *what-in-the-world* he's talking about!

That's where this book comes in.

I'm a Florida Bar Board Certified Wills, Trusts & Estates attorney who also happens to be a CPA. Back in 2004, Lorin Arundel and Ken Rasi asked me to write an estate-planning column for their award-winning Sanibel Island, Florida weekly newspaper, *The Island Sun*. We named that column "Will Power" (get it?!), and it has developed quite a following. COMMON CENTS ESTATE PLANNING is a compilation of some of the best "Will Power" columns that I've written in the past few years.

Each column is its own independent topic, written in layman's terms. I try to provide my reader a frame-of-reference to understand a legal, tax or financial point. Many of my columns are based on real world situations I've seen in my law practice (the names and facts have been changed for obvious reasons—chief among them attorney/client confidentiality). While growing up, my family did not have a lot of wealth, but we have a very rich family history, and I also draw on those experiences to relate to various topics.

With the help of my fantastic editor, Jean Boles, we arranged the columns in broad categories. The columns that deal with the tax law, for example, can be found in Chapter Seven, while those that consider problems that you may not have thought about when leaving assets to beneficiaries are bundled in Chapter Two.

This book isn't intended to follow a "how to plan your estate" format so much as it is intended to be read in snippets (aka bathroom breaks), similar to how you would read "Chicken Soup for the Soul."

While I realize that an estate planning book isn't going to rate high on the New York Times best-seller list, my hope is that I can give you real world advice that serves to provide comfort and clarity when considering your legal, tax and financial concerns.

You may also be surprised to learn how properly planning your estate can save you a lot of money during your lifetime, rather than just benefiting your loved ones at your death. Many of my clients, for example, have residences in Florida as well as in another state. You'll learn in Chapter Four how declaring Florida residency can save you significant tax dollars during your lifetime, and why those of you who are not Florida residents but who own a home in Florida should consider it.

One final point—while I strive to keep all of my columns up to date and try to provide current information, there is always the possibility that the estate, trust and tax laws have changed since the date of each column. For that and related reasons, this book is not intended to form an attorney-client relationship and should not be considered legal advice pertinent to your unique situation. You should always check with a qualified professional before implementing any course of action.

I welcome your comments, criticisms and especially your kudos! You can contact me by visiting my firm's website: www.sbshlaw.com.

Follow me on Twitter—@FLTrustLaw, or as follows:

Craig R. Hersch
Florida Bar Board Certified Wills, Trusts & Estates Attorney; CPA
Sheppard, Brett, Stewart, Hersch, Kinsey & Hill PA
Attorneys at Law
9100 College Point Court
Fort Myers, FL 33919
239-334-1141
hersch@sbshlaw.com

Thank you for taking the time to read this book. I hope by doing so it will clarify a lot of lawyer lingo and encourage you to take another look at your estate-planning documents.

Chapter One

Will and Trust Basics

The 10 Things Your Estate Planning Attorney Wished That You Knew

f you read enough periodicals, you'll see a lot of lists. So I thought I'd create one for you from an estate planning attorney's perspective. I came up with the list describing what I wished my clients were aware of *before* we sit down together to discuss their estate plan:

1. Even though we live in the United States of America, each of those states has different laws. It's therefore wise to update your estate plan any time you move from one state to another.

2. The tax laws and trust laws change quite regularly, as does your personal financial and family circumstances.

That's why it's important to review your estate plan at least every couple of years, even if you haven't moved to another state. It is unwise to create an estate plan and leave it in a drawer for many years, as that can lead to unintended consequences.

3. It's important to tell your attorney EVERYTHING—and I mean EVERYTHING—even though such disclosures might be embarrassing. Remember that your conversations are governed by attorney/client confidentiality. If you conceal something materially important, such as an illegitimate child, it could open your estate to challenges after your death. Complete honesty with your attorney is for your own best interest.

4. Life insurance is not totally tax-free. While in most circumstances life insurance is INCOME tax-free, unless more sophisticated estate planning is put into place, it is NOT ESTATE tax-free. The value of the life insurance might be included, for example, in the surviving spouse's estate, which may trigger estate tax upon the surviving spouse's death. Worse, if there is no surviving spouse and the life insurance is paid to children, there could be an immediate estate tax liability. An irrevocable life insurance trust is one way to get around that problem.

5. Durable Powers of Attorney cease at death. Many people wrongfully believe that a Durable Power of Attorney allows the designated holder of the power to write checks and to pay bills after the grantor of the power has died. Once the person has died, their will (or trust) takes over. The holder of the Powers of Attorney should no longer write checks or otherwise act for the deceased. A Durable

Power of Attorney is primarily useful during periods of incapacity.

6. You shouldn't name your oldest child as your Durable Power of Attorney, personal representative (executor) or successor trustee of your estate simply because they are the eldest of your children. You should, instead, look for the most trustworthy and responsible person to fill those roles. If that is your oldest child, then so be it. But if your youngest child is the most responsible, or if someone else is better qualified to fill that role, then you should name that person.

7. The offices of successor trustee of a trust and personal representative of a will are filled with obligations, responsibility and liability. In other words, they are more of a job than they are an honor. Many people name one of their children or a family member to fill this role, because that person might be offended if they weren't named. What most people don't realize is that the law imposes all sorts of duties and obligations on a trustee and a personal representative, and if they don't fulfill all of the legal requirements, that person might be held personally liable to the other beneficiaries of the estate, to creditors, or to taxing authorities—including the IRS.

8. Not signing a living will is more dangerous than signing one—even if you believe that the doctors will pull the plug to free up the hospital bed for the next patient. The living will is your direction of what you want to have happen if you are deemed to be in an end-stage terminal condition or in a persistent vegetative state with no hope of recovery. You can direct, for example, that food and water tubes shall never be removed. The living will does

not require you to direct that they always terminate life support. But without a living will, there is no direction from you at all. That's how you end up like Terri Schiavo. She never signed a living will. The result was her husband and parents fought in court over what her wishes would have been. You may recall even the United States Congress got involved in her case. No one wants that kind of political circus over their final affairs. Sign a living will and tell the world what you want if you find yourself in a condition where you can't speak for yourself.

9. A revocable living trust does not always avoid the probate process. The only way to avoid the probate process is to actually retitle your assets and accounts into your revocable living trust. Attaching a schedule of your assets to the trust is not enough. You actually have to sign deeds transferring the property into your trust and retitle your bank and brokerage accounts into the trust.

10. Revocable trusts do not offer any creditor protection during your lifetime, because you have complete and free access to your trust assets—that means that they are your assets and you can do with them as you please. So, if you have a creditor who is trying to get to those assets, that creditor can get to your assets because you can get to them. If you want to protect assets from predators and creditors, you have to engage in more sophisticated planning.

I hope that you enjoyed reading the top ten things that I wish my clients knew going into our first meeting. With this knowledge under your belt, you're ready to get the most out of any meeting with a good estate planning attorney!

Do I Need A Trust?

This question is one of the most common questions I encounter in my practice. That question goes something like this, "I'm not a millionaire and my estate is not taxable, so I don't need a trust, do I?"

Whether you would benefit from a revocable living trust does not really have any relation to whether your estate might be subject to tax. A revocable living trust helps you if you should become disabled, for example. In the event of your disability, or if you are simply unable to manage your investments or pay your bills because of age or infirmity, the successor trustee of your revocable living trust can step in and do these things for you.

Revocable living trusts are also private documents. In contrast to wills, which are filed with the probate court after your demise and are available for anyone to review, trusts are not filed with any public court in the event of your disability or in the event of your death.

Further, new Florida statutes enhance the privacy of your revocable trust when transferring assets into your trust. Brokerage firms have, in the past, requested a copy of your trust when you transferred your brokerage account into the trust. The new Florida statutes provide that the brokerage firm may rely upon a brief "certificate of trust" and a "trustee's affidavit" to verify the trust and trustee.

Many of you already know that trusts help avoid the probate process for the assets that have been transferred into the trust. If you own real property in more than one state, trusts help avoid not only the domiciliary proceeding here in Florida, but also avoid the necessity for an ancillary proceeding in the states in which you own real property. If you own a home in Indiana, commercial real estate in Ohio, and your primary residence is here in Florida, a revocable living trust could help your family avoid a probate process in three states.

The types of assets that you own also speak to whether a trust may assist you and your family. If most of what you own is in an IRA account, for example, then you have a beneficiary designation and a trust may not be as useful.

The ages and relative condition of your beneficiaries speaks to whether a revocable living trust would benefit you or your family. If you have minor children or grandchildren, for example, it is easy to create provisions inside of a trust that take care of them until they become old enough to handle their inheritance. If you want to provide asset protection features for your surviving spouse, children or grandchildren, trusts are often easier than wills.

If you are concerned about someone challenging your will, then a trust could benefit your family. Trusts are harder to challenge than wills are because you operate under the trust during your life, as opposed to a will that doesn't have legal significance until your death. Since you have been operating under the provisions of your trust for your lifetime, the theory goes that you had a greater understanding of the trust contents and that it was likely consistent with your intent.

So all of the above reasons speak to the benefits of a revocable living trust without consideration to whether you are a millionaire or have a taxable estate.

With $5+ Million Exemption Are Revocable Trusts Still Relevant?

In 2014 the federal estate tax exemption increased from $5.25 million amount to a whopping $5.34 million. This means that a married couple can shield a combined $10.68 million from federal estate tax.

So does this mean the end of revocable living trusts? Why would one create a trust or keep an existing trust active?

The answer is this: revocable living trusts are more viable, useful and valuable than ever.

Of course, you would expect a board certified wills, trusts and estates specialist to say that, wouldn't you? Well, please give me a few paragraphs to offer evidence in support of my proposition.

First off, estate tax planning is probably low on the totem pole as to the unique capabilities that trusts offer. One can easily draft estate tax planning into a will absent a trust.

Trusts still shine over wills as well as durable powers of attorney, since trusts can offer both lifetime benefits to you, as well as planning benefits to your loved ones who follow. Here are a few examples:

Probate Avoidance. Many people confuse probate with taxes. Probate is not synonymous with taxes. Probate is a legal, court supervised process that, in Florida, requires you to engage an attorney. In a probate process your will is filed and accepted by the court as your last will and testament, your personal representative (executor) is appointed, assets are inventoried and filed with the court, accountings filed, creditors notified and paid, and finally, distributions made to the beneficiaries. This court supervised process is avoided through proper revocable trust planning, which includes the transfer of one's assets to the trust;

Multiple State Probate Avoidance. For those who own real property in two or more states, probate might occur both in your domiciliary state and in any other state in which you own real property. By placing all of your real property into a revocable living trust, your loved ones avoid having to pay attorneys and court filing fees in those states;

Privacy. When you die, your will is filed with the probate court. The probate process described above is a public process, meaning that anyone can visit the probate court (or even go online) and view most of what has been filed. Any person claiming to be an "interested party" can review your will, inventory, names and addresses of your beneficiaries and so on. In today's electronic age of identity theft and fraud, it's usually a good idea to stay as private as you can, especially when loved ones are in a vulnerable state after a loss;

Protection. While your own revocable trust offers no protection against your own creditors since you effectively own and control all of the assets inside of your own trust, when you die your trust can establish testamentary trusts for the benefit of your spouse, children, grandchildren and other loved ones. These testamentary trusts built inside of your revocable living trust can offer your loved ones valuable legal protections against future creditors, predators or even from their divorcing spouses. Further, having a trust eliminates the need of placing assets in joint name with a loved one to avoid probate. It is extremely dangerous to place assets in joint name—those other than your spouse—for a variety of reasons, including gift tax, vulnerability to the joint account owner's creditors and the likelihood that the joint account circumvents your estate planning wishes.

Centralized Asset Management and Disability Protection.

Normally, the person who creates a revocable trust is also the trustee of his or her own trust, meaning that he or she controls all of the trust assets. But if one should develop an illness such as Alzheimer's disease or dementia, your trust names a successor trustee of your choice who can seamlessly step in and manage your assets for you. You can name your spouse, a child, a bank or trust company, or any combination of those parties to act. The important point is that you are in control of the process. You get to name and control the parties who will manage your financial affairs and make these decisions.

Income and Gift Tax Planning. Revocable trusts are income tax neutral during your lifetime, meaning that they don't cause extra taxes to be paid nor do they save you any income taxes. Upon your death, however, your trust could establish testamentary trusts for your loved ones that contain "sprinkle" powers enabling income to be distributed to the beneficiaries most in need, which could result in lower marginal income tax rates. Further, the distribution of that income is not a gift, which preserves the $14,000 annual exclusion gift option.

I could go on, but hopefully, I have made my point. Trusts accomplish goals that wills simply cannot, and even in those areas where wills might be able to match the benefits of a trust, the ease of administrating the trust over a will is usually well worth the time and expense of creating and maintaining the trust.

Difference Between Durable Power Of Attorney And Revocable Trusts

In this article, I'm going to explain the differences between using a Durable Power of Attorney when its grantor becomes incapacitated as opposed to using a Revocable Living Trust.

These differences can best be related through two different residents at the Kings Crown Pavilion at Shell Point Retirement Center, "Lucy" and "Sarah." The Kings Crown Pavilion is where residents here move when they require full assisted living, and many of them suffer from memory loss and related disorders.

Lucy had a revocable living trust that named her son "James" as her successor trustee. When Lucy established her revocable trust, all of her bank and brokerage accounts were transferred into her trust. She served as her own trustee for many years until her diagnosis and subsequent move into the Pavilion. At that time she resigned as her own trustee, resulting in James taking over that role.

The transition was seamless. Lucy signed her resignation document which was then forwarded to her banks and brokers. James was now listed on the accounts as trustee. He has the ability to write checks for his mother, pay her bills, roll over certificates of deposit, direct the financial planner for Lucy's investments and do all the things that Lucy would have done had she remained capable. While James lives in a Midwestern city, he did not have to travel to Southwest Florida to sign any documents or meet with any financial advisors or bankers. It was all taken care of over the telephone or through written communications.

Sarah, on the other hand, did not have a revocable living trust when she moved into the Pavilion at Shell Point. Sarah believed that since she did not have a taxable estate, she would circumvent the need for establishing a revocable living trust by designating all of her accounts as "Transfer on Death" to her children. She did, however, have a Last Will & Testament, as well as a Durable Power of Attorney document that named her son "Robert" as her agent.

When it became apparent that Sarah would no longer be capable of writing her checks, paying her bills and managing her investments, Robert decided that he would have to begin serving under the Durable Power of Attorney document. The banks and brokerage firms all wanted originals of the Durable Power of Attorney. Since Robert only had one original (as that is the norm) he didn't know what to do.

Robert was advised to record the original Durable Power of Attorney on the Lee County public records and obtain as many certified copies as he needed for each different financial institution. So that's what he did, and most of the banks and investment firms accepted the certified copies.

The banks and brokerage firms, however, all wanted Robert to complete paperwork and to provide personal identification verifying his identity before they would put him on the accounts. This required Robert to personally visit each financial institution where Sarah had an account. Sarah was one of those investors who looked for the best CD rate in town, so she had certificates of deposit scattered among several banks.

Robert had to fly down from his hometown in the northeast to accomplish these frustrating tasks. Several banks said that they needed to send the Durable Power of Attorney document up to their legal department before Robert would be installed as a signor on the account.

You can see the difference between using a Durable Power of Attorney and a Revocable Living Trust when the grantor becomes incapacitated. I'm not here to say that Durable Powers of Attorney are unworthy. They are an important document that everyone's estate plan should include. Even those with trusts need a Durable Power of Attorney document so that your loved ones can transact business on assets outside of the trust (IRA accounts are a good example of such an account).

Placing assets and accounts in joint names with loved ones is also not a good idea to circumvent a trust. I've written on that topic before. My website has videos and blogs on the dangers of joint accounts.

The moral of the stories of Lucy and Sarah is that revocable trusts are not just probate and tax avoidance vehicles. Trusts can serve as valuable tools when our loved ones become incapacitated, as they are much easier transitional devices than are powers of attorney.

But then again, trusts aren't for everyone. If you don't have a trust, you should have an up-to-date Durable Power of Attorney. The laws on powers of attorney have recently changed, so in either event it's important that you confer with your advisors to ensure that your documents are up to date and right for your situation.

Difference Between A Will And A Revocable Living Trust

Occasionally, I am asked a basic estate planning question that I will review here, and that is the basic differences between estate planning with a will as opposed to estate planning with a revocable living trust.

First, let's start off with the will. Many people wrongfully believe that if they have a will then their estate will avoid the probate process. Actually, all wills are subject to the probate process. Probate, you may recall, is not a tax. It is the legal process wherein your last will is admitted to court, your personal representative is appointed, your estate is inventoried, your creditors are cleared, taxes are paid and ultimately, your beneficiaries receive their inheritance.

Every aspect of the probate process is administered in a probate court. This means that your will's contents and all of the other aspects regarding your estate are mostly open to the public. Anyone can go down to the courthouse and review the probate filings. In some counties, the probate filings are also available on the internet.

You may argue that your father, mother, spouse or other loved one died with a will and their estate did not go through a probate process. This might be true if everything was owned jointly. While in some estates joint ownership of assets might be a wise thing to do, joint ownership of assets often leads to more problems than it solves.

Visit my firm's website, www.sbshlaw.com and click on the Video Learning Center link to watch a video about the perils of joint ownership if you want to learn more about why placing all of your assets in joint name is generally not a wise idea if you are doing so to avoid the probate process.

Whereas wills are only useful upon your death, revocable living trusts can help you during your lifetime. A revocable living trust is a legal agreement made between a Settlor (you) and your trustee (also 'you') how to hold, invest and distribute the trust assets both during your lifetime and upon your death.

Many wrongfully assume that if they create a revocable living trust then they'll lose control over the assets that they've put into the trust. But this is not usually the case. You are usually your own trustee, meaning that you control the assets. Because revocable trusts can be changed, you also have the ability to amend the trust at any time, meaning that you normally have complete control over all of the trust assets during your lifetime.

Generally speaking, you usually transfer most of your assets into your trust upon its creation. Failure to fully fund your assets into your revocable living trust could end up in a probate administration on those assets. This is why it is so very important to make sure that the titles on your bank and brokerage accounts, as well as the legal title on the deeds to your real estate indicates the trust (by way of the trustee of your trust) as the proper owner.

If you should become disabled, your trust names a successor trustee who can step in for you to write your checks, pay your bills and manage your investments. Your successor trustee can be your spouse or other loved one. You may also name a bank or financial institution to help with these duties if you wish, although this is not a requirement.

Whenever you have a revocable living trust, you usually also have a will, but the will doesn't usually say who gets what at your death. Instead, it "pours into" your trust. These are known as "pour over wills."

One of the advantages to a revocable living trust is that they are private and are usually not subject to court supervision. While Florida law imposes requirements that your successor trustee must satisfy in the event of your death, most of those requirements do not require court filings. There is no trust inventory filed with a court, for example.

To learn more about the differences between wills and trusts, go to my firm's web site and click on the Video Learning Center link: www.sbshlaw.com.

Making An Irrevocable Trust More Flexible

N o one likes something that can't change with the times. Especially now. Things change so rapidly that we appear to live in a "throw away" economy. Remember the Sony Walkman? Replaced by the iPod. Even now the iPod is threatened by music streaming services like Pandora and Spotify.

Blockbuster Video stores used to be in nearly every Publix shopping center. They were run out of business by Netflix, Redbox, Hulu and Xfinity On Demand.

When I was a young kid there was really no such thing as mutual funds. Only the wealthy could afford to have financial advisors who helped them build individual stock and bond portfolios. Today, financial service products abound that meet the needs of everyone from the uber-rich to the middle class.

The Brady Bunch was considered such a unique blended family situation back in the 1970s that America tuned in to watch the antics. Today, Brady Bunches are commonplace.

Tax laws change. Trust laws evolve.

So what's my point?

Irrevocable trusts. They're a dangerous necessity in some estate-planning situations. As opposed to Revocable (or "Living") Trusts where the grantor can change anything that he or she wants as long as he or she is alive and competent, irrevocable trusts, by design, cannot be changed by the grantor.

The reason that irrevocable trusts can't be changed is because they are used to make "completed gifts" to remove assets from an estate, or to protect assets from the reach of creditors or predators like divorcing spouses. Irrevocable trusts are necessary to get charitable income and estate tax deductions as well. If the trust in question were revocable, it could not accomplish any of those benefits.

When implementing an irrevocable trust, one must be very careful. Once you've named the trustee, that selection can't be changed by you as the grantor. So if you named "Friendly Local Bank" as Trustee, and that bank was bought by "Unfriendly International Bank" that charges high fees and provides little service, the beneficiaries could very well be stuck.

Once you've determined which beneficiaries get what share, it is written in stone. When you draft a document to conform to today's investment strategies and tax laws, it might be obsolete in a few years.

Ask a friend or family member who is a beneficiary or a trustee of an inflexible irrevocable trust, and you may hear gripes, or worse—horror stories.

So what is one to do? Live with the inflexibility?

No. There are alternatives. The client and attorney can discuss including "escape hatches" to be built into the irrevocable trust that allow for flexibility. Consider how you might include flexibility in a document that irrevocably names a trustee, for example. Let's say that Client wishes to name Trust Company as Trustee. To ensure that Trust Company remains good and vigilant, Client can create a provision inside of the irrevocable trust that names an independent party who can remove and replace the Trust Company with another or with a family member.

The irrevocable trust can grant "powers of appointment" to certain beneficiaries that allow them to change who is entitled to income and principal from their share. This way, if an unexpected death occurs, or a beneficiary experiences a bankruptcy that threatens the inheritance, or if a beneficiary develops drug or alcohol problems, the terms of the trust can be "amended"—not by the grantor—but by a trusted independent individual or beneficiary, as circumstances warrant.

A "Trust Protector" can be named and powers granted to this individual who would have the ability to modify the trust to comply with changing tax laws. Generally speaking, the Trust Protector should not be a trustee or a beneficiary of the trust to prevent unintended tax outcomes.

There are countless other strategies to make irrevocable trusts more flexible. You see my point. Careful thought should be put into the selection of the independent parties named inside of the document, including the powers that one grants to those parties.

There is always the possibility that the parties you select abuse their authority. If they did, then they would have to answer to the beneficiaries. Anyone serving in an independent role would have a fiduciary duty to the trust beneficiaries when acting. In other words, they would have to act in the best interests of those affected. Paragraphs expressing the grantor's intent go a long way here.

As you can imagine, a well-drafted irrevocable trust is anything but "boilerplate." It pays to put the thought in before assets are transferred, rather than waiting for problems after.

Estate Planning Lessons From Tony Soprano

By now, most of us have heard about the tragic death of James Gandolfini, the actor who portrayed mafia boss Tony Soprano in the HBO hit series. Many of you may have also heard about how his Last Will and Testament seemed to include quite a few questionable decisions.

These questionable decisions include several items, among them: his estate didn't take advantage of the marital deduction to the extent necessary to defer a significant sum of estate tax; he left millions to an infant daughter in such a way so that she will have full access and control over all of the funds by the tender young age of 21 without supervision; and he left amounts to his sisters in an estate tax disadvantageous way, meaning that when his sisters die the assets will likely be estate taxed again—which could have been avoided.

Whether these "mistakes" were the fault of the attorney or the client making poor decisions over his attorney's objections is not the focus of this discussion. What I wish to talk about is how the media (and now everyone else) knows the intimate details of Mr. Gandolfini's private estate affairs.

How could this be? Aren't our wills and the inventories of our estates private?

I've written in past columns that wills are not private. When we die, our wills are filed with the local probate court. Anyone can go down to the probate court (or in some cases look the file up online) and review a will to see who was left what and how it was to be distributed. While inventories (our assets subject to probate) are not supposed to be subject to anyone's review, in Florida all one has to allege is that they are an "interested party" to have access to this very private and sensitive information.

Revocable trusts, in contrast, can perform the same function as wills (direct the disposition of one's assets upon death), but because they are not required to be filed in a court, they add a very important level of privacy. Revocable trusts allow for the management of the assets in the trust name by the successor trustee without involving a court.

So long as the assets are properly transferred and titled in the name of the trust prior to the trust maker's death, everything should avoid public scrutiny.

In virtually all cases, clients who draft their dispositive plans in revocable trusts also have wills, commonly referred to as "pour over" wills, because they catch assets that haven't been funded into the trust at death and then "pour" them into the trust. These wills are often abbreviated, simply providing that any assets in the estate should be distributed pursuant to the trust. Thus, even if a probate estate is opened to take care of assets that haven't been properly funded into the trust at death, the only document available for public inspection is a simple will saying nothing about the disposition of one's assets.

For those who are in the public spotlight especially, privacy about one's affairs is paramount. Former CEOs and company heads should take a lesson from Mr. Gandolfini's estate experience if they don't want newspapers, business magazines, internet bloggers and trade journals commenting on their most delicate affairs.

We commoners also have an interest in privacy. If one has a disinherited family member or has a former spouse who might take advantage of discovering financial and legal details of one's estate, a trust is most preferable to a will for obvious reasons. Moreover, there are scammers out there who can use the public information from our probate court files to try to prey on our loved ones during a vulnerable time.

I've found that those who resided in the northeastern United States typically have wills, even though trusts might offer more benefits. It's my understanding that probate is not an onerous, time-consuming process as it is here in Florida. In fact, I have had conversations with several attorneys from up north who don't like trusts and view them as simply revenue devices for attorneys who recommend them.

Privacy is not the only benefit of having a revocable trust. Ease of administration in the event of incapacity of the trust's maker is yet another highlight trusts offer over wills. Hopefully, the James Gandolfini case will open both the eyes of practitioners as well as their clients as to the many benefits that revocable trusts provide.

Who's Who And What's What

Every profession seems to have its own language, doesn't it? Whether its medical terminology, computer technology or legal matters, the layperson can easily get lost in each profession's everyday words.

As an example, I was in my doctor's office the other day and he was talking to me about my cholesterol. He mentioned HDLs and LDLs and which molecules should be bigger and which molecules should be smaller. I don't remember which was "good" and which was "bad." It all seemed like Greek to me. I walked out of there with a prescription and a blood work order.

All I knew is that I'd be fine but we had to monitor my cholesterol, and that my doctor was happy that I keep myself in reasonably good shape and take fish oil pills.

That's when I was reminded that as foreign as medical terminology is to me, to most of my clients, trust and estate terminology is just as confusing.

So I'd thought I'd review some very basic "who's who and what's what" in revocable living trusts. The terms "Settlor" or "Grantor" and "Trustee" are used quite often, and I also realize that clients are often embarrassed to ask what those basic terms mean.

So let's find out.

When we're talking about a trust we need to have a person who "creates" it. In other words, the trust document contains the words that describe someone's wishes. That someone is referred to as the "Settlor" of the trust. A synonymous term is the

"Grantor" of the trust. Some attorneys like to use the term "Settlor," while others prefer "Grantor."

All you need to know is that they mean the same thing. A trust is a legal document that dictates how the assets of the trust are to be held, managed and distributed. The Settlor/Grantor is the person who decides what those terms will be, how they will be carried out and who is charged with the responsibility of carrying them out.

If you think of a trust as a "bus route," then the Settlor is the city planner who dictates the route. Imagine the City Planner drawing a bus route that begins on Main Street, turns right on First Street and then turns left on Maple Avenue. When you are the Settlor of your trust you are the one who dictates its terms. You dictate the route.

All buses also need a bus driver. That is the Trustee. The Trustee doesn't set the bus route; instead, he is only supposed to drive the bus on the route. He is not supposed to deviate from the route. That's the trustee's job—to drive the bus. More specifically with a trust, the trustee is charged with the responsibility of managing the trust investments and carrying out the terms of the trust.

In a revocable trust the Settlor is usually also the Trustee at the onset. But the Settlor may become ill and unable to serve as his own trustee. At this point, the successor trustee takes over. Think of it as the second shift on the bus route. The driver who piloted the bus all morning ends his shift and then the night shift bus driver takes over.

The same holds true with a revocable trust. We all have a nightfall when we can't serve as our own trustee any longer. At this point, the next trustee steps in for us.

Even though the trustee changes, the Settlor never changes. Whether or not the Settlor is alive, disabled or dead, that person will always be the Settlor. But when you examine a trust and it refers to the "Trustee," that person might be the Settlor, or it might be someone other than the Settlor, depending upon where in the timeline you are.

Contrast the revocable trust (one that can be changed) to an irrevocable trust (one that cannot be changed). In an irrevocable trust the Settlor usually isn't the trustee at the beginning. This is because the purpose of an irrevocable trust is to transfer assets to someone else and exclude those assets from the Settlor's estate for tax purposes, or it might be established for asset protection reasons.

In an irrevocable trust, the Settlor cannot also act as his own trustee since IRS rules would include the irrevocable trust assets in the Settlor's estate, because as trustee, he retains dominion and control over those assets. If the purpose of the trust is asset protection, again, the Settlor usually does not act as his own trustee, because as trustee he has too much dominion and control over those assets. Therefore, in order for an irrevocable trust to work, the Settlor must usually select an independent person to act as the Trustee from the very beginning.

I hope this discussion helped you understand who's who and what's what in a trust. Now if only someone would explain why good cholesterol molecules are supposed to be small and bad cholesterol molecules are supposed to be large? Or is it the other way around?

Difference Between Trustee And Beneficiary

When you deal with your estate plan once every decade or so, it's easy to get lost in the vocabulary. This occurred to me the other day during a conversation with a client who was upset that one of her daughters was not listed in her documents as a successor trustee if the client became incapacitated or died.

I was befuddled since this very same client told me how irresponsible this particular daughter was. In fact, the client said that she didn't want this daughter to have any control over the client's bank or brokerage accounts. So I first confirmed with her that we were talking about the same person.

"Well, yes" client answered, "I don't want her to control any of my money, at least while I'm alive."

"So why are you upset that she is not going to serve as your trustee?" I asked.

"Because I still want to treat all my children equally!"

This is where I explain that being a trustee is not an honor, nor does it bestow any more of a beneficial interest on the person acting as trustee. Instead, acting as a trustee is a job. It is laden with a lot of responsibility.

Whoever serves as your successor trustee must have the ability to interact with your financial advisor to determine what your asset mix should consist of. In fact, your trustee is held to the "prudent investor" standard under Florida law. Violating that standard could lead to a lawsuit where the other beneficiaries of the trust recover damages against the trustee.

If stocks or bonds need to be sold in order to have cash to pay for in-home nursing care or other convalescent care expenses, your trustee is the one who makes decisions which assets should be sold to do that. If you need to move out of your home for care, then the family member that you have named as your trustee will have to decide whether to have your finances continue to carry the expenses associated with owning the home or whether it would be prudent to sell it.

These are not easy decisions.

Your trustee will file your tax returns. He or she will interact with your CPA as well as your attorney when deciding legal matters associated with your estate. When you die, your trustee will have a fiduciary duty to your creditors, taxing authorities and the other beneficiaries. If your trustee violates these fiduciary duties, then he or she can be held liable and have to pay an attorney out of their own pocket to defend the claims or to satisfy any judgments if they are deemed to have acted negligently.

Just because someone is a trustee does not mean that the amount that they are entitled to as a beneficiary will change. If Suzy is a 25% beneficiary of the estate, she does not receive any additional beneficial interest when acting as the trustee.

She may get reimbursed for her out of pocket expenses associated with fulfilling her trustee duties, such as air fare, car rental, hotel expenses, overnight express charges and the like. She will also be entitled to take a trustee's fee for her time. The fee that she takes is usually well earned, and it is taxed as ordinary income much like a CPA's or attorney's fees would be taxed to them as ordinary income.

Many family members graciously perform their duties without taking a fee. More often than not, his or her siblings will not appreciate the responsibility required and may expect the child you have selected to act as trustee to do it all for free—even though the duties can be enormously burdensome.

It is therefore vitally important when naming a trustee that you select someone who will devote the requisite time and attention to these important matters, and who will be comfortable interacting with your professionals. Someone who is confident, diligent and detail oriented makes for a fine trustee. They don't necessarily have to have any background in law, accounting or taxes. As long as they know how to interact with your team of professionals, it usually works out fine.

As you can see, it really isn't a matter of being "fair" to one child or another. I would go so far as to say that not only have you not bestowed an "honor" upon the family member that you select as your trustee, rather you have handed them a job—a big job, at that.

So don't worry about being equal. Select the family member who is the most likely to do the job right.

Amending Your Will Or Trust

They say a woman's prerogative is to change her mind. My wife, Patti, exercises her rights almost every time we eat out at a restaurant. Did you ever see the movie "When Harry Met Sally?" If you remember the way Sally ordered her food "I like this but with that on the side, and leave off those…" then you know how Patti orders.

I'm guilty of changing my mind when I react quickly to one of my daughter's requests. "Dad, can I…."

"NO!" I shoot back before she can even get the question out.

Then, I think, maybe I answered too quickly. So I go back and ask her why she wants to go somewhere, or do that thing, and after thinking about it from a calmer perspective, I find myself more willing to consent.

We all change our minds from time to time, don't we? When you want to change what you have in your will or trust, you have to be very careful. New clients will visit with me in my office and bring me their current wills and trusts. When I examine them, I'll often find that they've crossed through various provisions and written in new ones.

What many people don't realize is that when you cross out a provision in a legal document such as a will or trust, those cross-outs and revisions are generally not legally valid. This is because any change to your will or trust has to be signed with the same formalities as the original document. This means that you need to have the requisite number of witnesses, and if you want the document to be "self proved"—meaning that after your death your family doesn't have to find the witnesses and get them to attest to your signature—then you also need a notary public.

Florida law also provides, more or less, that the witnesses and the testator have to all see each other sign the document. The testator can't, for example, sign in the presence of one witness, then go to another witness later and get the second witness to sign separately. That would usually be considered an invalid signing.

When you try to change your will or trust on your own with cross through notations and notes on the side, you probably aren't signing these new provisions with the requisite formalities. What these new provisions will do is only "cloudy up the waters," which may lead to litigation between the beneficiaries.

Sometimes I've seen that those that have created those cross-outs actually had a couple of witnesses sign. They think this will validate the handwritten changes. The problem with this thinking is that there is no other evidence that all of the legal formalities were followed. Were the witnesses in the room with the testator when she signed? Did she sign at all or were there just notations? Were the witnesses together? Who are these witnesses, as we will have to have them testify when the parties try to determine who the rightful beneficiaries may be? And on and on.

A beneficiary who sees that he or she may get more from the estate if the cross-through notations are legally effective may try to figure out a way to get them validated. This is usually a long shot, but stranger things have happened in a court of law. The likely result is that the parties will fight it out for some time, but the cross-through notations will be thrown out.

But this may not detour an aggressive beneficiary who could benefit.

That kind of litigation can get very expensive. The trustee for the trust or personal representative for the estate will have their own counsel, as will each of the beneficiaries—who are generally separately represented. Discovery will take some time, and eventually a trial may be conducted.

All of those hours that all of the attorneys spend on the case will likely deplete the amount that all of the beneficiaries would have received. This is where "the lawyers win" and everyone else loses.

So if you have a legal document that you have marked up, it's generally a good idea to visit with your estate planning attorney and have a valid amendment or codicil drawn that will remove all doubt as to your intent.

Don't Name Specific Accounts In Your Will

From time to time a client will direct me to write a will or trust that gives specific accounts—such as a bank or brokerage account—to a specific beneficiary. The direction usually sounds something like this: "I want to give my Raymond James brokerage account #456789 to my son, Bob, while I want my daughter, Suzy, to get all of my certificates of deposit that I hold at The Sanibel Captiva Community Bank."

Wrong. Don't do it that way.

First, let me start with the reasons that I hear—the logic a client might offer—behind the request. Sometimes my client inherited the account from another relative and wants to pass that account down to one of her beneficiaries. Other times it's because the client believes that the investment strategy that worked so well for the client during his lifetime with this certain account will also work for the intended beneficiary. Or perhaps the client believes that by bequeathing a property to one child he can balance the scales by giving away a bank or brokerage account of similar value to another beneficiary.

I've heard all those reasons and then some. I stand by my original statement. Don't write your will to bequeath specific accounts to specific beneficiaries.

Allow me the opportunity to review some scenarios that illustrate my point.

Assume that Mary's will says to give her son, Bob, her Raymond James brokerage account #456789. The value of the account when she writes her will is $650,000. Mary's will also directs that her daughter, Suzy, is to inherit all of her certificates of deposit at various banks that coincidentally add up to $650,000. Her will says to split everything else up equally between Bob and Suzy.

The reason Mary made these bequests is because she knows that Bob has more risk tolerance and would enjoy receiving the investment assets and that Suzy would feel more comfortable inheriting the cash assets.

Several years go by. Mary's broker changes firms and now works at Wells Fargo. When the broker left Raymond James, he asked Mary to follow him. Because Mary trusted her broker and had no special relationship with the Raymond James firm, she did, in fact, move her account. But now her account is at a different firm and is a different number.

If Mary dies, and doesn't change her will, is Bob still legally entitled to the new Wells Fargo account? Remember that Mary's will says that the Raymond James account is what Bob is supposed to inherit. Not the Wells Fargo account. It's entirely possible that Suzy still gets the certificates of deposit, but that the Wells Fargo account is treated as a remainder asset that is supposed to be divided equally between Bob and Suzy.

Does your answer change, by the way, if Mary left half of her assets in the Raymond James account and the other half migrated to Wells Fargo with her new broker—and she never changed her will?

Let's take it a step further. Assume that Mary never changes brokerage firms. Now let's also say that Mary becomes disabled and that she has named Bob as her durable power of attorney agent. Mary needs expensive in-home nursing care. So as her durable power of attorney agent, Bob starts spending down her cash assets. When Mary dies, her certificates of deposit are worth half of what they were at the time that Mary made her will. So now Suzy receives a devise that is only half that of what Bob is going to receive, assuming that Bob is entitled to the brokerage account.

Now let's stay with the assumption that Mary never changes brokerage firms—she still has the Raymond James account—but let's also say that when $150,000 of her certificates of deposit matured, Mary wasn't sure what to do with the money. Her Raymond James broker came up with a good idea to invest in a bond mutual fund that would pay a higher rate of interest. So Mary took the $150,000 certificate of deposit money and added that to her Raymond James account.

Mary later becomes disabled and then dies without changing her will. So now Bob's Raymond James inheritance increased by $150,000 while Suzy's certificate of deposit inheritance decreased by that same amount.

What if Bob, as her durable power of attorney agent during Mary's illness, moved the money when the certificates of deposit matured? Would your answer change if Bob had no knowledge of what Mary's will said? What if Bob was only a stepson and not a blood sibling of Suzy? Would that change your opinion? How do you think a court would rule? Better yet, how much in legal fees will Bob and Suzy pay to sort that mess out?

Take another example, assuming the stock market crashes and Mary never changes her will.

You should, by now, understand why I said that you shouldn't leave specific accounts to specific beneficiaries. Too much can happen between the time that the will is written and the actual administration of that will that could thwart the testator's intent.

Instead, you could accomplish much the same intent by thinking of your estate as a pie. Your will could state—in percentages—how large a piece each beneficiary should receive of that pie. "I direct my personal representative to distribute my liquid assets equally between Bob and Suzy. Without limiting the discretion of my personal representative, to the extent possible I direct my personal representative to distribute cash assets to my daughter Suzy and investment assets to my son Bob. In making these distributions, however, my overriding intent is to treat Bob and Suzy equally."

I could give you a dozen more reasons why you shouldn't leave specific accounts to specific beneficiaries. As always, consult with your own professionals when making these important decisions.

Joint Accounts With Children Are A Bad Idea

Should you put your bank and brokerage accounts in joint name with one or all of your children? In almost all cases the answer is an emphatic "No!" Because I see this so often, I thought that I'd spend this section discussing why it's not a good idea.

First, when you title an account in joint name with someone else, you are actually making a gift of half of its value. So if Claire puts her brokerage account worth $1 million into joint name with her daughter, Susan, she just made a gift of $500,000 to Susan (half of the value of the account). Because the most anyone can gift tax-free is only $14,000, titling an account worth more than $28,000 would require the filing of a federal gift tax return. In my example, Claire would have to file a return that would either reduce her gift and estate tax exemption, or, if she's already used up her exemption she may actually have to pay gift tax.

Second, if Claire's daughter, Susan, is experiencing any legal or financial problems, Claire may have put her account at risk. If Susan is going through a divorce, for example, a forensic accountant may discover the asset and it might be at jeopardy, depending upon circumstances. The same holds true if Susan has creditor or bankruptcy problems.

Third, titling the account jointly will likely thwart Claire's estate plan. Assume that Claire has a will that says that upon Claire's death all of her assets are to be divided equally between her three children. If the account is titled jointly with rights of survivorship with Susan, Susan would inherit the account outright despite Claire's contrary intention in her will. Even if the account is held jointly as tenants in common, Susan owns half of it and the other half would be distributed in thirds according to Claire's will.

Susan might be altruistic and wish to share the account equally with her siblings. But she might have a gift tax problem herself. If she tries to divide the account that she legally owns, she is making a gift in excess of the $14,000 annual gifts that she can give tax-free.

Fourth, accounts owned jointly do not enjoy the full "step-up" in tax cost basis that would otherwise occur. Assume that Claire owns 1000 shares of ABC Company Stock that is worth $100 share but she paid $10/share many years ago. If Claire sold all of her shares she would recognize a $90,000 capital gain. But if Claire dies still owning the shares, her children inherit them at the date of death value for tax cost basis purposes. So if her beneficiaries sold the shares shortly after her death for the $100,000, there would not be any capital gain and therefore, no capital gain tax to pay.

But if Claire places the account in joint name with Susan during Claire's lifetime, on Claire's death Susan only gets a one-half tax cost step up. In this case, Susan would recognize a $45,000 capital gain if she sold the shares for $100,000. ($100,000 sales price less $5,000 basis in half the shares and $50,000 basis in the other half of the shares).

Hopefully, you are convinced that placing assets in joint name with children isn't a good idea. So what should you do if you want your child to be able to transact business on your accounts, particularly if you become disabled and unable to manage your own affairs?

This is where revocable living trusts really shine. Claire can create a revocable living trust and name herself as her initial trustee but also name Susan as her successor trustee in the event of a disability. Susan can then transact business on all of Claire's accounts that the trust owns. It is not a gift to Susan since she is acting as a fiduciary for her mother. On Claire's death the trust avoids probate and rightfully distributes the accounts to all of Claire's children (if that is her wish).

Another alternative is a durable power of attorney. Claire can sign a durable power of attorney that would name Susan as her attorney-in-fact to transact business on all of Claire's accounts. You should know that the Florida law governing durable powers of attorney changed significantly on October 1, 2011. If you have a durable power of attorney created before that date, you should consult with your estate planning attorney to determine if yours needs updating.

The bottom line is that you shouldn't put accounts and assets in joint name with your adult children. There are reasonable alternatives that don't carry all of the disadvantages associated with joint accounts.

Even Young People Need A Will

A young, recently married cousin of mine called me recently. "I don't need a will do I?" she inquired. "My husband and I have only been married a few years and we really don't have many assets."

"You do have a young son, though, right?" I asked knowing the answer. "How old is little Nathan now?"

"Nathan is two years old," she replied.

"What happens if you and your husband are killed in a car accident? Who would you want to take care of Nathan until he grows up?"

"Well, I think my sister would be a good choice..." my cousin said thoughtfully.

"But what if one of the grandparents wants to raise him? Wouldn't you rather tell the world who you think is best suited to take care of him in the event that you and your husband can't?"

"Yes, but can't I just do that in a letter?" she asked.

"You might try. But generally speaking, those kinds of wishes should appear in your will," I said.

"You also said that you don't have much in the way of assets," I continued. "But do you and your husband carry any life insurance?"

"We do."

"How much?"

"Well, we have $1 million on his life, and another $500,000 on mine."

"Who are the beneficiaries of the policies?"

"We've named each other."

"And after each other, who have you named?"

"Well, Nathan of course!"

"That could pose a problem," I said. "Nathan is a minor. If you and your husband both died, then a formal court guardianship would have to be appointed. The life insurance company won't pay benefits directly out to a minor. If you had a will or a revocable trust, you could instead name your estate or the trust as the beneficiary. In that document you would name a trustee to handle the money and make distributions for Nathan's benefit."

"But I don't want a trustee! I don't want a bank to get involved," Cousin protested.

"A trustee doesn't have to be a bank. It can be a relative or trusted friend," I said.

"But without first setting up an estate plan, you don't really have any options with your insurance policy. That is, until Nathan attains age eighteen. Even though he would be an adult then, my guess is that you don't want an eighteen-year-old to control $1.5 million of life insurance proceeds, plus any other amounts that you have accumulated."

"So I guess we need a will, huh?"

"Yep. At a minimum. You probably could use a trust given your situation."

Trusts Are Boilerplate, Right?

Today we're commonly asked to sign a lot of forms. I go to the doctor's office and I sign forms before I can get an exam. I sign forms when I rent skis at the mountain resort. When I get my car serviced, I sign a bunch of forms. Before the vendor sets up the inflatable castle with the water slide feature for my kid's birthday party, I sign forms.

Do I read them? Not all the time. If I won't sign the form I typically won't get the service I am after.

So it shouldn't surprise me when I am reviewing a trust with one of my clients for him to question, "This is just all boilerplate language, isn't it?"

Well no, it's not.

A well-drafted trust should be tailored to a specific client's goals and concerns. That trust should also look different depending upon the type of assets that the client owns, the way in which he owns those assets, his marital and family status, his income and estate tax status and a host of other variables.

Allow me to offer a few examples to illustrate what I mean. Let's compare two fictional characters, Bob to Ted. Both are married and have $2 million of assets. Bob is in his first marriage and his children are of that marriage. Bob's net worth consists mostly of his Florida homestead and stocks and bonds.

Ted, on the other hand, is in a second marriage. Ted lives in a home that is owned by his second wife. He wants his wife to benefit from his financial assets, but then he wants those same assets to revert back to his children upon his wife's death.

Do you think that Bob and Ted's trusts look alike? If they do, they're likely not visiting with a qualified estate planning attorney. These two situations scream for different types of provisions.

I can almost read your thoughts, dear reader—"Well that's well and good, but compare two people with very similar situations, won't they have the same provisions?"

They very well may, but then again, let's look at an illustration. Here we're going to compare Amy and Cathy. Both are widows. Both have assets approximating $3 million that consist of a Florida home and stocks and bond accounts. Both want their children to inherit the assets following their deaths.

$1 million of Cathy's stocks and bonds, however, are held in a rollover IRA she inherited from her husband. Cathy's trust should look very different from Amy's trust because Amy's stocks and bonds are not held inside of an IRA account. Cathy's attorney rightfully includes special tax apportionment provisions that are designed to allow Cathy's children to not have to draw down any part of the IRA to pay estate taxes. Without these provisions, Cathy's children may have to invade the IRA to pay estate taxes, resulting in income tax on the withdrawal as well as a loss of the opportunity for tax-deferred growth.

Now let's assume that Amy and Cathy have exactly the same assets in the exact same amounts. Do they have the same trusts? What if Amy is concerned that one of her children may be going through a divorce, while Cathy does not share that concern about her children? In that event, their trusts will look different in that Amy will build in protections to ensure that the inheritance she leaves her children will not be affected by the divorce.

What if Amy's children are working professionals who are subject to potential malpractice claims, while Cathy's children aren't fiscally mature with money? Different provisions? You bet!

I could go on, but I'm sure you get the picture. Here's another question to consider: Are all attorneys who draft these types of trusts equally qualified? Don't we all plug these variables into some computer program, and out spits a trust? I'm sure you've heard the adage that applies to computers—garbage in means garbage out. If it were that easy I invite you to pay $75 for one of those "do it yourself" trusts that you can purchase on the internet.

There are differences between attorneys. One distinction in Florida is to consider whether the attorney is board certified in wills, trusts and estates. To become board certified means that the attorney has satisfied special criteria with the Florida Bar, including having a certain number of years of practice in the specialty, a review of references, completing additional hours of advanced specialty continuing education, a Bar conducted background check and passing a thorough written examination. An attorney who meets these criteria must be recertified every five years to maintain his board certification.

There is a difference. Before you begin your own estate planning or before you update your existing plan, consider the qualifications and experience of the attorney that you are working with.

The conversations and information that you share with your estate planning attorney should be geared to what is most important to you and what outcome you would like to see. It should address not only your goals but also your concerns. Then be sure to spend the time to thoroughly review the drafts of your documents and ask any questions you have before signing them.

Ruling From The Grave—Or Protecting The Inheritance?

The client sat across from me in the conference room. "I don't want to rule from the grave," he began.

"What do you mean by that?" I asked.

"Just what I said," he replied. "When I'm gone, I want the kids to get everything outright with no strings attached."

"That sounds good," I said. "When your children die do you care if they leave the inheritance that you left to them to their children or to their spouse?"

"I want them to leave it to their children, of course. What if they die first and their spouse remarries? Then the money could end up outside of my family!"

"Yes, true. But if you leave it to your children outright and their will says everything to their spouse, as most wills do, then that's what's likely to happen."

"I never thought about that," he said.

"And wouldn't you want to protect the inheritance that you leave your children in case any of them get divorced?" I asked.

"Yes."

"And if any of your children have any creditor issues—like deficiency judgments from an upside down mortgage that was foreclosed—you wouldn't want a bank to find out about their inheritance and go after it would you?"

"Obviously not."

"Didn't you say that one of your children—your daughter that owns that software business—is actually a lot wealthier than you are?"

"Yes, she has a lot of money."

"If you left her inheritance outright to her with no strings attached, then you might exacerbate her estate tax problem. If you left it in a continuing trust, on the other hand, you could protect it from any creditors and predators as well as divorcing spouses; plus, it can be outside of her estate for estate tax purposes."

"But I don't want her to have to go to a bank or trust department and beg for her money," he exclaimed.

"She wouldn't have to," I explained. "You could name each of your children to be the trustee of their own continuing trust share. Your children could decide how their share is invested, they can distribute the income to themselves, or to their children or even their grandchildren one day. You could even let them decide who they leave it to in their own will."

"But what if I want their inheritance to one day go to their own children?"

"Then you can have me draft their trust share provisions so that's what is supposed to happen. This is all very flexible. You have me build what are called 'testamentary trusts' inside of your own revocable living trust. The testamentary trusts do not get funded with your own trust assets until after you pass away. But the whole structure is built inside of your own trust."

"Are there any tax problems?"

"Not really. IRA and 401(k) assets might pose certain problems that we would need to plan around, since those have an income tax element when they are distributed. But all of your other assets would work just fine."

"What if one of my children wants to withdraw money from their trust share to buy a house or build an office building? Can they withdraw the money to do so?"

"We could put in a trust provision that would allow them to do so, yes," I answered. "But the better thing for them to do would be to have their trust share buy the house or build the office building. That way the asset remains protected under the trust umbrella."

"But what if they wanted to later sell the house or building?"

"Your child could do that too," I said. "Remember that as trustee they control the trust investments and can buy and sell as they please."

"Frankly, it sounds too good to be true," my client said. "I always thought by creating trusts for my kids in my estate plan that I'd be ruling from the grave."

"Not really. This isn't ruling from the grave so much as it's creating opportunities that otherwise wouldn't exist. Your children can't create their own trusts that would have these features in them. Only someone else can create a trust that would have these asset protection and favorable tax elements. And the parent is the logical person to create it in their own estate plan."

"You learn something new every day."

Putting Everything In The Right Box

With three daughters at home (two of them teenagers) you might think that our house is a continual mess of clothes, shoes, backpacks, electronic gear, school books, papers and what not.

And you would be right.

Patti and I are constantly badgering the kids to put everything in its place. Folded laundry goes in the dresser. Books up on the shelf. Backpacks in the closet. It's a never ending battle that we're losing day by day.

"Clean up your room," Patti demands, "because the cleaning people are coming tomorrow!"

"Why do we have to clean our room for the cleaning people? Isn't that their job?" belligerent daughter(s) respond.

Sigh.

My mother's curse from thirty five years ago has come true. "I hope that you have kids one day that…"

I'm sure we'll be hexing our children similarly.

But the point of this is that many of you are more like my daughters (and perhaps your children when they were young) than you care to imagine. You haven't put everything in its proper place either. Yes, your home may be neat and immaculate—that's not what I'm referring to.

How do I know that you haven't put everything in its place? I know this from my estate planning practice. What am I referring to, then?

What I'm referring to are your assets. You may have a revocable living trust, but have you actually titled your bank accounts, brokerage accounts, real estate and other possessions into it? Simply making out a list and attaching that list to your trust is insufficient to legally change title. You actually have to change the title on the account itself, or on the deed itself. If you fail to do so there's going to be a probate on those assets—even if you have a revocable living trust.

You might think it's simple to put everything in its place. In reality, it's not. Depending upon a variety of factors, including whether you are in a first or second marriage, and whether you create testamentary trusts for children and grandchildren, you may need to divide your assets between your two trusts. Which assets should go into which trust? You will want to consider the relative liquidity of each trust as it is generally a bad idea to have one trust with illiquid assets and all of the liquidity in the other trust. In second marriage situations, where the equity from the assets is intended to follow bloodlines after the death of the second spouse, this process usually requires more additional thought and careful planning.

If you don't have a spouse, then it might be less complicated. But you still may need to create new boxes other than your trust.

Consider the client who has rental real estate. She wants to segregate the liability with that real estate from her other assets, so that a slip and fall or other calamity doesn't somehow entitle a plaintiff to get to her other assets. So she may want to create a separate box that is owned by her revocable living trust to hold the real estate in.

Your estate planning attorney, CPA and financial advisors may also help you with the different types of boxes that you already own. The IRA should be considered its own box—with its own beneficiary designation. Who is named as the beneficiary of your IRA may affect the other boxes that you have created—and how they are designated.

Same situation for annuities and life insurance policies. Each can be considered its own separate box and should usually be considered as a part of the grand plan. From where should taxes be paid? How about expenses? Is there a specific purpose for the insurance policy, such as for a small business buy-sell arrangement? Are there written legal documents in place to account for these arrangements?

Is one child expected to take care of another? That's actually a topic for an entire section on its own. But if you have that expectation, which assets are designated for that purpose? Is there a "box" (often in the form of a testamentary sub-trust built into your estate planning documents) to take care of your intent?

These are just a few of the reasons you may want to meet with your estate planning counsel to make sure everything is up to date and "put away."

It's easy to shove everything under the bed and forget about it. Obviously, that's not a smart thing to do.

After all, the cleaning people will be coming one day.

Chapter Two

Beneficiary Matters

Conditional Inheritance?

This just in from the "reaching out from the grave" department: Can you impose conditions on your grand-children's inheritance, such as requiring them to marry someone within your faith or else they lose the trust funds? The Illinois Supreme Court ruled that you can impose such restrictions.

Looking at In re Estate of Feinberg, Max Feinberg created a trust in which he declared that any grandchildren or lower descendants who marry outside of the Jewish faith are to be treated as if the grandchild predeceased the grandparents, thereby denying the grandchild a share of the inheritance unless the spouse of such descendant has converted to the Jewish faith. The parties to the litigation call this "the Jewish clause."

An Illinois circuit court held that this Jewish clause was invalid and an appellate court confirmed, both finding the clause unenforceable and against public policy. Generally speaking, courts will find such constraints against public policy if they either encourage divorce or discourage marriage itself.

One of the judges of the appellate court disagreed, stating that the clause should be held valid. "Max and Erla had a dream...to preserve their 4,000 year old heritage," Justice Alan J. Greiman noted.

Max and Erla Feinberg were survived by five grandchildren. All of the grandchildren married, but only one married a Jew. Several cases erupted against the estate plan. They were consolidated into one case and the question about the Jewish clause went to the appellate court.

One of the grandchildren, Michele Trull, who had married a non-Jew, sued the co-executors of the estates. Those executors happened to be Michele's father, her aunt and uncle. Michele claimed that the three had engaged in a conspiracy to evade estate taxes and had misappropriated millions of dollars from her grandparents' estates. Apparently the amounts left in the grandchildren's shares exceeded the Feinberg's generation skipping tax exemption. So the executors sought to enforce the Jewish clause to pull amounts back to the children's generation, to which the executor's belonged.

The executors of the estate sought to have Michele's case dismissed because the Jewish clause deemed Michele to have predeceased her grandparents and therefore she had no interest in the estate.

The appellate court's opinion explored the public policy argument voiding the Jewish clause. Such a clause is invalid if it encourages disruption of a family relationship, discourages formation or resumption of such a relationship, or seriously interferes with a beneficiary's freedom to obtain a divorce or exercise his or her freedom to marry.

It is conceivable that such clauses "could just as well result in the courts being required to enforce the worst bigotry imaginable," Justice Quinn noted. "Courts are not well suited to decide all the various questions that might arise in the enforcement of such conditions. What would happen if one of Max and Erla's grandchildren initially married a non-Jewish person but subsequently married a Jewish person? Would the grandchild be resurrected upon the second marriage?"

Justice Greiman, on the other hand, who dissented, examined a multitude of cases from outside Illinois. Most were decided in the 1950s or earlier and sided with enforcing such a clause. According to those cases, "partial restraints on marriage are valid unless they are unreasonable, and therefore conditions on gifts prohibiting a beneficiary from marrying a specific individual have been upheld."

Given the heated exchange between justices Greiman and Quinn, the Illinois Supreme Court agreed to hear the case and reversed the lower and appellate court's rulings, holding in a unanimous ruling that the Jewish clause was valid and enforceable.

"Although those plans might be offensive to individual family members or to outside observers, Max and Erla were free to distribute their bounty as they saw fit and to favor grandchildren whose life choices they approved," Illinois Justice Rita Garman wrote.

The appellate court's concern as to whether the clause "encouraged heirs to divorce and remarry to claim an inheritance" was rejected by the Illinois Supreme Court. "Erla did not impose a condition intended to control future decisions of their grandchildren regarding marriage or the practice of Judaism; rather, she made a bequest to reward, at the time of her death, those grandchildren whose lives most closely embraced the values she and Max cherished," Garman wrote.

James Carey, an attorney representing Michele Trull, said his client "was disappointed with the Supreme Court's decision." Steven Resnicoff, co-director of the DePaul College of Law's Center for Jewish Law & Judaic Studies, hailed the court decision as consistent with Illinois public policy. "It's not just a Jewish clause. It's a Catholic clause; it's a Muslim clause," Resnicoff said. "It's not uncommon that people want to encourage their children to follow in their footsteps."

I Love My Son (Daughter) In-Law, But…

"Henry" recently visited with me. "I love my son-in-law as if he was my own son," he began, "but my daughter's marriage to him has been rocky at times, and I'm worried that when I die he's going to take the inheritance I leave my daughter. What can be done to ensure that what I leave behind benefits her?"

I suggested that Henry consider leaving the amounts to his daughter in further trust as opposed to an outright distribution.

"I don't want her to beg for her inheritance, though. My aunt was left a trust and had to beg the bank every time she needed money, and it was HER money," Henry said.

"That situation might come true if you name a bank or trust company as the only trustee, and give that bank full discretion over when you daughter gets income or other assets from the trust," I said. "But what I'm suggesting is to make your daughter her own trustee, or perhaps name a friendly co-trustee with her. While naming a bank or trust company might give your daughter professional management over the trust, if this is what you want, I would suggest to give your daughter or some other person the ability to remove and replace the bank or trust company. But in any event, you can always name your daughter as the only trustee of his or her share."

"But if she's her own trustee, won't she have the ability to do whatever my son-in-law asks?" Henry worried. "What if he wants her to invest in the next big internet company and she blows it all?"

"That's always a possibility if she has full discretion over the trust funds," I answered. "This goes to how much you trust your daughter. You were going to give her the money outright before anyway. By leaving it to her in a trust that she controls you can protect the inheritance you leave her from creditors, predators and even divorcing spouses."

"How does that work. If she has control, won't the assets be subject to those dangers?"

"The more control you give her, certainly the more likely creditors will be able to attack the assets. But by taking some preventive measures, such as naming an independent co-trustee, or naming her children—your grandchildren—as co-beneficiaries who may also be entitled to income, you can better protect the trust assets. When there are other discretionary beneficiaries, your daughter will, as trustee, have a duty to protect the trust assets for their benefit as well."

"But even so, my daughter's rights to the trust will be mandatory, right? In other words, I want all the trust income to be distributed to her."

"Well, if she is the trustee, she can determine when it's best to make distributions from the trust. So I might suggest that you make your daughter a discretionary beneficiary as well."

"If we make her kids as a current beneficiary, when they get older, can't they demand trust money from her? I want her to have enough for her retirement and not necessarily give it all to the grandkids."

"We can build language into the trust that indicates your primary intent is your daughter. You can also give your daughter something known as a 'power of appointment' so that she can dictate where the trust assets are distributed when she dies. There are several ways to limit your grandchildren's ability to make demands on their mother."

After several more minutes of give and take on this issue, Henry decided to leave his daughter amounts in trust as opposed to an outright distribution. There are also other benefits to doing this.

Do I Want It Simple Or Do I Want It Right?

Nothing is easy or simple these days, is it? Turning on the television isn't simple anymore. I'm still trying to figure out my Comcast Xfinity remote control, and I've had it a few years now! I can't seem to make an airline reservation without having to input all sorts of superfluous information—only to be told that I'm getting a middle seat without paying any extra. Back in the day, I used to be able to replace the alternator in my car if I had to. Now, I don't even know where under the hood that contraption might be.

We all crave simplicity. We all want to go back to the days when things were simpler.

So it's understandable when someone says, "My estate plan is going to be simple." Who wants a complicated will or trust? No one does. And there's nothing wrong with that. Until, of course, you look at the situation. Then you have to ask yourself, "Do I want it simple or do I want it right?"

I once had a client tell me that their estate plan should be simple when they were on their fourth marriage, had four children, two of whom were a product of the first, the second a product of the second and the third a product of the fourth. The kids were decades apart in age. Most of this fellow's net worth was tied up in a closely held business, but he did have large retirement accounts that he wanted his spouse to benefit from, and whatever was left at her death would be distributed to his children.

And, he owned an Italian villa that had been passed down through the generations in his family.

Simple? Far from it! But it doesn't take that complicated of a situation to require an estate plan that needs something more than a simple will. Retirement accounts such as 401(k)s and IRAs are a perfect example of this.

Consider the individual who has a significant portion of his net worth in an IRA. He wants his spouse to benefit from the IRA for the rest of her life, and he wants his children to receive what's left over after her death. He doesn't want his wife to be able to change the beneficiaries after he dies.

That can become a big problem. Normally, the man would name his wife as the outright beneficiary of the IRA account. Upon the man's death, his wife then takes the IRA account and rolls it over into her own name. Now it is her IRA account. Who he had on the account as his contingent beneficiary (his children) doesn't matter anymore. She needs to name both a primary and contingent beneficiary on her account.

So suppose that she gets remarried. She might name her new spouse as the primary beneficiary of the IRA account. Do the children who were the formerly named beneficiaries have any recourse? No!

What if she keeps his children on as her primary beneficiary and gets remarried without a nuptial agreement? Can her new spouse claim rights to the IRA account on her death, even though the new spouse is not the named beneficiary? You betcha!

So what are the alternatives? One alternative is to name a trust as the beneficiary of the IRA rather than the spouse herself. Are there any problems with that? Of course there are! First, the trust must meet five certain tax law requirements or else all of the income in the trust that hasn't been taxed yet will be taxed in the year following the original IRA owner's death. That could result in the loss of forty percent or more of the IRA account to taxes right off the bat.

Assuming that the trust does qualify under the tax law for continued income tax deferral for the surviving spouse's lifetime, there remains the problem of Required Minimum Distributions (RMD). The trust must withdraw an increasingly large percentage of the IRA each year. The RMDs will be larger than they were for the original owner because a trust beneficiary has a more aggressive withdrawal schedule. What this translates to is that if the surviving spouse lives a normal or longer life expectancy, even with the trust, the IRA may be totally consumed before her death and his children will get nothing.

All of these issues must be considered when creating an estate plan with IRAs. And that's just one issue. Florida homestead presents similarly complicated scenarios, as will a variety of other types of assets that people commonly own. All of these issues can be addressed with a good result—but more thought usually has to go into the planning to make it all work out.

So like most things in our modern society, there's nothing simple about most people's estate plans anymore. It really breaks down to, is the estate plan going to be simple, or is it going to be right?

Are You Really Doing Them A Favor?

When the news broke that one person holds the winning $400 million Powerball lottery ticket, my mind immediately went to several other lottery winners I know who had died penniless. This occurred despite all of the best intentions (or not) of those surrounding them. Similar news stories appear from time to time about professional athletes who sign mega-million dollar contracts, only to go entirely broke when their athletic career ends.

How does this happen? It's no secret that silly mistakes are made when sudden wealth descends upon those who don't have any experience handling fortunes. Wealth is often wasted on depreciating assets like boats and cars. Friends offer "great business deals" or "the next big internet company" for a "small investment" and so on.

So let me pose you a question. When one bequests a substantial estate to their loved ones, how is that really any different from the (inexperienced in handling wealth) lottery winner or the professional athlete? More importantly, why is it that many who have wealth to bestow are not fond of naming a professional trustee to help their loved ones become accustomed to managing that wealth—even if for a definite period of time?

Allow me to illustrate with an example. Auntie leaves in her will a substantial sum of money to her nephew, who despite being a hard-working young man in his thirties, hasn't had any real experience with sums of money. When Auntie was working with her attorney to write her will, she was asked whether she wanted to name a professional trustee, such as a bank or trust company to help her nephew manage and budget so that he wouldn't make unwise decisions.

"No, I don't think that's necessary," Auntie proclaimed. "He's a smart and responsible young man, so I think that he'll be able to handle it."

While this might be true, I would suggest that Auntie isn't doing her nephew any favors. Like the lottery winner or suddenly wealthy professional athlete, her nephew is going to be barraged with investment advice, deals that he can become a part of, temptation to make big-ticket purchases for those things that he otherwise couldn't have afforded until Auntie's death—and a number of other issues that go along with sudden wealth. Nephew has no experience to speak of in dealing with investment advisors, lawyers and accountants. It's going to be a whole new—and often overwhelming—experience for him.

Naming a professional trustee such as a bank or trust company could help cushion the transition from having little to inheriting sudden wealth. Since Auntie has vast experience dealing with investment professionals, lawyers and accountants, she could choose to name her team in her legal documents to help her nephew get accustomed to managing his new wealth.

The time period immediately following Auntie's death is probably the toughest for nephew to navigate. There's the admin-istration of the trust, including the separation of its assets into the different sub-trusts that may be created for tax and other purposes. Tax returns will have to be completed. Due to the step up in tax cost basis of the assets (and the corresponding reduction in unrealized capital gains) and the different long-term goals that Nephew may have, the investment mix should probably be reviewed and adjusted. Nephew will probably want to create a budget of his expected income and expenses to map out his financial future. So there might be real value in having experienced hands assist with the wealth transition.

Unfortunately, many believe that naming a corporate trustee is an "all or nothing proposition," when in fact there are several "middle ground" options available. Rather than permanently naming a trustee to manage nephew's wealth, for example, Auntie can name a professional trust company for a period of years. After the time period is complete, her legal documents can give her nephew the ability to remove and replace the trust company.

She can choose to always require a professional trustee, or she can allow him to remove the trust company altogether and serve as his own trustee at some point in the future. If Auntie decides to have nephew always have a corporate/professional trustee, she can give her nephew the ability to change who that corporate trustee might be for any reason. All of this is possible with proper drafting inside of her legal documents.

Auntie probably also wants to create a default estate plan for nephew inside of the trust in case he never gets around to prepare an estate plan of his own. By giving nephew a "power of appointment"—which means that he can change the default plan and give the assets at his death to those of his choosing—she can both create the emergency plan and give nephew unbridled discretion of how his estate will be handled at his death.

When dealing with any degree of wealth, these are important things to consider. Leaving everything outright with little or no direction, while seemingly appealing, may be causing more problems than it solves.

Matryoshka Dolls Explain Testamentary Trusts

I remember when my sister, as a young girl, would play with my grandmother's collection of matryoshka dolls. Those are the wooden dolls of decreasing size, placed one inside of the other. The outer layer is usually the painting of a woman wearing a dress and a babushka, with figurines inside that are either male or female characters, the smallest usually looking like an infant carved out of a single wood chip.

The matryoshka doll is a good analogy for an estate planning technique that attorneys frequently use but that many of their clients don't quite understand—the "testamentary trust."

Think of a "testamentary trust" as the inside doll of one larger than it. The "outside," or main element, is usually a will or a revocable living trust. If I create the Craig Hersch Revocable Trust, then that is the biggest matryoshka doll. Inside of my main doll might be a bunch of smaller dolls—the "testamentary trusts."

When the grantor of that trust dies, the next inside trust comes out, which is a testamentary trust. "Testamentary" refers to "after death," meaning that the revocable trust may split into one or more testamentary trusts that can continue on for a period of years or the lifetime of the beneficiaries who follow the person who originally created the trust.

Let's say that George creates a revocable living trust. At his death, a "testamentary" marital trust is created for his wife, Barbara, and it benefits her for the rest of her life. When Barbara dies, two more testamentary trusts are created to benefit their children, Sam and Sarah. Like the matryoshka doll, the trusts keep dividing.

But the testamentary trusts are not "new trusts" that require new language. They always existed inside of their "parent" trust, but they didn't spring into life until the trust before them "died" or was "taken apart" so that the new trust becomes the governing language.

Many people, including those who work in the financial services industry, get confused by testamentary trusts. When George dies, for example, my office might call the bank and tell them to change the account to the marital trust created for Barbara. It's easy for them to get confused. "Where is this marital trust?" they might ask. Or, "We need a copy of the marital trust" when, in fact, they always had the copy of the marital trust because it was embedded inside of George's trust—which they knew about from the beginning!

As each testamentary trust is established, the title on the accounts changes and a new taxpayer identification number is obtained. Like the matryoshka doll, it's a new trust that came from inside of the old one, but it is a completely different "person" in that it might have different provisions and beneficiaries. That is why the banks and brokerage houses have to change the title to the accounts that are now divided between the testamentary trusts.

You might wonder why anyone would use a testamentary trust to begin with. Why don't you just divide all of your estate and leave everything outright to your children? Testamentary trusts are useful in that they can serve to protect the assets that you are leaving your children from the threat of a divorcing spouse, creditors and predators.

Assume the example where a son got foreclosed and the bank obtained a deficiency judgment on the mortgage balance. If you leave an inheritance outright to him, the bank may be able to force collection on their judgment. Another example would be your daughter, the doctor, who is in the middle of a malpractice case when you die. There, the inheritance you leave her might be at risk. Testamentary trusts can be built to mitigate these problems.

In years past, testamentary trusts got a bad rap. Many named banks as trustees that didn't perform well or were loathe to distribute any of the money to the trust beneficiaries. Those days are past. A good estate- planning attorney can draft a trust that gives its beneficiaries control over the investments and distributions of the trust. You don't even need a bank or trust company.

Testamentary trusts can also be drafted to accomplish income tax savings amongst its beneficiaries that cannot otherwise be achieved when an estate is distributed outright. There are all sorts of benefits to drafting testamentary trusts inside of your revocable trust or will, and many of these benefits have nothing at all to do with estate taxes.

So when your attorney starts talking about the use of a testamentary trust, think about the old, wooden, matryoshka dolls. They're not quite as beautiful or as much fun, but they can sure add some life and good benefits to your estate plan.

The In-Laws

From time to time when drafting up wills and trusts, I have a client tell me that they want to split their estate into shares for each of their children, but they don't want the estate to go to their daughter-in-law or to their son-in-law. Instead, they would prefer that whatever is left of the inheritance would go to their grandchildren.

The intent is perfectly reasonable. If your son dies, and if his inheritance goes to your daughter-in-law, who then remarries, it's possible that your hard earned estate will one day end up with some other family that you don't know.

So when I get direction to bypass the in-laws, I will often ask my client if they are talking about what would happen if their son/daughter predeceases or if they are talking about a situation where their child survives my client and then dies.

"What does this matter?" is a question I often hear in response to mine.

"Well, let's say that your son survives you," I begin. "If you leave his share of the estate outright to him, then he now owns it and can leave it to whomever he wants. So if his will gives everything to his wife, then she's likely to inherit what you left him."

"We love our daughter-in-law," my client might respond, "but what if she remarries and leaves everything to some new husband? We don't want that. We'd prefer that our grandchildren receive what's left."

"In that case you shouldn't leave everything to your son outright, instead you should leave it in a continuing trust for his benefit," I add. "You can make him the trustee of his own share, but instead of it being subject to his will, you could add a provision that if he dies and if there is anything left of the share, then it is to benefit your grandchildren. That way you give him control as trustee and as primary beneficiary, but you can direct it at his death rather than giving his will complete control over what you left him."

Before the client instructs me to do just that, I throw something at them that they may not have ever considered.

"If you leave the assets in a continuing trust, you might want to give your son a power of appointment over the assets so that he can direct who gets them in his will."

"Why would we do that? Then we're right back where we started! If he gives everything to his wife, then what's the point of creating a trust share for our son that would go on to our grandchildren?"

"That's a good question," I say. "But consider this—what happens if your son has hit hard times economically and dies unexpectedly? Then there might be considerable sums held in trust for the grandchildren, leaving their mother destitute. You wouldn't want that either, would you?"

"Probably not." Client says. "So what do we do?"

"A power of appointment does not have to be an all or nothing proposition," I advise. "You could give your son the power to appoint some portion of his share, but it must be appointed into a trust for his wife that continues for her lifetime. In other words, you could limit how much of his share he can redirect away from the grandchildren (who would be the default beneficiaries) and to his wife, but you can also ensure that upon her death it goes back to your bloodline."

The power of appointment might say something along these lines: "I grant to my son the limited power to appoint up to half of the remainder of his trust share to his wife, provided that he exercise the power in such a manner as to direct such sums into trust, paying his wife income for her life, and then the remainder of the share at her death will revert to my grandchildren."

I explain that the actual wording of the will would be more "legal" in nature, but that would be the gist of it.

While it's easy to simply go with default language that would distribute all of a deceased son's share to that son's children, that might not be the right thing to do, especially when your child is in a long-term marriage and your grandchildren are of that marriage. Every family's situation will be different, so it is important to consider the ramifications of your default beneficiaries should something unexpected happen.

Sharing Isn't Always So Easy

The concept of sharing doesn't seem to be innate among most of us, and this becomes apparent when you watch little kids with their siblings or their peers. From a very early age "MINE!" seems to be a word that is used often in struggles over toys, food and whatever else the little devils want at the moment.

So it shouldn't surprise us to learn that sharing an inheritance can be problematic. I'm not talking about an estate that is divided into equal shares for each one of the beneficiaries. That's an easy division that often doesn't result in any problems.

Instead, what I am referring to here is when someone creates something known as a "pooled trust" that is supposed to benefit a certain class of beneficiaries. A common example of a "pooled trust" is when an educational trust is created for a person's children or grandchildren.

Allow me to explain by example. "Henry" rightly values education. "You can give a man a fish or teach a man to fish," Henry likes to say, so he wants to create a fund of money that will be used to educate his grandchildren. Currently, Henry has five grandchildren, ranging in age from 16 down to 2, but there may be more in the future.

Henry directs me, his estate planning attorney, to create in Henry's will a trust that will achieve his goal. "How much are you going to leave to the educational trust in your will?" I ask Henry.

"Let's say I would like to direct $500,000 to the educational trust at my death," he replies. "I'd like that amount to be spent on my grandchildren's education. The money is to be used for books, tuition and room and board to the extent possible."

"Are you planning to make lifetime gifts to your grandchildren who are already in college?" I ask, pointing out that his oldest grandchild is only two years away from starting college and that we expect Henry to still be around at that time.

"Yes, I do," Henry replies.

"Will there be a maximum amount that the trustee can direct towards any one grandchild?" I ask.

"I never thought of that," Henry replies.

"What if, for example, the oldest grandchild goes to Harvard? That might consume the entire trust and there would be nothing left for any of the younger grandchildren."

"You're right," Henry says, scratching his chin. "Well, maybe we ought to put a limit on the amount that any one grandchild can receive."

"How much is that limit?" I ask.

"I don't know," Henry replies.

"There are other questions that the trust has to address as well," I point out. "Are the funds solely to be used for a college education? What if a grandchild doesn't have a propensity for book learning but might be good at a vocation? Can the funds be used for a vocational education? Is there an age limit? Can a 30-year-old grandchild seek money for his or her education? Is there a degree limit? Can the funds be used for a bachelors and a master's degree? What if the grandchild wants to fund his own bachelor's degree but wants the trust to help with post graduate studies?"

I continue pointing out issues that must be addressed in the document, "Does a grandchild have to show progress towards a degree? What type of progress must they demonstrate, and do they lose the ability to access trust funds if progress is not demonstrated?"

"Wow. There's a lot that this trust must address," Henry says.

"There's more," I go on. "Must they attend an accredited college or university? What happens if they drop out for a year or two and then return—do they lose the ability to access trust funds for their education? At what point must the trust terminate? We don't know how many grandchildren may yet be born, so is there a date certain that the trust terminates? If so, who gets whatever is left at that point?"

"What if we left a lot of this up to the discretion of my trustee?" Henry asks. "We could put a general statement of what my intent is and then let the trustee sort things out as the grandchildren begin attending college."

"That might work," I tell Henry, "but here you have to be careful who the trustee is. Is it going to be one of your children, who also have children of their own who may qualify as a beneficiary? What if that trustee is accused of favoring his children over the others? What safeguards are we going to put into the trust for that?"

"We could always name an independent trustee, such as a bank or trust company," Henry rightly points out.

"Yes, a corporate trustee may be appropriate here," I continue, "but usually you need to have a minimum amount to make the administration of the trust relative to the fees worthwhile. Also, what do we tell the trustee about their duty to preserve amounts, not only for grandchildren who currently attend college, but for those younger ones—and even the unborn—that aren't yet in college? Does the trustee have a duty to preserve money for those future beneficiaries? The trustee doesn't want to get sued if the first four or five grandchildren consume the entire trust leaving nothing for the rest of them—some of whom we don't even know yet!"

"You make this sound like an insurmountable task!" Henry objects.

"Whenever you have a trust that is pooled for a class of beneficiaries you run into these issues," I explain. "The task is not insurmountable, but for the trust to work properly these and other issues should be dealt with to the extent possible so that whoever administers it will know what you would have done if you were alive and self-funding the educations, given the same set of facts and circumstances."

As you might imagine, a pooled trust, such as a pooled educational trust, takes a great deal of thought and careful drafting to work out properly. Otherwise, you might have a lot of beneficiaries claiming "MINE!" too often and too loudly.

Who Should Own The Life Insurance?

I see a common problem among spouses who own each other's life insurance policies. It would seem perfectly reasonable for a husband to own a life insurance policy on his wife's life, where he is the primary beneficiary, and vice versa. I'm here to tell you that when spouses own each other's life insurance policies, practical problems arise.

Take the example where wife owns the policy on husband's life. In this fact pattern, it is not uncommon for wife to be the primary beneficiary and their children to be named as the contingent (alternate) beneficiaries if wife predeceases husband.

Assume we have that example and now assume further that wife predeceases her husband.

Remember that wife is named as the owner to the policy that insures husband's wife. Since she is now deceased, wife's estate now owns the policy. The only way to transfer the insurance policy to husband is for him to open a probate estate and transfer the policy to himself, assuming he is the beneficiary of her estate. This can be costly and time consuming.

Husband may not care to open the probate and instead keeps the policy in wife's name. When husband dies the children are still the beneficiary, since the primary beneficiary (wife) predeceased husband. The children would simply need to produce both of their parents' death certificates to make a claim on the policy proceeds.

So what's the problem?

There are a few problems, actually. Let's say that husband wants to borrow against the cash surrender value of the policy during his lifetime. He won't be able to do it without probating the policy and transferring it into his own name.

Assume further that wife has a taxable estate. The cash surrender value approximates the value of the policy for estate tax purposes. If that cash surrender value needs to be tapped in order to pay any estate tax that may be associated with the value of the policy, there is no way to do that without opening up a probate and transferring the ownership of the policy.

Take another scenario where one of the children predeceases their father. In this case husband may want to name alternate beneficiaries on the policy for the child who died. But he can't change the beneficiaries because he does not own the policy— wife's estate does. He would have to probate her estate and take ownership of the policy through a court process in order to update the beneficiary designations.

So how should married couples own their life insurance policies? It is important for married couples to consult with their estate planning attorney to ensure that the ownership of the life insurance policies fits into their estate plan. Generally speaking, you commonly find four different options.

The first option is where the insured owns their own policy. In other words, husband owns the policy on his life and wife owns the policy on her life. If husband dies, for example, there is not going to be any probate on the ownership of the policy since the beneficiary now makes a claim for the policy proceeds.

Another option is for the married couple to create irrevocable life insurance trusts (ILITs). ILITs are commonly used to remove the value of the life insurance from the couple's estate for federal estate tax purposes. ILITs may also be used for asset protection purposes.

A third option is for the insured's revocable living trust to own the policy. Since the trust assets avoid the probate process, dealing with the policy is not a problem.

Yet another option is for the children to own the policy. The danger here is that the children have the ability to change the beneficiary of the policy. This could result in the surviving spouse not receiving the insurance proceeds. There are also gift tax issues, as when the children own the policy each premium payment constitutes a gift to the children.

Determining the ownership of a policy is only the first step. The married couple must next name the policy's beneficiary. This might be more complicated than it first appears. Couples who have revocable living trusts or ILITs often name the trust as the primary beneficiary, or sometimes the trust is the contingent beneficiary, depending upon the family's estate plan.

Don't overlook common mistakes and planning pitfalls when designating the owner and beneficiary of life insurance. It doesn't hurt to put some careful thought into the process.

Don't Name Minors As Beneficiaries To Insurance, Annuities & IRAs

" Joe," a widower, recently passed away owning an IRA and life insurance policies that named his daughter as a primary beneficiary, with his daughter's children (Joe's grandchildren) as contingent beneficiaries. Unfortunately, Joe's daughter predeceased him, so his grandchildren stepped into the role as primary beneficiary.

When the children's father went to collect the IRA and life insurance benefits for his children, the financial firms said that they wouldn't pay the benefits directly to the children. This is due to the fact that the children were minors, and they cannot legally sign for the money. The children's father offered to sign on their behalf, as the legal guardian.

Not good enough under the law.

The financial firms are concerned that if the father were to collect the proceeds and were to use them for his personal benefit, then the grandchildren could later successfully sue the financial firm for recovery. Believe it or not, this concern is well founded in the law.

So how does a minor beneficiary collect the benefits from a life insurance policy, IRA, annuity or other similar financial instrument that names the minor as a beneficiary? The usual course of action is to file a legal guardianship with the court. The child's parent can be named as the guardian over the property (in this case "property" refers to the insurance and IRA monies), and the court will oversee the distribution of the proceeds. The guardianship will last until the minor child becomes an adult.

Every year the guardian of the property will have to petition the court to spend the money on behalf of the minor beneficiary. The guardian will also have an obligation to file formal accountings with the court, detailing income, expenses and distributions.

Sounds time consuming and expensive, doesn't it? One can certainly see how a guardianship proceeding will serve to protect benefits that could be improperly consumed by a child's parent or other guardian, so the law makes sense.

But isn't there an easier way?

There is. The easiest way to avoid an expensive court administration over the minor beneficiary issue is much the same method used to avoid probate. I'm talking about the use of trusts.

Assume, for example, that Joe, instead, created a trust. Instead of naming his grandchildren as contingent beneficiaries to his IRA and life insurance policy, he names his trust. The trustee that he appoints in the trust following Joe's death (could have been the grandchildren's father, could be some other trusted friend, relative or even a bank or trust company) would have the legal authority to collect the insurance proceeds and IRA monies and would then distribute those monies to or for the benefit of the grandchildren pursuant to the trust provisions.

If Joe were to want those proceeds held until the grandchildren reached college, and to pay for the college education using those proceeds, Joe could specify this in the trust.

Because the trustee of the trust has a fiduciary responsibility under the law to the trust beneficiaries, the financial firms can make the payment to the trustee without fear of their own liability under the law. Instead, the legal liability transfers from the financial service firm to whoever is serving as trustee of the trust proceeds for the grandchildren.

When dealing with IRA accounts, the trust that serves as the beneficiary needs to be drafted with a careful eye towards preserving the tax-deferred benefits. Often the trust needs to have special provisions concerning the beneficiary's "required minimum distributions" (MRD).

You may be aware that owners of IRA accounts have MRDs upon attaining the age of 70½. What you may not know is that EVERY beneficiary of an IRA account (including Roth IRAs) also will have MRDs—even if the beneficiary is younger than 70½. So the trust needs to include the five requirements for a beneficiary to be considered "identifiable" under the tax laws, and therefore be entitled to preserve the tax free growth associated with the IRA account.

I won't bore you with the five requirements here. If you would like to read them for yourself, look up Treasury Regulation s.1.401(a)(9)-4. Then tell me how long it took you to get cross-eyed!

Failure for any trust to meet those five requirements often results in the IRA income being wholly taxed in the year following the IRA owner's death. This is often a very bad tax result.

So if you have named minors as beneficiaries or as contingent beneficiaries to life insurance, IRAs or annuities, you should consult with your estate planning attorney to ensure that all of these issues have been addressed.

Anti-Lapse Statute Excludes Granddaughters from Estate

For those of you who believe that you can write a will just as effectively as an attorney and save a lot of money, allow me to present to you a case out of California that points out how important it is to know all of the law surrounding estates and trusts. Not using an attorney well versed in estate law could lead to—and often does lead to—unintended consequence. You be the judge if the law worked correctly or if this would have been an unintended consequence of a contingency not thought of at the time the will was created.

In re: Estate of Nellie G. Tolman, the deceased left a will that bequeathed a $10,000 gift to each of her granddaughters, Deborah and Laurie, with all of the rest of her estate to her daughter, Betty Joe Miller. The value of Nellie's estate was roughly $1 million. Deborah and Laurie were the daughters of Nellie's deceased son, Lloyd. Each of the bequests to Deborah and Laurie stated that the gift would "lapse" if they failed to survive Nellie.

So Nellie's will basically left $20,000 to her granddaughters who were from her son's side, with everything else to Betty Joe, Nellie's daughter.

Unfortunately, Betty Joe also predeceased her mother. Nellie's will did not say what would happen to Betty Joe's share in the event that Betty Joe predeceased. In other words, the gift of everything else (the bulk of Nellie's estate) did not say that the gift lapses in the event Betty Joe predeceased her.

Interestingly, Nellie's will did provide the following: "Except as otherwise specifically provided for herein, I have intentionally omitted to provide herein for any of my heirs who are living at the time of my demise, and to any person who shall successfully claim to be an heir of mine, other than those specifically named herein, I hereby bequeath the sum of ONE DOLLAR ($1.00)."

Since Betty Joe predeceased Nellie, the court had to determine who was entitled to Betty Joe's share. Betty Joe had a son, Michael, who was Nellie's grandson. Betty Joe also had a daughter who predeceased her, with three children of her own.

The granddaughters alleged that the language in the will should be read to mean that everything that would have gone to their aunt, Betty Joe, should instead go to them, and not to Betty Joe's descendants (Michael and the three grandchildren of Betty Joe). They read the language to mean that Betty Joe wanted to specifically disinherit Michael and Betty Joe's three grand-children.

The California appellant court said, "not so fast, Deborah and Laurie!" California (like most states) has something known as an "anti-lapse" statute. That statute provides that unless a contrary intention appears in the will, an heir at law's descendants will step into the shoes of the heir at law as if she survived, taking in her place.

What this means in this case is that Betty Joe's share is not split amongst her nieces and her child and grandchildren. Instead, Betty Joe's share is treated as going to her lineal descendants; in other words, one-half goes to Michael (her son) and the other one-half goes to her deceased daughter's children—Betty Joe's three grandchildren. Deborah and Laurie share nothing of Betty Joe's share.

If Nellie had wanted Betty Joe's share split amongst all of her descendants (including Deborah and Laurie), she would have to specifically say in her will that Betty Joe's share would "lapse" in the event she predeceased Nellie, and would have named where that share would otherwise go.

So the anti-lapse statute effectively worked to leave the amount intended to Betty Joe to instead go to Betty Joe's heirs.

Was this a fair and proper result? No one other than Nellie would know what she would have wanted. But that's what happened. And it happened because of a statute, and not necessarily what was written (or not written) in the will.

My Bubby's Silver Dollar

While in my experience as an estate planning attorney, families rarely fight over inheritance, but you might be surprised to learn that when such fights do occur the conflict isn't usually over the money or stocks or property.

Rather, it's the things.

Like Mom's diamond engagement ring. Dad's baseball card collection. The ladle Grandma used to cook her soup.

And the reason that these things become so important is that they have a lot of emotion attached to them. As last Sunday was Mother's Day, I thought that I would share with you something that was given to me a long time ago that illustrates my point.

I was close to my great grandmother, who I affectionately called my "Bubby." I probably got special treatment, not only because I was her first great grandchild, I was also her only great grandson. My parents had named me after her deceased husband, Charles, and my Hebrew name—Gidalyah—was also his. Not only that, but my Bubby and I celebrated our birthdays together, as hers was March 5th and mine March 4th.

On New Year's Eve of 1976, (when I was all of 12 years old) my Bubby babysat my sister and I while my parents went out to celebrate. After my sister went to bed, my Bubby and I sat together on her easy chair to watch Dick Clark ring in the New Year. Shortly after the ball dropped, she reached into her pocketbook, taking out an 1890 Indian Head silver dollar coin.

She went on to explain (in her Germanic-Yiddish accent) its significance. "When I was a very young girl, my father fled to

America to escape the pogroms in our native homeland of what was then Austria. He didn't have enough money to secure passage for my mother and me, and had to work several years in his new homeland to earn the money necessary to bring us to New York."

She told me of her fear that when she got to America her father wouldn't recognize her or love her. Her mother told her that was nonsense, of course, but in those days overseas communication (delivery of letters) was difficult and rare. She described seeing the awe-inspiring Statue of Liberty as her ship sailed into Ellis Island, and the fear that during the immigration processing she would be diagnosed with tuberculosis or some other disease and not allowed entry.

Finally, she made it through the ordeal, after which she was reunited with her father, who she described as a large man with a booming laugh and big, furry beard. He scooped her up in his arms and gave her this 1890 silver dollar—which was an American coin dating to the year of her birth. Back then, at the turn of the century, a silver dollar was a lot of money!

"This silver dollar signifies the riches that America brings us in our new life together!" he exclaimed. My Bubby kept that silver dollar with her every day of her life.

At that moment she handed it to me. "Here, my dear Craig, I want you to have it," she said. I tried to refuse but she insisted. Later that year my Bubby would die of cancer—none of us knew that she was even sick that New Year's Eve—and I still think of her daily. She was a sweet, loving and kind woman.

I framed that silver dollar along with a picture of my Bubby and I, celebrating one of our birthdays together. Today, more than 35 years later, it hangs in a prominent place in my home, and my children all know its story. In fact, my family purchased a place for her name on a plaque on Ellis Island. It was an emotional moment for me when visiting Ellis Island with my wife and children and telling them this story, and seeing her name there.

While anyone might purchase an 1890 Indian Head silver dollar on the open market for $50 or $60, it is invaluable to me. It ties me to my heritage—to my ancestors—and symbolizes the struggles, hopes and dreams that they lived and died for. My Bubby's silver dollar reminds me of the risks that they took, leaving everyone and everything that they ever knew for a land that offered promise—despite the fact that they hadn't yet learned to speak English—all so that their progeny could thrive.

As far as inheritances go, I've never expected to receive much in the realm of money or property from my family. They're not very wealthy people. But we do have a rich heritage, and I've inherited something of far greater value—a piece of my history.

The Divorcee's 10-Point Estate Planning Checklist

Divorce is often a nightmare which disrupts all aspects of one's life. Getting through it is difficult enough, but then most new divorcees often don't take the final steps to shore up their estate plan. That is why we're going to review a ten-point checklist for every newly divorced person—especially those who have kids at home:

1. **Make sure the life insurance is up to date** and that your new beneficiaries are listed properly. Don't name kids as beneficiaries! This will put the insurance proceeds straight into a conservatorship where a judge will supervise their financial lives until they are 18, and then they'll get the proceeds in one fell swoop.

2. **Create a trust** which will sidestep the probate process, keep the management of the kids' assets private and in your control, prevent the loss of those assets to your kids' future creditors and predators, and reduce the estate taxes that may take valuable resources away. When creating that trust, **name a trustee** that will have your kid's best interests at heart, and one that can work well with their surviving spouse—your ex-spouse.

3. **Don't leave your assets to your kids outright and don't leave too much.** There is nothing more damaging to a child's life purpose than having too much disposable money at their fingertips.

4. **Don't cheap out on an estate plan.** Whitney Houston did that. Apparently, she went online to create a will that is a disaster. It doesn't protect her assets from her daughter's creditors, estate taxes and probate. Spend the money to get it done correctly. It isn't really that much in the scheme of things.

5. **Make sure you have enough disability insurance.** Nothing will diminish your wealth and put you in the poor house quicker than not being able to earn a regular income. Most people don't carry nearly enough disability insurance, and social security disability in all likelihood won't cover a fraction of what you need to maintain any semblance of your current lifestyle.

6. **Name a guardian in your will for your minor children and ask your ex who he has named.** You might be able to agree on who would care for your kids if you both should die. If you and your ex disagree on who should fill that role, there could be a nasty court fight that would only eat into what you are leaving your children.

7. **Check to make sure all life insurance and retirement account designations are up to date.** You may still have your ex named as the primary beneficiary. Under many state laws your ex may be treated as predeceasing you even if they are so named—but this may lead to other problems. You don't want minor children to be named as beneficiaries (see item #1 above), and many plan agreements default to your estate if you have no alternate beneficiary named. In the case of IRAs and 401(k) accounts, this will result in the immediate recognition of taxable income of the balance of the plan.

8. **Have your ex-spouse sign an ERISA waiver.** In some cases—particularly if you die before you are remarried—your ex-spouse may maintain rights to your retirement accounts unless they sign certain waivers after your divorce.

9. **Update your health care directives** such as your living will and health care surrogates, and don't name your children as your agent unless they are over the age of 18 and are emotionally

mature enough to deal with the weighty decisions that come with the territory.

10. **Before you remarry, get good legal advice.** Unless you enter into a good nuptial agreement, your new spouse may have rights to your home and assets even if you don't include him or her in your will. If you have created a whole estate plan to take care of your children, then it behooves you to protect that plan from those who could thwart it.

Once you've completed your divorce it makes sense to visit with competent estate planning counsel to ensure that your intentions and assets are protected.

Who Are Your Heirs?

In today's world of "Assisted Reproductive Technology" (ART), do we really know who our heirs might be? I recently attended The Heckerling Estate Planning Conference, which is a weeklong preeminent continuing education course for professionals who practice trust and estate law. One of the sessions featured Miami Attorney, Bruce Stone, who lectured on how reproductive technology affects wills and trusts.

I was surprised to learn that nearly one out of every 100 new births today is a product of ART. Couples are waiting longer to have children, working against their biological clocks. It is therefore not uncommon for ART facilities to harvest and freeze a couple's eggs and sperm in case they want to have children at a later time but can't.

Stone described a client meeting that included not only the husband and wife, but also one of their adult sons. When Stone described the will and trust documents to his clients and got to the "per stirpes" provisions, he explained that if one of the couple's three sons predeceased them, then that son's children (the couple's grandchildren of that son) would take the share of their predeceased son. If, at the time of the death the son had no heirs, then the other surviving sons would split the estate.

That's when the son dropped a shocking revelation.

"Wait a minute," he said. "My wife and I have embryos frozen in case we would want to have a child someday. What happens if I died, but my wife hasn't transferred one of the embryos in utero yet? We might not want to ever have children, but if I were to die suddenly, we've discussed the possibility that she may decide to carry one of these frozen embryos."

The room sat in shocked silence. When all parties gathered themselves to discuss the possibilities, much emotion poured out.

Florida law states that if an heir is "in-utero" when its parent dies, then it stands in line as a per stirpes heir. Once it is born, it is then entitled to the share of the deceased parent. Stone explained that the unborn child would actually have to be in the womb at the time of the adult son's death in order to be considered an heir.

"But what if my wife decides to wait some time and then have the child? Can it not be considered my legal heir at that time?"

Stone explained that the state law may be circumvented with proper legal drafting inside of the will or trust. In other words, if the clients put a provision that would call an after-born child a direct heir, then it can certainly be considered one.

But this presents all sorts of problems. Consider a family that has three sons. The will is drafted to allow one of the son's wives to conceive a child after the son's death and have that child considered to be a legal heir, so long as the after-born child's DNA is that of the son.

Assume that the son predeceases his parents. When his parents die, there are two sons who survive them, but their daughter-in-law has not decided whether to go ahead with the embryonic transfer. There could be a question of how long the personal representative (the executor) must keep the estate open and not make distribution to the two surviving sons, because no one is sure if they are entitled to 1/3 each (since the predeceased son's heir could be born at some point in the future) or 1/2 each (assuming that the wife either won't go through with the procedure at some point in the future, or even if she does, whether the procedure will be successful)?

ART presents other problems. Consider the child who donates sperm to a sperm bank to earn some extra money in college. Could a child conceived from such a donation take a rightful share of the estate? State laws generally protect against this scenario, but not all state laws are similar. Different fact patterns may also affect the outcome.

To what extent should someone who has made, or is making an estate plan, ask his or her children whether an ART heir is possible? How long should a class of beneficiaries remain open, if at all, to accommodate this new technology?

Reports indicate that the percentage of ART children born when compared against those normally conceived will continue to increase over the coming decades as biological technology improves.

It would seem that clients should begin to open up these rather delicate issues with their adult children to ensure that their estate plan doesn't have unintended consequences. Further, if there's intent to accommodate the wishes of an adult child who is having difficulty conceiving, then those wishes should be conveyed to the estate planning attorney so that they can consider the possibilities and draft detailed provisions to satisfy the intent.

Chapter Three

Estate Planning for Second/Blended Marriages

The Ties That Bind

We're all familiar with the refrain "you can choose your friends but not your family," which usually refers to the fact that we often prefer the personalities of our friends over those of certain relatives. Imagine how much more this holds true when you throw in relationships, money and inheritance into the mix.

As second marriages become more common, estate plans increasingly must deal with step-parent/step-children relationships. Estate planning attorneys encourage the use of "split interest" trusts in these situations. A split interest trust refers to one that provides for one party then terminates in favor of another party. When you have second marriage situations the split interest usually means that the surviving spouse receives benefits until his or her death, then the trust terminates to the deceased's children.

You may have heard of a "QTIP" trust, which stands for "qualified terminable interest property" trust. Features of the trust include income payments to the surviving spouse, with principal invaded when the income isn't sufficient to provide for the surviving spouse's health, education, maintenance and support. So the trust "qualifies" as a marital trust—allowing it to be tax deductible as a marital deduction for estate tax purposes—even though the trust terminates at the death of the surviving spouse in favor of the deceased's children.

These types of trusts are promoted as satisfying the estate planning concern to provide for one's spouse while ensuring whatever is left after his or her death goes back to one's children instead of to the spouse's family.

Consider, however, that the surviving spouse's interest and the children of the deceased interests are adversarial to each other. I don't necessarily mean adversarial in the sense that the parties don't get along. What I am referring to is that the interests are legally adversarial. Every dollar that the surviving spouse receives from this trust during the rest of her life is one dollar less that the children will inherit.

But it goes beyond that. The surviving spouse wants the trust to maximize her income for the rest of her life. The children, however, would like to see the trustee invest in growth assets so that when they finally inherit the amounts they will have grown between the death of their parent and their stepparent. The trustee of a split interest trust has a fiduciary duty to both the income recipient (surviving spouse) and the remaindermen (the children).

Even if the trustee is the surviving spouse, she can't consider her interests solely, or she could be held liable to her stepchildren.

This situation is exacerbated when the surviving spouse is only a few years older than her stepchildren. Here, although one's intent could be to provide for both a surviving spouse and children, where the age differences are compressed, the children may not inherit until they are well into old age.

There are alternatives. Where one is insurable, one could consider investing in a life insurance policy that names one's children as the direct and immediate beneficiary. Allow me to illustrate through example:

Assume that Ben is divorced, age 55, and has two children who are 30 and 28. Ben marries Susan, who is 42. If Ben leaves his estate in a classic split interest trust benefiting Susan for the rest of her life before it distributes to his children, Susan and Ben's children are tied together economically for the rest of Susan's life. Since the children are only a little more than a decade younger than Susan, they are unlikely to enjoy any inheritance until they are well into old age. If Ben's children are both male, it is not outside of the realm of possibility that Susan survives one or both of them.

Let's say that Ben, noting these possibilities and wanting his children to enjoy something after his demise, decides to purchase a life insurance policy that names his children directly. Ben could have his sons own the policy directly, but the risk there is that they "cash out" the policy before his death, or otherwise do something with the policy that Ben wouldn't want them to do.

Instead, Ben decides to create an irrevocable life insurance trust to own the policy. Ben funds the policy with a single premium amount, so he won't have a long-term annual commitment to fund the premiums. Now Ben knows that despite Susan's potential for longevity he can be assured that he provided for his sons in the manner that he wanted.

This may also serve to smooth the relationship between Susan and her stepsons in that Ben was able to provide for Susan, and her trust can now be built with more flexibility so that she may not be as beholden to Ben's sons as before. The sons don't care because they received an immediate inheritance and they were told by Ben that they may not receive any more amounts. While Ben may still use a QTIP trust, he could build in provisions that allow Susan to change the ultimate beneficiaries (through powers of appointment), so the sons aren't vested beneficiaries to the QTIP. This takes some pressure off Susan as to the rest of her inheritance.

This is but one solution to the step-children/step-parent inheritance dilemma. These situations require careful thought. I'm hopeful you can see from this discussion that even though a plan may make sense from a tax perspective it may not necessarily work from a human perspective. If you have a similar situation you may want to bring up your concerns with your estate planning attorney.

Second Marriage Estate Planning Issue—Spouse vs. Kids

A cousin of mine has been married a few times and has children from different unions. Over a holiday dinner he asked me to help him with his estate plan. "It's real simple," he began.

"Simple?" I answered. "Your situation is far from simple my friend!" I replied pouring a glass of cabernet for him and for me.

"How so?" he asked. "I want to leave everything to Lauren, and then when she dies I want it all split between my kids," he said, sipping from his glass.

"I understand the intent," I said, "but you should understand that carrying out that intent is far from easy."

"Seems easy to me," he replied, shrugging his shoulders.

"Okay, cousin, let me ask you a few questions," I began. "You say that you want to leave everything to Lauren. But if you do that, let's suppose that she remarries and leaves everything that you left her to her new husband. Your kids get nothing in that scenario."

"Well, I don't want to leave it to her *outright!*" Cousin said. "I want to leave it in one of those trusts that sounds like an ear cleaner!"

"A QTIP trust?" I laughed.

"Yeah, one of those," he said. "Why's it called a QTIP trust?"

"It stands for 'qualified terminable interest property," I said, knowing that most people don't care and neither did my cousin. "It's a way that you can leave assets in a trust for your spouse that terminates in favor of your kids or whoever else you want as the ultimate beneficiary after her death. A QTIP trust generally qualifies for the federal estate tax marital deduction."

"Too much information!" Cousin laughed holding his palms up at me. "But yeah, that's the type of trust that I want for Lauren. She gets the income from my investments, and at her death the principal will go to my kids."

"What if the income is insufficient for her needs?" I asked. "Especially in today's market—yields are very low. You may only get a couple thousand dollars a month of income on $1 million of principal."

"I suppose she can invade the principal if she needs it," Cousin said finishing off his wine. I poured him another glass while nursing my own.

"For what purpose? Who decides how much of the principal she will need? Should her other sources of income be considered? Must she deplete her own resources before she gets to invade the principal of what you left her?"

"What—are you interrogating me?" Cousin said, getting a little agitated.

"No," I said, smiling, trying to diffuse his anger, "But these are real questions that your will and trust should speak to or else after your death Lauren will be arguing with your kids in court over these same questions."

"The kids won't have any right to say anything!" Cousin said.

"Yes they will! Under Florida's law—as in most states—your children are called 'qualified beneficiaries,' meaning that they have a right to annual accountings of the trust assets held for Lauren. They can also question the trustee's decisions as to whether and how much Lauren should receive under the terms of the trust."

"I'll just make Lauren her own trustee," Cousin said belligerently.

"You could do that," I said, "but then she'll be wearing two hats. She'll wear one hat as the beneficiary of the trust and the other hat as the trustee. She'll certainly have more control over the assets, but it won't change the fact that she'll still have a fiduciary obligation as the trustee to treat your children fairly."

"Fair is all in the eye of the beholder," Cousin said.

"Until the beholder is taken to court and challenged to justify his or her actions," I countered.

"Whose side are you on anyway?" Cousin asked. "I thought you were going to help me with this."

"I am going to help you. The way that I help you is by pointing out all of the issues that we should think of to put into the document. Ultimately, that more than anything will help you accomplish your intent. So bear with me. Even though these are not easy decisions to make now, it will all help in the future when the plan is actually put into action."

"Wow," Cousin exclaimed, rubbing his temples. "There sure is a lot to think about."

"Yes there is," I replied. "And we haven't even talked about the complex homestead rules and how that affects your estate plan!"

"I think I'll save that for another day," Cousin said, laughing slightly.

"Yeah, there's a lot of stuff to talk about that, we'll save that for later."

"I guess my estate's not so easy," Cousin said with raised eyebrows.

"That's what I was trying to tell you!" I said, raising my wine glass. "Cheers!"

It Seems So Simple—But It's Not!

A client and his second wife were in my conference room recently, explaining what he wanted in his trust document. "It's really quite simple…" he began.

Twenty years of experience has taught me a few things. One is, when someone starts out by stating how simple their situation is, or how simple a request is—it's usually not.

This client wanted to create a trust that distributes $50,000 a year to his wife for the rest of her life. Everything else was to be distributed to his children immediately upon his death.

"How much should I carve out from your estate to hold in trust for your wife?" I asked.

"I already told you," he said. "I simply want $50,000 a year to go to my wife with the rest of it immediately to my children."

"But I have to start with some amount, and that amount has to be more than $50,000," I explained.

He looked puzzled. "This is so simple," he said. "You're making this too complicated!"

While I acknowledge that lawyers tend to get caught in the minutia, I had to get my point across so he could see what I was talking about.

"Suppose you had $1 million of liquid assets at your death," I began. "If it yielded a 4% return, then it would produce $40,000 of income, which is insufficient to pay your wife the $50,000 you want her to get."

"That's right," he said, "But I wouldn't want you to hold the entire $1 million in trust for her. I would want my kids to get some of that immediately at my death."

"So that means that you would want your trustee to distribute some of the principal to your wife every year to make up the $50,000. But we would have to start with an amount that would be held in trust first."

"Why?" he asked, wrinkling his nose.

"Because otherwise we wouldn't know how much your kids should get immediately at your death. Suppose that you said one-half of your liquid assets were to be immediately distributed to your kids. Assuming you have $1 million of liquid assets, then $500,000 would go to them and the other $500,000 would be held in the trust to generate the $50,000 annually to your wife."

"But that wouldn't be enough for her. If that money was held in a money market account earning less than 2%, it would last just over ten years," he calculated, "and she might live longer than that."

"Now you're seeing my point!" I exclaimed. "We need to start out with an amount that is sufficient to pay the amounts that you want distributed over your wife's lifetime. If we knew how many years she was going to survive you, and we also knew exactly how much your investments would yield over that time period, the calculation might be a bit easier. But since no one knows either variable, it's difficult to determine."

"I didn't think it was that complicated," he acknowledged.

"Throw in the factor that over time inflation will eat into the purchasing power of that $50,000 and you have another variable that you might not have counted on."

The client looked discouraged. Something that he thought was so easy really required a lot more thought to accomplish then he had originally anticipated. And that's more common than not with estate planning. I used this hypothetical situation to illustrate the point. Many times, it's actually more involved than my explanation above.

Another variable that comes into play is the decision over which assets should be used to fund the income bequest to the surviving spouse. If the client owns an IRA but has investments outside of the IRA, for example, then the net amount (after income taxes are calculated) might make a real economic difference to the surviving spouse.

Another variable is whether the couple had a nuptial agreement. Absent a valid nuptial agreement, the surviving spouse might have rights against the decedent spouse's estate over and above whatever he decided to leave her in his legal documents. If the surviving spouse were to exercise her rights against the estate, it could work to thwart the entire plan.

There are planning opportunities available to meet the needs of this particular couple. But in order to create a plan that works to meet their needs and intent, many variables should be reviewed to ensure the solution picked has a reasonable chance to succeed.

Estate Planning Is An Art As Much As It Is A Science

We all want everything to be simple and easy. It's either this or that. Good or bad. That's human nature. "My estate plan should be simple," clients will say.

But it's not always simple or straightforward. Take a situation where a man is in a second marriage and wants to leave assets to his spouse so that she will have sufficient income for the rest of her life, but on her death he wants the equity to pass on to his children and grandchildren, who are not of this marriage.

Simple? Not always. Yes, there is something known as a "QTIP Marital Trust." He can leave the assets to that trust and it will pay his wife income for the rest of her life and then pass the assets on to his children. But that's just one choice of many. Allow me to lay out some of the complexities of this situation.

Does the man want his wife to get the only the income or should she have the ability to tap into the principal of the trust if she needs to? In today's low yield environment, a healthy $1 million trust may only generate $30,000 or $40,000 of income in the best of circumstances. That might not be enough income, depending upon resources, lifestyle and needs.

The trustee has a legal duty to balance the needs of the remaindermen (the children) against the needs of the spouse, unless the trust is drafted in such a way as to favor one over the other. In other words, the trustee cannot just invest in the highest income producing assets without looking at growth prospects for the remaindermen beneficiaries. Having to invest in both income and growth will limit the amount of income that a typical marital trust may generate.

Suppose, knowing this, that the man therefore directs his attorney to draft the trust so that not only income is available to the surviving spouse, but also principal for her health, maintenance and support. Fine. Who will be the trustee who makes that decision? Is it the surviving spouse herself? Might her decision to invade principal cause conflict with her stepchildren? Is the invasion standard to be tied to any other assets or income that she has available to her? How should this language be drafted to balance her needs against those of the remaindermen?

What if the man wants his wife's Marital Trust to terminate if she remarries after his death? He can include that type of provision, but then the trust won't qualify for the federal estate tax marital deduction. The deduction may or may not be necessary depending upon a variety of factors, such as whether the man has a taxable estate, or whether he wants his children to enjoy a step-up in tax cost basis at his wife's death, minimizing capital gains taxes.

Now consider the situation where the man's liquid assets are mostly in IRA or 401(k) accounts. Routing those types of assets through the standard QTIP Marital Trust may not make much sense at all. If the trust does not meet the five "identifiable beneficiary" requirements under the Treasury Regulations, then the entire amount of his IRA or 401(k) could become taxable in the year following his death. This could have catastrophic consequences on the estate plan.

Even if the QTIP Marital Trust does qualify his wife as an "identifiable beneficiary" under the Treasury Regulations, the trustee must still withdraw the IRA based on wife's Required Minimum Distribution schedule, no matter her age (even if she is less than 70 years of age at her husband's death). If she lives to a normal life expectancy, then the entire IRA would be distributed.

If the Marital Trust acted as a "conduit trust," giving her the withdrawal each year, then there would be nothing left for the man's children.

IRAs and 401(k)s naming trusts as beneficiaries are difficult to understand. The distribution from the IRA is generally all taxable income. But for trust purposes, some of it is "income" as some of it is "corpus" or "principal."

If the man wants to accumulate some of the corpus in the trust to preserve it for his children, that corpus (as a taxable income distribution) is taxed at the highest marginal income tax bracket (39.6 percent plus 3.8 percent Medicare Surtax) on amounts over approximately $14,000, due to trusts' compressed federal income tax rate schedules.

You can now see how difficult satisfying a seemingly simple direction such as "give her the income and upon her death I want it to go to my children" can be. There are solutions to these dilemmas, but each one depends largely upon the goals of the individuals involved and their own facts and circumstances. Now you might better understand why I say that estate planning is often just as much an art as it is a science.

Wrong Way To Look At Prenuptial Agreement

"Harry" and "Sally" were interested in marrying, as they had cohabitated for many years but had not tied the knot. Both were retired; Harry was widowed and Sally's former relationship had ended in divorce. Harry and Sally had separate assets, with Harry's estate being the larger of the two. Harry wanted to enter into a prenuptial agreement with Sally before taking his vows. Sally was offended at the idea. They had been through multiple sets of attorneys—mostly divorce lawyers— unable to come to an agreement that would then open the door to a beginning of a new stage in their lives.

So they continued to cohabitate, both wanting to marry but at a standstill as far as the nuptial agreement went.

"You're looking at the prenuptial agreement all wrong," I suggested when they came to visit. Both of them seemed puzzled at my thought. I continued, "You're looking at it the way a divorce attorney would look at a prenuptial and not the way an estate attorney would look at it."

"What do you mean?" Harry asked.

"So far, you've described a scenario where Harry's attorneys were trying to give Sally as little as possible in the event of a divorce or Harry's death. At the same time, it appears that Sally's attorneys were trying to do the exact opposite—get Sally as much as possible in either event."

"Isn't that to be expected?" Sally asked.

"I suppose so," I added, "but it's no surprise that when you come at a situation from opposite ends of the spectrum, it's harder to agree where the middle is. What if we started at a point that you both consider the middle and work from there?"

Harry and Sally seemed to like that approach.

"So let's look at the reasons you're wishing to enter into a nuptial agreement first, and see if we can work into what you both might consider a fair middle ground," I said.

During our discussion I discovered that they both had valid concerns about the future of their relationship. Harry wanted a life companion that would be there for him "in sickness and in health, til death do they part." He was concerned that when the going got tough, Sally would bail. Without a nuptial agreement she might take half of what he owned in that event, and she wouldn't have lived up to their bargain.

Sally was worried that even if she was there until the end, there was nothing that would prevent Harry from leaving everything to his children and nothing to her. While she recognized that Harry's children should be entitled to as much as half of his estate at the time of his death, he had promised her that he would be there financially for her in her elderly years.

I began by asking, "What would both of you living up to your promises look like?"

Harry and Sally described a scenario where they stay together until the end. If Harry died first, Sally would want the income from half of his estate, along with a life estate in the home where they resided together. She would expect Harry's estate to dip into principal if she needed it for important emergencies such as health, maintenance and support—if her assets were insufficient for those purposes.

Harry agreed with Sally's thoughts.

My next question got tougher. "So let's look at what the penalty should be if either of you doesn't live up to your promise of 'til death do us part.' What happens if you get divorced before that time?"

After some discussion it was agreed that there would be a sliding scale starting at 10% and moving its way up to 35% of the estate for Sally if they got divorced. The scale would be based upon the number of years together. It didn't rise to 50% because that was the amount agreed upon if they lived up to each other's promises. There had to be some kind of penalty for the failure to get to that point.

Provided they stayed together to the end, Harry agreed that Sally would get a life estate in the residence plus a marital trust for fifty percent of the value of his estate, excluding the residence, if she survived him. The remainder of his estate would be distributed to his children. He was willing to put this promise into the nuptial agreement, draft a new will and trust to evidence his promise, and attach it to the agreement as an exhibit.

In order to have a valid nuptial agreement, both sides had to be represented by separate attorneys, and that's what we did to actually draft the agreement. But before we got to that point, this initial meeting was critical. What I tried to do was change the way that Harry and Sally viewed the nuptial agreement. Rather than it be an adversarial zero sum game process, I tried to turn it into a more detailed understanding, describing each other's expectations surrounding their marriage.

During the course of our one meeting we were able to come to a middle ground that made them both happy. I don't think that middle ground could have been achieved had we not talked about the reasons that they wanted to get married, what they felt their expectations were of one another, and how meeting those expectations should be rewarded (or penalized) if they were met or not.

Harry and Sally were both relieved and thankful once we got this emotionally trying mess out of the way. I hope that if you find yourself in a similar situation, you can look at it like Harry and Sally were able to and come to a reasonable middle ground.

How To Use Annuities To Benefit Spouse/Step-Child Relationship Within An Estate Plan

The estate planning complexities surrounding second marriages with blended families are largely under-estimated, not only by clients, but also by their attorneys. Since second (and even third) marriages are becoming more common, it is not unusual for a married couple to each have adult children from prior marriages. When you link these parties in an estate plan, sometimes things can go terribly wrong.

When completing estate plans in second marriage situations, the challenge includes how to provide for one's surviving spouse for the rest of her or his life, while at the same time preserving assets and equity for one's children. The typical response is a "Marital" or "QTIP" trust that pays the surviving spouse income and may also provide for discretionary principal distributions for the spouse's health, maintenance and support. At the surviving spouse's death, the remaining assets of the Marital Trust are then distributed to the children.

While such Marital Trusts are useful tools to accomplish these goals, careful and deliberate consideration should be given to a variety of factors that may exist. If, for example, one's spouse is closer in age to one's children than oneself, there is the distinct possibility that the spouse survives the children, effectively removing them from the line of inheritance. While grandchildren may reap those benefits, this may not be consistent with the testator's intent.

Even where the spouse is not close in age to the testator's children, there are other emotional, familial and financial issues to consider. Marital Trusts, by definition, economically bind the surviving spouse to his or her stepchildren. The parties may enjoy a superb familial relationship, or they may not. But once the "glue" that holds these parties together has died, the relationship may become a purely economic one.

And whether the parties acknowledge it or not, the economic relationship is adverse. Every dollar that step-parent spends from the Marital Trust will one day result in the children receiving one less dollar (or perhaps even less when one considers the opportunity cost of compounding interest). Whoever the trustee is has a difficult job of balancing investments inside of a Marital Trust. The surviving spouse wants to maximize income while the children call for growth. Difficult decisions confront the trustee when considering whether to distribute additional amounts that the surviving spouse may request when home repairs, new cars or other major expenses loom.

IRAs, 401(k)s, pensions and profit sharing plans (I'll just blanket all of these types of accounts by calling them IRAs) pose an even greater challenge. Naming a Marital Trust as the beneficiary to IRA accounts may only serve to result in higher income tax costs, since the Required Minimum Distributions will eventually exhaust the account over time if the surviving spouse lives long enough. The alternative is to simply name the surviving spouse as the primary beneficiary.

But when the surviving spouse is named as the primary beneficiary, he or she can roll over the IRA into their own IRA. Now the surviving spouse has the ability to name whomever they want as their beneficiary. There is no guarantee that the children of the first deceased spouse will inherit anything from the IRA account at the surviving spouse's death.

When IRA accounts are a significant portion of one's estate, one may consider an annuity as an alternative. Annuities, by definition, are "wasting assets" in that their distributions consist not only of earnings (interest and dividends) but of return of capital (principal). As such, the "income stream" distributed by annuities tend to be higher than simply income that may be earned on investments.

Depending upon the situation, one might be able to divide up one's IRA account into separate accounts to take care of a surviving spouse and children immediately upon death. In other words, one portion may include an annuity inside of the IRA that guarantees an income stream to the surviving spouse. All parties know and recognize that this portion of the IRA will likely be fully consumed and not end up with the children. The advantage to an annuity over simply bequeathing investment assets is that the annuity company guarantees the payout over the surviving spouse's lifetime, no matter how long he or she lives.

The balance of the divided IRA account can name the children as direct beneficiaries. Using this approach, the children don't have to wait until their stepparent's death before receiving at least a portion of their inheritance. The surviving spouse/step-parent, on the other hand, has an income stream that won't be scrutinized, since the children would have no expectations of receiving any amounts from that portion of the estate.

There are many nuances to this approach that need to be carefully considered with legal, tax and financial counsel. Nevertheless, the thought of "unbinding" a surviving spouse to his or her step-children is worth considering, and may result in better familial relationships into the future, since the parties are not tied to one another economically as they otherwise would have been.

IRAs And The Second Marriage Dilemma

Holiday season is tough enough for most families, and can be even more difficult for those in second marriages. Who is visiting where on Thanksgiving and does that mean that they're spending Christmas with the other side?

Then comes the actual holiday, complete with out-of-town relatives. Everyone really wants to get along and try his or her best not to do something that upsets the step-mother/father/son/daughter.

All of those emotions become exponentially trickier when you consider estate planning in these second marriage situations. Depending upon the type of assets that make up the estate plan, the situation can go from difficult to downright mind numbing.

Take IRA assets, for example. IRAs present a uniquely challenging problem that requires much more thought than what usually goes into completing the brokerage firm's IRA beneficiary designation.

Recall that when money is contributed to an IRA you get an income tax deduction. The IRA grows tax-deferred until amounts are withdrawn. Each withdrawal results in the recognition of taxable income.

This goes on for the rest of your life. When you die, your IRA account names a primary beneficiary and it may also name contingent, otherwise known as alternate beneficiaries. Many people don't realize how the IRA account may not end up with the loved ones in the manner that you originally intended.

Consider the example where Jim names his second wife, Alice as the primary beneficiary of his $700,000 IRA account with Jim's children, Tom and Tina as the alternate beneficiaries. Alice is not the mother of Tom and Tina; instead, she has her own son, Frank. When Jim dies and is survived by Alice, who is named as the primary beneficiary to the IRA account, she can "roll over" the IRA into her own IRA account.

At that time Alice is free to name anyone she chooses as the beneficiary of the account. Alice can name her son, Frank, as the beneficiary if she wants, which would effectively disinherit Tom and Tina. It doesn't matter that Tom and Tina were the contingent beneficiaries to the original IRA account.

Nor does it matter that Jim's revocable trust creates a marital trust for Alice with the remainder to Tom and Tina at Alice's death. That's because the IRA isn't governed by Jim's will or revocable trust. The IRA has a beneficiary designation that governs how the IRA is devised.

Suppose that Jim, realizing this fact, decides to name his revocable trust as the beneficiary of his IRA. Jim's intent is to flow the IRA through his trust that benefits Alice for the rest of her life and then distributes the remainder to Jim's children, Tom and Tina. Jim doesn't necessarily want Frank to benefit from his IRA one day. He wants Alice to receive enough income to live off of, but then wants the balance to go to his children.

The problem here is that by naming Jim's revocable trust as the beneficiary to his IRA, there could be adverse income tax consequences, and Alice may not have enough income to live off of.

The IRS imposes complicated rules when a trust is named as the beneficiary of an IRA, and many revocable trusts won't qualify to defer the income tax treatment of the account during the surviving spouse's (Alice's) lifetime. In order to stretch the tax deferred treatment over Alice's lifetime, the trust must qualify Alice under some very strict regulations known as the "identifiable beneficiary" rules. Failure to do so results in disastrous income tax consequences, triggering all of the income that hasn't been taxed yet.

In this case, Jim's entire $700,000 IRA could be taxed as ordinary income to his trust in the year following his death, resulting in the loss of 35% - 40% of its value to taxes. Further, the balance (let's calculate that to approximate $420,000) may yield something less than 4% under current interest rates, generating a measly $16,000 of annual income for Alice.

Assuming that Jim's trust does actually qualify Alice as an "identifiable beneficiary" under the complicated IRS rules, that doesn't necessarily solve the problem. Because Alice is the eldest of Jim's trust's three beneficiaries (Alice, Tom and Tina), the minimum required distributions are calculated under Alice's age on the IRS tables. Consequently, if Alice should live a long life, it's possible that the entire IRA will be distributed to Alice over the course of the rest of her life.

So even if Jim was successful in creating a trust to benefit Alice for her lifetime (and that trust successfully complies with the identifiable beneficiary rules), because the required minimum distributions are based on Alice's age, Tom and Tina may not inherit much, if any from the account.

There are several possible solutions to this dilemma. One is to create a special type of trust that will qualify Alice as an "identifiable beneficiary," where Alice's trust share is designed to withdraw amounts necessary to maintain her standard of living.

At the same time, that special trust may create separate trust shares for Tom and Tina. Here, the IRA may be shared by all of the beneficiaries during Alice's lifetime, by splitting it into separate accounts. If there is any remaining amount in Alice's share at her death, that share can be directed back to Tom and Tina.

Another is to name all three beneficiaries as primary beneficiaries for a fixed percentage of the IRA, and allow them to all go their separate ways. Alice is free to name her own beneficiary of her own share. While Tom and Tina may not ever inherit the portion that designated Alice as the primary beneficiary, this "unties" the beneficiaries from one another.

There are many variations on these strategies. What I want to leave you with here is the importance of thinking through what's most important to you and to your family to maintain family harmony while achieving your estate planning goals.

Poorly Drafted Trust To Support Residential Expenses

In the past year I've reviewed half a dozen or more poorly drafted trusts that set out to pay for residential expenses after the owner spouse dies when the surviving spouse intends to remain in the home. These trusts often created more problems than they solved, so I thought that I'd review this issue here.

In most, the fact patterns are similar, usually involving a second marriage where the owner spouse would want his or her surviving spouse to continue to live in the residence for the remainder of his or her lifetime, and the owner spouse wants his or her estate to pay for the taxes, maintenance, association fees and other routine expenses associated with the residence.

Typically, you find these arrangements in second marriage situations where the parties otherwise want their own estates to benefit their own children. In other words, his estate benefits his children and her estate benefits her children. The owner spouse would like for the surviving spouse to reside in the residence, but then the owner spouse wants his or her own children to either own the residence or receive the proceeds from its sale after the surviving spouse dies.

So the problem language found in the will or trust may look something like this:

"I leave my residence in trust for my spouse to reside rent free for the rest of his or her lifetime. I direct my trustee to pay for all ordinary and necessary expenses associated with the residence, including but not limited to property taxes, insurance, association fees and annual assessments. My trustee shall then distribute the remainder of my estate to my two children, outright and free of trust. When my surviving spouse dies the trustee shall sell the residence and distribute the proceeds of the residence between my two children."

What do you find wrong with these provisions? At first glance they appear to satisfy the decedent spouse's intent, don't they? But consider this—from what funds is the trustee supposed to pay the annual expenses? The provisions of the trust do not indicate how much money or assets should be carved out to pay for the expenses associated with the residence. If the remainder of the estate is distributed between the decedent spouse's two children, what is left over to pay for the ongoing expenses?

In order to properly satisfy the decedent spouse's intent, it would be wise to carve out an amount of assets and/or money to be held in continuing trust to generate the income necessary to satisfy the intent of paying for the residential expenses before the rest is divided between the children.

This issue can be more difficult to properly draft than one might first imagine. No one knows how many years the surviving spouse will live, nor does anyone know how over that time period inflation will affect taxes, insurance, fees and assessments. Whatever amount that is carved out from the estate to be held in further trust would presumably generate some growth and income.

Because of the compressed income tax rate schedule that affects income that is accumulated inside of trusts, it is usually best to make an actuarial assumption when determining the amount of carve-out necessary and assume that both income and principal will be used to satisfy the first decedent spouse's intent.

There are a variety of other issues that may apply. What happens if the surviving spouse remarries? Is the home then sold and the proceeds distributed to the children? If so, then the value of the residence likely won't qualify for the estate tax marital deduction. If one has a taxable estate, there could be estate taxes due on the first spouse's death. Are those taxes to be paid from the other assets, thereby depleting what the children initially are to receive? If not, from what source are the taxes to be paid?

What if the surviving spouse wants to sell the home and move into something smaller? In order to do this, there should be a direction in the trust instrument that allows for this possibility. But the trust should continue to own the new property. What happens to the excess proceeds? If they are to be distributed to the children rather than held in a qualifying marital trust, you encounter the same estate tax issue discussed above.

The Florida homestead rules play into this issue as well. If the parties do not have a valid nuptial agreement that waives Florida's descent and devise statutes, then the provisions will fail as an invalid devise. There you have other problems between the surviving spouse and the decedent's children that I have written about in other columns.

While fashioning a will or trust to satisfy one's intent is certainly possible, all of these issues must be carefully addressed or significant legal and tax problems will likely arise amongst your loved ones.

Power Of Appointment Dangers

Normally, when one has a revocable living trust, that trust becomes irrevocable upon the death of its Settlor. This makes sense, since the Settlor is no longer alive to amend the trust.

But there are situations where you might want to allow a close loved one the ability to change the trust provisions. This is common between spouses. "At my death, my trust becomes irrevocable—except I give my wife the power to change the beneficiaries or how those beneficiaries receive the trust assets."

Why would you want to do this? There could be a long period of time—several years or even decades—between the death of the first spouse and the second spouse. During that period of time a lot can happen. What if one of the children develops a drug or alcohol problem? You could imagine different scenarios where you would want to give your spouse discretion to change the trust and how it is distributed.

But you usually don't want to give total discretion. You wouldn't want your spouse, for example, to direct the trust assets away from your children towards a new spouse that they married following your death. So the power of appointment may be limited to a certain class of beneficiaries.

An interesting case was recently decided on this very issue. In *Timmons v. Ingrahm*, a decedent was survived by his spouse and two children he had adopted from a previous marriage. The surviving spouse also had four children herself from a previous marriage, none of whom was adopted by the decedent.

In his will, the decedent created two trusts, the family trust and the marital trust. The marital trust provided that upon the surviving spouse's death, the remaining principal would be "poured over" into the family trust to be distributed in accordance with its terms. The family trust provided that upon the surviving spouse's death, the trust assets were to be divided into as many equal shares as there are children of the decedent. Here, the will expressly defined the decedent's children as to include his two adopted children and the surviving spouse's four children (even though the four children were step-children and not legal descendants).

The family trust also allowed the surviving spouse, who was also a co-trustee, a limited power of appointment concerning "all or any part of the principal of this trust, free and clear of any trust to and among my then living *living descendants* in such proportions and subject to such trust and conditions as she may direct. This limited power of appointment may be exercised by said wife even to the point of completely exhausting the entire corpus trust of this trust estate."

Based on this language, the surviving spouse executed a limited power of appointment that attempted to grant all of the principal and income of the family trust to her four children to the exclusion of the decedent's two adopted children.

The two adopted children sued for breach of fiduciary duty and accounting, challenging the attempt to disinherit them. They argued that the surviving spouse could only exercise her limited power of appointment in favor of the decedent's "lineal descendants" and that the surviving spouse's four children did not qualify as such.

After the parties filed cross motions for summary judgment, the trial court ruled in favor of the co-trustees, which would have effectively disinherited the decedent's two adopted children. They appealed.

In reversing the trial court's decision, the appellate court held that the term "lineal descendants" did not apply to the surviving spouse's four children, who were stepchildren of the decedent. The appellate court also looked at the decedent's intent and did not find that he intended to give the surviving spouse the power to disinherit his two children in favor of her four children. Therefore, the appellate court ruled that the surviving spouse's exercise of the power of appointment was invalid.

Despite the ruling, this case should serve as a warning that powers of appointment pose dangers to your intent. While, generally speaking, such powers serve a useful purpose to allow an otherwise irrevocable trust the ability to "change with the times," who you give a power to and what conditions you impose should be carefully considered.

Chapter Four

Florida Specific Planning Issues

The Snowbird Tax

I guess that my workshops that describe the benefits of Florida residency, including the potential income tax savings, have made word all the way back to St. Paul, Minnesota. In response to the flock of snowbirds who maintain residences here and there, Governor Mark Dayton wants to tax the investment income of those who spend more than 60 days in the land of ten thousand lakes, even if they are no longer legal residents of the state.

I jest, of course, about my workshops, but this is potentially serious business. The new tax would hit part-time Minnesota residents' unearned income. So even if one doesn't spend the requisite six months and a day in the state to qualify as a taxable resident of Minnesota, they must file a Minnesota state income tax return if this new law gets passed.

Floridians who enjoy watching their former hometown Twins during spring training and then go back to their Minnesota lake residences to play with their grandchildren during the hot summer months would apparently be baked economically by the Governor's scheme.

Minnesota, like other northern states that impose income taxes, has watched their wealthier residents take flight to Florida, where no state income tax is imposed. This means a big difference when considering unearned revenue sources of many retirees, such as dividends, interest and capital gains.

Earned income in states that impose a state income tax (such as salaries) can't be avoided, regardless of the individual's state of residence. But most retirees don't have any more earned income. Instead, their income is derived from their savings. So this plan attempts to tax those part-year residents on the theory that they consume state services, even if they are only there the months of July and August.

How might Minnesota rein in those crafty snowbirds that have legal residences here in Florida? The State Department of Revenue has its ways. They could subpoena phone records, credit card statements, restaurant receipts and a host of other breadcrumbs that Minnesota Hansels and Gretels leave behind when they spend the summer months in their former home state.

This discussion leads me to wonder whether a snowbird tax might legally be avoided anyway. Consider, for example, a scenario where those who own summer residences in Minnesota gave the residence away to their children and simply rented them back during the months that they wish to reside there.

The law must make a distinction between a partial-year resident and a simple visitor, or else I would suppose that it would cast too wide a net or fail on constitutional grounds.

When the estate tax exemptions were lower, this strategy may not have worked well, as the gift might consume too much of the available exemption. With the increased federal gift tax exemptions available, however, it would seem possible to gift away a Minnesota residence into a trust or family partnership of some kind and then rent the residence for the term that one would like to use it.

So long as a former resident remains outside of the property tax rolls, I would guess that the state would have a hard time claiming any form of residency that would allow them to impose the income tax. But the details of Governor Dayton's plan are not yet ironed out, so tax attorneys like me will have to wait to review the fine print.

States are coming up with increasingly desperate measures to balance their budgets. Governor Dayton's tax grab includes a proposal to increase Minnesota's already high personal income tax rate to 9.85% on income above $150,000 for singles and $250,000 for married filers. This would rank Minnesota's income tax rate among the top six in the nation.

Look for other states to follow suit. These are going to be interesting times, but luckily many of the new federal tax laws are going to give estate planners leeway to give their clients options that would otherwise not be there in a more restrictive estate and gift tax environment.

Florida Homestead Peculiarities

With the deadline for declaring Florida homestead fast approaching on March 1st, many new residents are busy making their applications. There are several good reasons to do so. First, you get the property tax exemptions that save several hundred dollars off a typical annual property tax bill.

Another benefit includes the Save Our Homes Property Tax assessment cap. Once you have declared Florida homestead status, no matter the increase in the assessed value of your residence, it can only be increased 3% annually. In other words, even if your residence increases 6% over the course of a year, the amount that the taxable assessment can increase is limited to 3%. Over the course of several years, the Save Our Homes assessment cap can result in tens of thousands of dollars of property tax savings.

While it is generally a very good thing to declare Florida as your primary residence, there is an estate planning danger that you should be made aware of. My experience is that most attorneys from other states who do estate planning aren't aware of the Florida descent and devise rules. These rules govern to whom you can leave your Florida homestead in your will or trust.

Simply stated, absent a nuptial agreement that expressly waives the Florida homestead descent and devise rights, you must leave your house to your spouse. While this isn't a problem for most married couples who own a home jointly with rights of survivorship, consider the couple who have a residence here and another one in another state and who have separate wills or trusts.

In many of those situations, the attorney will suggest that the homes be split between the two trusts. In other words, the husband's trust might own the Florida residence while the wife's trust owns the other residence. The attorney would recommend this to split up the amount of assets between the two trusts in an effort to utilize both spouse's exemptions from estate tax.

But here's the issue— if your will or trust was implemented prior to 2012 (or even thereafter depending upon how your attorney chose to utilize your estate tax exemptions), when you die and your Florida home becomes part of a "testamentary trust," such as a credit shelter (commonly referred to as A/B trusts), then you have an "invalid devise" under Florida law. Even though the testamentary trust is held exclusively for the surviving spouse, it is not an outright bequest to him or her.

When you have an invalid devise, then Florida law doesn't care what your will or trust says. Your surviving spouse has a choice. He or she can elect to take a "life estate" in the residence or an undivided one-half interest in the residence. The children of the deceased spouse get the rest. This is true even if you wanted only one child to get the residence after the death of the spouse, or if you wanted some other distribution to occur. The law totally disregards what you have in your estate plan when you have an invalid devise.

This can be dangerous for the surviving spouse. He or she owns the residence with the deceased spouse's children. In second marriage situations, this can be especially troublesome.

The surviving spouse won't be able to sell the house without the children's permission, or without their signatures on the deed. They have to split the proceeds of the sale of the residence even if they do agree to sell. Further, if one of the children has a creditor problem, then that could cloud the title to the property.

Keep in mind that these issues did not arise until Florida homestead was declared. Everything about the estate plan was just fine. Nothing in the plan changed. But when the residence became Florida homestead, then all of these other issues automatically arose.

This is one of the reasons why it so vitally important to make sure that your estate plan is up to date when you change from another state's residence to becoming a Florida resident.

Don't get me wrong. The advantages of becoming a Florida resident are many and usually outweigh these homestead descent and devise problems. Florida has no state income tax. Florida doesn't impose an estate tax or an inheritance tax. There are no intangible taxes. Generally speaking, it is economically advantageous to become a Florida resident.

But when you do, just make sure that you keep your estate plan up to date. The descent and devise rules can be accounted for and even circumvented with proper planning. But if you don't adjust your estate plan and leave it in the drawer until something happens, that is when you could run into trouble.

So make sure that you declare your Florida homestead before March 1st, but at the same time, seek qualified counsel to make sure your estate plan is up to date.

So Where Are You From?

So where are you from? And if you own a residence in Florida and haven't declared Florida residency yet, why haven't you? In case you haven't heard, living here can substantially decrease your tax bill. In contrast with forty-four (44) other states, Florida doesn't impose a state income tax.

In 2014, fifteen states (CT, DE, DC, HI, IL, ME, MD, MA, MN, NJ, NY OR, RI, VT and WA) impose an estate tax, while seven states (IA, KY, MD, NE, NJ, PA and TN) levy an inheritance tax. Two states even tax gifts (CT and MN), and four states sock it to generation skipping transfers (HI, NY, MA and VT)!

By making your Florida residence your legal homestead, not only can you shed many of the taxes discussed above, you may also enjoy a property tax break due to the "Save Our Homes" property assessment cap that serves to limit each county's tax appraiser's ability to increase the assessed value of your homestead for property tax purposes.

Especially if you own a residence both here and somewhere else—and your current state imposes income, estate, inheritance or gift taxes—why would you remain a legal resident of that other state? The answer isn't necessarily that you don't spend enough time here in Florida. In fact, Florida really doesn't care how long you stay here, so long as you take the necessary actions to establish residency, which typically includes registering as a voter, obtaining a driver's license, declaring Florida homestead and disassociating yourself from the residency of your former state.

And that's where most of the issues arise. It's really not so much whether you can establish Florida residency under Florida law—

that's the easy part—it's really all about whether you can successfully disassociate yourself under the statutory provisions of the state from which you formerly legally resided.

One important note of which everyone should be aware: if you have "source income" that is earned in another state, then that income will likely continue to be taxed in that state, regardless of your residence. A classic example of source income is that income earned in your employment or business activity in that state. Another example would be rental income from real estate located in that state.

In contrast, you may save considerable tax sums from interest, dividend, capital gains, IRA, 401(k) and similar accounts should you successfully break from your former state of residence. Breaking from that state doesn't necessarily mean that you should sell your residence there. You just need to be aware of the rules that each state has created to determine who they consider a resident for tax purposes.

New York, New Jersey and Pennsylvania are examples of states that consider an individual a resident if that person spends more than 183 days in the state. They may also consider where your spouse and minor children spend a considerable amount of time when deciding whether you fit under their taxing umbrella. Minnesota recently considered some of the most draconian residency laws that beg to be challenged in court. By and large, the individual states don't want to lose tax revenue—especially to their residents who own homes in tax-friendly Florida—and they are looking for any and all means available to retain their citizens as state taxpayers.

I'm often asked how the states determine how many days you're actually there. With today's technology, there's a number of means available. If a former resident has filed his last state income tax return, and the state decides to audit whether he has established residency elsewhere, it may decide to subpoena credit card, cell phone records or even flight receipts.

To remove yourself as a taxpayer from a northern state, you may want to consider a two-step process. The first step is to take the necessary actions to become a resident of Florida, with the second step including taking steps to abandon your former legal residence. When becoming a Florida resident, in addition to declaring homestead, obtaining a voters registration and driver's license, one should consider changing your address for passports, Medicare, Social Security and tax returns, as well as keeping a log of your travel.

When abandoning the old state residence, as long as you don't have any "source income" in that state, filing a final state income tax return appropriately marked "FINAL" at the top of the return would be appropriate. If there is such a thing as a homestead declaration in your other state, you should renounce that declaration (which is also a Florida requirement). You would want to change your primary physician to Florida and change your legal documents, among other things.

If you decide to join those of us who agree that Florida is a great state in which to reside, you will have plenty of company. Florida recently overtook New York as the third largest state by population, behind only California and Texas. We welcome nearly 1,000 new residents every day.

So I ask again, if you own a residence here but are legally domiciled in a state that imposes its own income tax, estate tax, inheritance tax and/or gift tax in addition to what you pay the federal government, why aren't you already one of us?

Top Reasons Minnesotans Become Florida Residents

You might think that being the warm weather spring training home for the Minnesota Twins, with stars Delmon Young and Joe Mauer, would lure cold Minnesotans into becoming Southwest Florida residents. But there's another famous Minnesotan who is likely to cause a mass exodus from the Land of 10,000 Lakes to the Sunshine State.

Who could that be? The answer is Governor Mark Dayton, who proposed a plan that would make his state's wealthiest residents among the nations highest taxed, while attempting to erase almost half of the state's $6.2 billion deficit.

The Governor's plan includes a new 10.95% income tax rate, a 3% temporary income surtax on people with taxable incomes over $500,000 and a new property tax on million-dollar homes. The taxes are part of a two-year $37 billion budget proposal that includes cuts for state-subsidized health care and nursing homes and more money for schools. Minnesota State House Speaker Kurt Zellers called the plan "feeble and pathetic," saying that it would give Minnesota the nation's highest tax rate.

That would be quite an accomplishment according to a Wall Street Journal editorial. In it, the Journal reported that New Jersey currently harbors the highest tax rates in the nation, including a top marginal combined federal and state death tax rate above 54%! Maryland, New York, Delaware, Illinois, Indiana, Ohio, Massachusetts, Pennsylvania and a host of other states have top marginal combined death tax rates above 44%.

So if you think that the death tax is no more—given the law passed at the end of 2010—think again. Because it's not just about federal taxes. Ever-hungry state revenue departments are looking for ways to bridge their ever-widening budget gaps. As the Great Recession has trimmed state tax revenue, state legislative bodies are looking for ways to collect more taxes, and increasingly are turning to those who may still have a buck or two—the wealthy.

And wealthy dead people are much easier to tax than are folks who still vote and write letters to the editor.

In contrast, Florida remains a tax haven. Florida does not have a state income tax, and the only way that one could ever be levied is if the voters amend the Florida Constitution to make it so. There are no more intangible taxes, as those were abolished a few years ago. Florida doesn't tax the deceased either, as there aren't any estate or inheritance taxes. Finally, claiming a homestead exemption on your Florida residence serves to reduce your property taxes and cap the increase in assessment of your homestead's value. (You can't claim a Florida homestead exemption if you already claim one somewhere else.)

For those retirees who split their residence between Florida and a northern state, it usually makes sense to consider Florida as the state of primary residence. While income that is earned in the northern state is likely to remain taxable in that state, unearned income (interest and dividends), inheritance and other assets could avoid an ever-increasing tax burden by claiming Florida residency.

How does one change residence? It's a facts and circumstance determination—and each state enforces different rules. Florida law simply requires intent to become and remain a Florida resident. But it's not Florida law that transplants should be concerned about; rather, it's the law of the state of their former residence.

Generally speaking, one would want to spend at least half of the year in Florida, and become registered to vote and licensed to drive here, among other things. If you would like a complete laundry list, go to my firm's website www.sbshlaw.com and click on "New Florida Residents Click Here" to watch a video and read a guide on Florida residency and estate planning. Alternatively, you can call my office and we'll be glad to send you the free guide and DVD.

With the likes of Governor Dayton occupying the Governor's mansion in the frigid north, it almost doesn't make any sense not to consider a change of residence. It might mean thousands of dollars of savings for you and your family.

The Most Expensive Fishing License Ever

As many of you head to your northern residence for the summer I thought that I'd leave you with an interesting story and a word of caution.

Several years ago I assisted a client to become a Florida resident and along with that we updated his estate plan. He was thrilled to avoid state income taxes and future state death taxes from his northern state of residence, where he continued to own a fishing cabin. Shortly after finishing his estate plan he headed north to his lake front cabin for the summer.

Sadly, he never made it back to Florida, as he suffered a heart attack and died. While assisting his family to administer the estate and trust, we received a claim from the northern state's department of revenue for state death taxes. I had anticipated a claim for taxes associated with the value of his cabin, because even if you are a Florida resident, if you own real property in a northern state that imposes a state death tax there might be tax on the value of that property.

Much to our surprise, however, the state death tax imposed was calculated on his entire estate, including his investments and other assets.

I objected to the amount of the tax, writing a letter to the state's department of revenue, explaining that the man had declared Florida residency. I showed evidence indicating that he took all of the necessary steps, including spending more time in Florida, registering to vote in Florida, declaring his Florida house as his primary homestead residence, getting a Florida driver's license and updating his estate planning documents to Florida law.

The response from the northern state department of revenue rolled off my fax machine. (This was back in the day when faxes were popular and everything wasn't attached to emails.) What they sent to me was a local fishing license that my client purchased at the general store near his lake residence a few weeks before his death. There were two boxes on that license to check. The first box said "In State Resident" with a fee of $15, and the other box said "Nonresident" with a fee of $25. The "In State Resident" box had been checked, and there was what appeared to be my client's signature on the appropriate line of the license.

That ten dollars savings resulted in the northern state declaring him an "in state resident" for tax purposes. They imposed state income taxes as well as death taxes on his estate.

I argued that by checking the "In State Resident" box my client hadn't declared his residency to the northern state, but instead obviously felt that since he owned a residence in that state (and presumably paid property taxes there), he would think that he would be entitled to pay the lower fishing license fee. In other words, I argued, "In-State Resident" doesn't necessarily mean primary residence—it could refer to a secondary residence.

The state department of revenue, obviously hungry for money, stuck to its guns. We consulted local counsel, continuing to negotiate the matter.

Eventually the family decided to settle, paying less than half of the original amount of tax levied. To fight further and try to get the tax eliminated would have required hiring litigation counsel in that state, which would have been very expensive. So the $10 savings on the fishing license cost the estate thousands of dollars.

The moral of the story is to be careful if you are a dual resident. Make sure that you don't do anything that might give your other state reason to tax you or your estate.

A good example of this is your estate planning documents themselves. Sometimes clients will ask me to forward documents to them while they are up north for signing. I usually believe that this is a bad idea. Aside from the fact that the witness and notary seals will show the northern state (rather than Florida) as the place that the documents were signed, sometimes they are not even signed properly and in accordance with Florida law.

The "self proof" clause at the end of the document requires, for example, that the witnesses sign in the presence of the testator (the person signing the will or trust) and that the testator sign in their presence. There is a definite order to the signing. If the formal legal requirements aren't met, then there is the chance that the document isn't signed correctly, resulting in problems later.

So as you head up north to escape the hot and humid Florida summer, be careful what you sign and how you sign things.

And enjoy the fishing.

Nose Bowl

When I was a freshman at the University of Florida, the pledges of my fraternity—Tau Epsilon Phi (TEP)—traditionally had an annual flag football game against the pledges of Pi Lambda Phi, called "Nose Bowl." The name of the game was in reference to the fact that both fraternities were predominantly Jewish, and although it would seem politically incorrect, the name had been around for decades and no one seemed to care.

In any event, winning the game was a big deal because the bragging rights for each pledge class hinged on whether they were victorious against its most hated rival. TEP's fall 1981 pledge class (the year before mine) won the game 24-0, so there was a lot for my pledge class to live up to. If your pledge class won the game you were likely to be inducted as brothers into the fraternity before Thanksgiving break. If your class didn't win, then your pledge class would often have to wait until just before finals before induction would occur.

This was a big deal since you didn't want your "hell week" (the week before induction when most of the crazier hazing took place) to interfere with studying for finals.

In the weeks leading up to the big game, the brothers made us pledges practice at all hours of the day and night. We were told to do wind sprints, push-ups, football drills—you name it. I always thought the practice for the big game was a veiled way to haze us pledges all semester anyway.

As the game day approached we discovered that Pi Lam had invited three very athletic looking African-American students into its pledge class. This was highly unusual since there aren't a whole lot of African-American Jews—Sammy Davis Jr. being one notable exception, although I'm not sure anyone would want him on their flag football squad. As it turned out, these particular African-American students had once played quarterback and wide receiver at prestigious high school football programs. We rightly felt that Pi-Lam had some ringers on their squad.

The president of our fraternity paid a visit to Pi-Lam's president to sort things out. There wasn't much we could do since all campus fraternities were free to invite whomever they wanted into their pledge classes without regard to race or religion. Despite our belief that they were ringers, there was nothing that would compromise their eligibility to play.

Which leads me to this estate planning topic, and that is who, in your will under Florida law, is eligible to serve as your personal representative (executor). You may be surprised to learn that under the law you cannot choose anyone that you want to be your personal representative. They must be eligible as defined by our laws. So who is qualified under the law to serve as your personal representative?

The answer is fairly simple and straightforward. Any person who is your spouse, child, adopted child, parent, brother, sister, uncle, aunt, niece of nephew or someone related by lineal consanguinity to such person, or a spouse of any such person. So basically if they are closely related to you by blood or marriage, then they will likely qualify to serve as your personal representative. It doesn't matter if they live here in Florida or in Timbuktu. They are eligible.

What about a good friend? Does a good friend qualify to serve as your personal representative? The answer is "yes," provided they reside in the state of Florida. If their primary residence is elsewhere then they won't qualify.

So your niece's husband who lives in Sri Lanka and whom you haven't seen or heard from in twenty years qualifies as your personal representative, but your best friend who knows everything about you, owns a home here in Florida but maintains her primary residence in Indiana does not qualify. Not surprise-ingly, someone who would otherwise qualify but who is a convicted felon, or who is still a minor won't qualify either.

What about a corporation? Would a Florida corporation qualify to serve as your personal representative? In most cases the answer is "No" because the corporation must have "trust powers" under Florida law to serve. Banks and trust companies will therefore qualify.

What if you named The First Community Bank & Trust as your personal representative but Mega National Bank later bought it? Do you have a named personal representative if you never changed your will and there is no more First Community Bank & Trust? The law says that in such a scenario, the Mega National Bank will become your personal representative, since they are the successor in interest to the First Community Bank & Trust.

What about charitable corporations and churches? Can they serve as your personal representative? In most cases the answer is no, they will not qualify because they don't have trust powers under Florida law. So you can't name your church to serve as your personal representative, even if you are leaving all of your assets to the church. But you can name your pastor, who resides here in Florida.

If you have a question about whom or what might be eligible to serve under your will, you should consult with your estate planning attorney.

As for the Nose Bowl game, even though Pi-Lam had their ringers in place, my pledge class won the game 26-0! We were soon thereafter inducted as brothers into the fraternity, and I did well on my finals that semester.

Hell week wasn't that bad either. As for the eligible ringers who failed to help Pi-Lam win, I later heard they were blackballed and never made it into the fraternity. Being eligible to play Nose Bowl apparently wasn't enough!

Beware When You Rent Out Your Florida Homestead

Florida homestead poses some difficult challenges from an estate planning perspective. Most people who move to Florida, who already have their will or trust prepared, ask their northern attorney if their estate plan is up to snuff for Florida law. Many times the attorney will tell them that it's just fine and dandy for Florida.

Don't believe them, particularly if you own Florida homestead.

The reason is that when you consider Florida to be your primary residence, your Florida home becomes your "homestead," whether or not you actually file a homestead application.

Filing such an application is advantageous, as there are exemptions available that reduce your property taxes, and you also qualify your residence under the "Save Our Homes" tax assessment cap, which limits the increase of your homestead's assessed value to only three percent per year, even if the value increases at a much faster rate.

Florida homestead, however, does not fit into any neat "estate planning box," as I have written about previously. If your will or trust has the standard credit-shelter trust/marital trust provisions, chances are that the disposition of your home is an "invalid devise" that can create estate planning havoc. If you would like a copy of my column on this issue just email me, and I'll send it along.

When you claim Florida homestead, you cannot have any other homestead claimed for any other residence. If you have a "homestead" in a northern state, for example, you must disavow the homestead status and any special exemptions that you receive in that state. Claiming two homesteads at once poses criminal penalties that you don't want to defend against.

Moreover, you cannot rent your homestead out and still claim homestead status. There has been some confusion on this issue, and I thought that it would be important to address it here since so many island properties are in the rental market.

Governor Scott signed into law Senate Bill 342 - Rental of Homestead Property, and it took effect on July 1, 2013. The new law amends Florida Statute § 196.061.

Under the old statute, enacted in 1996, a homeowner's rental of "all or substantially all" of his or her homesteaded property meant that he or she had "abandoned" the homestead and therefore lost the ad valorem tax protection, as well as the "Save Our Homes" property tax assessment cap.

The caveat to the law was that a homeowner turning his homestead property into such a rental after the first day of a given calendar year would not lose the homestead exemption for that calendar year, as long as the property had not also been rented the previous calendar year.

The new law clarifies the statute and limits the exception. Now, a property owner who rents out his or her homestead for more than 30 days per year for two consecutive years will lose the homestead exemption tax benefits on that property.

So if you rent out your homestead for more than 30 days per year for two consecutive years, you actually have an affirmative duty to notify the Property Tax Appraiser's Office that your home no longer qualifies for homestead status. Failure to do so can also result in criminal penalties.

If you rent your homestead property to third parties, you would want to perform a quick calculation to determine if the after-tax value of the rental income exceeds the property tax breaks that you achieve under the Florida homestead status. You would also want to determine if the creditor protection that Florida homestead status provides is valuable to you or not. You may know that the equity in your home is protected from almost all of your creditors (except those who have a mortgage or similar encumbrance on the property itself).

Finally, if you rent out your homestead property, and if you do disavow homestead status, you would want your estate plan to be adjusted to reflect the new status of ownership.

Can A Prenuptial Agreement Serve As A Will Substitute?

Brenda and Eddie decided to marry; each had a prior marriage that ended in divorce, and each had children from those prior marriages. Brenda and Eddie met and lived in the Chicago suburbs at the time of their marriage. After fifteen blissfully wedded years, both retired from their respective jobs to move to Florida. Since they both dreamed of spending time boating, they bought a beautiful property with Gulf access. Brenda and Eddie both contributed an equal (and substantial) amount of money to purchase the home.

Brenda had created a will before her marriage to Eddie that left everything to her two children. Likewise, Eddie's will was created before his marriage to Brenda and left everything to his three children. Both Brenda and Eddie desired to leave their respective estates to their children rather than to each other. Brenda and Eddie verbally agreed to this arrangement. They had attorneys draft a brief prenuptial agreement, but that agreement only waived their respective rights to alimony in the event that they divorced.

On the advice of their Illinois attorneys, when they bought the house in Florida they titled it as "tenants in common" rather than as "husband and wife" or "joint with rights of survivorship." Their attorney explained that should one of them die, by titling the house as "Tenants in Common," upon one of their deaths the equity of that portion of the home would follow to each of Brenda's and Eddie's respective families.

Since Brenda's will already left everything to her children, and Eddie's will did the same for his, neither party thought that it was necessary to update their wills after their marriage. They didn't intend to leave anything to each other, and their wills already left the assets to their respective children, so why spend money on creating new legal documents?

Big mistake.

When Brenda died her children discovered that under most state laws, including Florida's, there is a presumption that one spouse would have left at least a portion of his or her estate to the other if the Last Will and Testament was signed before the marriage and a new one wasn't created after the marriage. Since Brenda's will was signed before her marriage to Eddie, and Brenda never signed a new will after the marriage but before her death, Florida law presumes that had Brenda got around to making a new will, then she would have included Eddie.

The Florida attorney told Brenda's children that Eddie could claim an "intestate share" of Brenda's estate. "Intestate" refers to a condition where one dies without a will. Florida law provides that a spouse can claim fifty percent (50%) of the decedent spouse's estate as an "intestate share" when the decedent spouse has children. So in this case, up to fifty percent of Brenda's estate was exposed to a claim.

When the children pointed out that Brenda and Eddie had signed a prenuptial agreement, the attorney reviewed the agreement to determine if each party specifically waived their rights to each other's estates. In this case, the prenuptial agreement did not address spousal rights in the event of death.

The attorney explained that even if Brenda had created a new will after their marriage that excluded Eddie, without an agreement waiving each other's rights to each other's estates, Eddie could still claim a thirty percent (30%) spousal elective share. In other words, even if the presumption that Brenda would have included Eddie if only she had gotten around to creating a new will after their marriage is defeated (in that she did create a will but still excluded him), absent a nuptial agreement specifically waiving rights to the estate, Eddie could still claim up to thirty percent of Brenda's estate.

Even if Eddie lived up to his verbal agreement not to lay claim to any portion of Brenda's estate, there was nothing that would prevent one of his children, who held his durable power of attorney, from claiming it on his behalf. While this may seem far-fetched, if Eddie became incompetent there would be a real question as to whether someone holding a power of attorney had a fiduciary duty to Eddie to lay claim to his share of Brenda's estate. This would be even that much more problematic if Eddie never told the power holder of his intent and verbal agreement with Brenda.

To make matters even more complicated, under Florida's constitutional and statutory laws, unless the Florida spousal homestead rights are specifically waived in a prenuptial agreement, then the surviving spouse is entitled to a "life estate" in the decedent spouse's interest in the home.

While Brenda died believing that her children would be immediately entitled to half of the value of the Florida home that she helped purchase, that wasn't really the case. Eddie received a life estate in Brenda's interest in the home. While this might have been what Brenda and Eddie envisioned, problems can arise with this arrangement. Eddie can't sell the home without the consent of Brenda's children, and they can't sell the home without his signature.

Because Brenda's children had a "vested" interest in the home, if one of the children had a creditor issue, that could affect the title to the home and make it difficult to sell without satisfying the creditor.

When Eddie got sick and had to go into a nursing home, fights ensued between Brenda's family and Eddie's family over how much the home was worth and how much they should sell it for.

All of these problems could have been avoided through a carefully drawn up estate plan—not only after Brenda and Eddie's marriage, but also through an update upon their move to Florida.

Double Trouble

I recently conducted a very well attended estate planning workshop at the Sanibel Community House, and there were a lot of good questions posed during the workshop—a couple of which I thought that I'd review here.

One question covered my review of the concept of probate and revocable living trusts. I reminded everyone that unless one actually transfers their brokerage and bank accounts as well as their real estate into the trust, those assets would be subject to the probate process at death.

Listing those assets on a schedule at the end of the trust isn't sufficient to transfer them, contrary to what some may believe. You actually have to change the title to the accounts and deeds to the properties. In order for my brokerage account to be properly owned by my trust, it cannot be titled in the name of "Craig Hersch" but rather must read "Craig Hersch, Trustee for the Craig Hersch Trust dated January 15, 2000."

An attendee then posed the question about owning property in different states. Suppose that one owns a residence here in Florida as well as a residence in Ohio. What happens if those properties are not transferred into one's revocable living trust?

Generally speaking, you have the potential for double trouble. By that I mean when one owns property in different states there's likely going to be two probate administrations. One is called the "domiciliary administration" that occurs in the state in which you reside, and an "ancillary administration" in the other state that you own property. This may require two different attorneys, one in each jurisdiction, which obviously increases the costs of the administration.

I also reviewed one of the major problems that I see when individuals who already have revocable living trusts make Florida their primary residence. This has to do with the Florida homestead descent and devise rules—which govern who you can leave your homestead to.

Under Florida law, absent a nuptial agreement that specifically waives the Florida homestead rules, if you are married you must leave your primary Florida residence to your spouse. If you fail to do so, then you have an invalid devise.

Many who bought their home prior to becoming Florida residents may have placed their home into either husband's or wife's trust in order to balance out the value of each trust. This was common before portability came into effect under the tax law, to maximize the use of each spouse's estate tax exemptions.

Upon becoming Florida residents, however, even with no further action on anyone's part, the spouse who owns the Florida residence is likely to have an "invalid devise" under Florida law because their revocable trust usually will at death create a "credit shelter" or "bypass" trust benefitting the surviving spouse in order to consume the decedent spouse's estate tax exemption.

Even though the credit shelter trust benefits the surviving spouse, this is an invalid devise under Florida law, as it is not an outright disposition to the surviving spouse. The result of the invalid devise is that the decedent's will and/or trust is ignored. The surviving spouse has an option of receiving a life estate or a one-half interest in the homestead residence, with the decedent spouse's children receiving a vested remainder or one-half interest.

This can create huge problems. First, if one of the children is going through a divorce or has a creditor problem, this may cloud the title to the home. Further, the surviving spouse now needs the consent of all of the owners to sell the home, including agreeing to the sales price—which proceeds now must be shared with all owners. Moreover, despite what the trust says, even if in a blended family all of the children were to one day share in the ownership of the home, only the decedent spouse's children receive the benefits in my example. There are many more problems, including the possible loss of a portion of the homestead exemption among other things.

There are ways to accomplish the goal of using the value of the residence against the estate tax exemptions, but the standard credit shelter/marital trust formula generally won't do it.

The long and short of it is to avoid these problems when changing residence from a northern state to Florida, your estate plan should be reviewed and adjusted. This advice often contrasts with that of your northern attorney, who may believe that a simple amendment adjusting the applicable law of the trust to Florida is enough. It is not. This Florida homestead residence issue is quite ubiquitous and can be a big problem.

Chapter Five

Common Cents Estate Planning

Don't 'Should' On Me

My high school basketball coach used to warn us, "Don't 'should' on me."

He never wanted to hear that we should have run more wind sprints so that we weren't gassed at the end of games, that we should have practiced more free throws when we were tired so that we would be game ready for those inevitable moments as time expired, or that we should have done something more to prepare for our next opponent.

"IF YOU SHOULD ON ME," he would bark, "then I'm gonna ignore your whiny self and tell you that it's your own damn fault!"

I was reminded of my coach as I sat in a room at Lee Memorial reviewing documents with someone who had literally waited until the last minute to put their affairs in order. It's sad, really, and adds unnecessary strain to an already stressful situation. This person was visibly distraught that he had to make several important decisions as he lay in his hospital bed with tubes coming from all parts of his body and medical devices beeping in sync with his breaths and heartbeat.

I fully understand that most people don't want to deal with their wills, durable powers of attorney and health care directives. It's definitely no fun thinking about one's own health issues, nonetheless one's own demise. So it's easy to put these sorts of things off for later.

After all, humans aren't programmed to worry about such things. If we constantly focused on our own death, we might not find much point to living. Instead, we tend to focus on living in the moment, which psychologists tell us is the happiest and best way to conduct our lives.

But as responsible adults, most of us would like to give our loved ones the tools to help us if we should become infirm. We want our loved ones to be able to communicate with our doctors and caretakers. Without proper health care directives, our medical care providers and hospitals may not be able to legally discuss our condition with those that we trust to help make decisions for us because of the HIPPA law.

We want to empower those we trust to take care of our financial affairs if we should become vulnerable or unable to take care of them ourselves. Waiting too long to put someone in place with legal documents to take care of these matters puts our financial future at risk, which could lead to living out our lives in less than favorable conditions because poor financial decisions were made either by us, through our own infirmity, or by a loved one who wasn't properly instructed.

Finally, when we depart this world we want to leave our affairs as neat, tidy, organized and efficient as possible. We don't want any controversy over our intent to provide for spouse, children or other loved ones, and we don't want Uncle Sam to take any more out of our pockets than what is absolutely necessary.

But too many of us don't do the planning. It's estimated that less than 25% of American adults have their legal affairs in order. That means most of us haven't put a plan into place, or if we have one, it is terribly out of date.

You don't want to be the one who says, "I really should take care of that one day."

"I should have read through the draft documents that the attorney sent to me months ago."

"I really should have thought about those advance estate planning techniques before I got sick and it became an emergency."

Bad decisions are often made when you don't give yourself the time to consider all of your options. And don't fall into the trap of thinking that your affairs are simple, because they're often not as straightforward as you might think. Anyone who has any degree of net worth probably has a variety of different issues that should be properly addressed to put a good estate plan in order.

Because in the end, you don't want to "should" on those you care about most.

The Importance Of Teamwork

On a recent Sunday I rode 100 km (62.5 miles) in the Royal Palm Classic, a local bicycle tour starting in Buckingham Park that took the participants through North Fort Myers, Alva, Lehigh Acres and Gateway before returning to Buckingham. Of the 130 riders who did this particular loop, I finished fourth, averaging 21 mph. Not too bad for a 47 year old desk jockey!

But it wasn't without a lot of teamwork.

For those of you who follow bike racing, you know that at the beginning of a race a "peloton" forms, which is a large pack of bicyclists. It's easier to go fast when you are in the middle or in the back of a peloton, because wind resistance is a bicyclist's chief nemesis. Those in the front of the peloton "pull" the rest of the riders, meaning that they are acting as a windbreak, making it much easier for those behind them.

Cycling protocol demands that everyone take a turn at the front, so cyclists are constantly rotating from the front to back and then to front again. This way, those at the front are fresh, and those in the back are recovering from their pull. This allows the whole group to go faster over the course of many miles. Those that fail to take their turn at the front are called "wheel hogs." The pack will do their best to "drop" a wheel hog—put distance between the peloton and wheel hogs so they can't benefit from everyone else's work.

At some point during the race a few cyclists will break away from the peloton in an attempt to win. This happened that Sunday, when at the 40-mile mark, I saw one guy take off and then another guy sprint out ahead of the pack, trying to put some distance between themselves and the lead peloton. Feeling strong on Sunday, I took off after them, as did another fellow.

The four of us formed our own mini-group, rotating from front to back and then back up to the front again. Since there were only four of us we had to work harder since we didn't have as many bodies to break against the wind, yet we were able to stay out ahead of the peloton and win the race. If there were only one or two of us, that might not have been possible, since the wind resistance (that Sunday was a wind and rain-filled day) would have eventually worn us down over the last 22 miles. We might have been "reeled back in" as it is said.

The lessons of the peloton also apply to your estate, tax and financial planning. I've had prospective clients visit with me who have tried to do everything themselves. They did their own will online, they manage their own investments and they file their own tax return. They are a team of one.

This might work out for a while, but like the lone breakaway from the peloton, eventually the wind resistance of life will wear them down. An illness or disability leaves them vulnerable, since they are the only ones who know what they've done over the years. There is no CPA who knows about potential deductions, because they've never enlisted one. The family doesn't particularly know or understand the team of one's investment strategy, since it was never articulated to anyone else. They might not even know where all of the assets are.

When the team of one becomes disabled or dies, there is no estate attorney to help the family deal with a disability crisis, or to transition the management of financial affairs to another trusted one, or simply to guide the family during the administration of the estate in the proper and legal form. Worse, if there's a legal or tax mistake in the plan, there is no one there to discover it—until it's too late.

As it turns out, I was the weakest of the four riders that Sunday. On our final sprint to the finish I came in fourth. But because of our teamwork over the last 22 miles, I was still way out ahead (20 minutes as it turns out) from the lead peloton that came in after the four of us.

The same holds true for those that enlist the support of experts in finance, tax and law. They'll pay a price for the teamwork, but because those that are helping are so much stronger in their respective fields, the individual who builds a team of very good experts around him should find himself well ahead of the pack.

Documenting Your Intent

Most of the time our wills and trusts aren't controversial, or at least we don't think that they are. We might leave amounts either outright or in trust for our surviving spouse, and then when we're both gone it all goes equally to our children.

But sometimes it isn't so straightforward. We might be in a second marriage situation. In that case, we could decide to leave amounts in trust for our surviving spouse and then when he or she dies the remainder of what is left is destined to be distributed to our children. But every dollar that the surviving spouse spends is one less dollar that our children will one day inherit. Because he or she has only a step-relationship to our biological children, things could get a little testy when it comes to our money and assets.

Another instance is where we want to disinherit a child or other loved one. Perhaps the child has had alcohol or drug dependency problems that leave us afraid that when we die the child will squander their inheritance on booze or illegal substances. Or perhaps there has been a dispute in the family that has become irreparable. You'd rather leave the inheritance to the ones that you share a close relationship with, or skip the child entirely in favor of the grandchildren.

When we have more delicate interpersonal relationships that are going to affect our estate planning, it is imperative that we get the intent documented. It might be written inside of the will or trust itself, including the reasoning behind the bequests or lack of bequests. Or, sometimes it will make sense to write a separate letter explaining why we are choosing to do what we do.

Absent a clear narrative of our intent, others might try to fill in the gaps after our deaths as to why we did what we did. They could claim that we weren't in our right mind when we left such large amounts to our second spouse, or wrote the child out of the document.

Another popular challenge to a will or trust is the claim of undue influence. The complaining party could file a court action declaring that absent the influence of a party who otherwise benefited from our action, then we wouldn't have written the will or trust the way that we did.

Aside from worrying about challenges to the legal documents themselves, we have to guard against challenges to the way that our wills or trusts are administered following our passing. Allow me to explain by example.

Suppose that Bob leaves amounts in trust for his second wife, Mary. Mary is to receive the income from the trust for the remainder of her life, and she can take principal from the trust if the income is insufficient for her health, maintenance and support.

Suppose that Mary needs a new car. She withdraws amounts from the trust to pay for it. What if one of Bob's children challenges the withdrawal? The child says that Mary could have bought a less expensive model or even a used car. This would have preserved more of the trust for the children to inherit once Mary dies. What happens now?

Imagine that Bob included language in his trust that says this: "During Mary's lifetime, Mary shall be the primary beneficiary and her needs should be first considered, notwithstanding the effect that it may have on the inheritance of my children." Doesn't that kind of language strengthen Mary's position?

Now instead, let's add a scenario where Mary has plenty of her own assets. Bob still wants the trust to pay her income, but she should only invade the principal if she doesn't have sufficient assets of her own. Now Bob's trust reads: "During Mary's lifetime, the Trustee shall pay Mary the income from my trust. The trustee may also pay Mary from the principal of my trust for her health, maintenance and support, but in so doing the Trustee shall first consider Mary's other assets, income and resources available to her for such purposes."

Do you see how the two different provisions give all of the parties more clear direction on what Bob wants the trust to pay for and what Bob doesn't want the trust to pay for? You also see how each one of the provisions gives more specific direction than a generic clause that says: "Pay Mary the income and principal that she needs for her health, maintenance and support."

Statements of intent go a long way to not only thwarting a challenge to your estate planning documents in their creation, but also in providing clear direction to your loved ones which should result in warding off conflict between them.

Is Your Financial Planner Giving You Bad Legal Advice?

Most clients have more interaction with their financial advisors than they do with their estate planning attorneys. So it's not uncommon for a client to ask their financial advisor an estate planning question that is more legal in nature than it is financial. The financial advisor might feel comfortable giving a quick answer, but hopefully, he or she will refer the client to ask that same question to their attorney, or ask the attorney for them.

The problem is when they don't.

As an example, a client called me not too long ago wanting to update his estate plan. They hadn't been into the office in over ten years. The client and his wife had wills but no revocable trust. The client was convinced that all he needed to do was to update his will. When I reviewed the file I asked my legal assistant to send the client an organizer since I didn't have their balance sheet information.

When she did this the client told my assistant that he didn't need to fill out my organizer or disclose his financial assets. "My financial advisor told me that unless I have more than $3.5 million then I don't need a trust, so I don't want to disclose that information," he said.

Whether or not that is what the financial advisor said, that's bad advice. First of all, the $3.5 million figure has nothing to do with anything. The estate tax exemption today is roughly $5.25 million. So if the gentlemen thought that a trust isn't necessary unless you have a taxable estate, he is mistaken both as to the amount that constitutes a taxable estate as well as to the correlation as to whether having a taxable estate or not is relevant to the usefulness of a trust in his estate plan.

Whether or not you have a taxable estate is unrelated to whether a revocable trust may benefit you. One could have a net worth exceeding $10 million yet not need a revocable trust. Why? This is because a trust won't benefit you if most of your net worth is in life insurance, annuities and IRA accounts that name a beneficiary.

On the other hand, assuming that your net worth is less than $1 million you still might benefit from a trust. Consider an individual who owns residences in two different states (which coincidentally, the client in question did). For that individual, a trust might be extremely beneficial, as it would help to avoid the probate process in two states.

Anyone who owns real property in two different states at the time of his death is likely to have both a domiciliary administration in his primary state of residence, and what is known as an "ancillary" probate administration in the other state(s) in which he owns property.

The cost of two sets of lawyers in two different states is likely to be greater than the cost it would take to establish a trust inside of one's estate plan. So the financial advisor in this particular instance, who told his client that he doesn't need a trust because his estate is worth less than $3.5 million, really gave poor legal advice.

It's hard for a layman to know who to rely on when seeking estate planning advice. When should you consult your lawyer as opposed to your CPA and/or financial advisor? Sometimes the lines are blurred between their respective areas of expertise.

Generally speaking, I suggest that the financial advisor should be consulted on the issues surrounding your investments, generating income, savings, growth and such other related matters. Investment advisors may also know how to minimize taxes through various investment strategies.

But when it comes to creating the legal structure that holds those investments, I suggest consulting a qualified estate planning attorney. It's even a good idea to get your attorney and financial advisor in the room at the same time when discussing estate, financial and tax issues, since together, they can give a client a better view of the issues and potential solutions than either could individually.

Finally, I don't want to leave you with the impression that all financial planners try to give advice beyond the scope of their expertise. Most of the ones that I've dealt with are good at working as a part of a team.

The point that I'm trying to make here is to be careful when seeking advice that might be beyond the scope of what that particular advisor is credentialed to give.

Liquidity As An Estate Planning Issue

Most of us need a certain amount of money to pay our everyday bills. People who are in the workforce usually rely on their paychecks, and they try to keep a little extra on hand for emergencies. Financial professionals refer to the "extra" amounts on hand, such as savings or investments that can readily be turned into cash, as "liquid" investments. Retirees generally rely on their investments to earn interest and dividends for their income, and they also have assets that they might liquidate in an emergency.

But what happens when you die? Does the need for liquid assets remain? It certainly does.

For those of us that are married, liquidity is needed for our surviving spouse. Liquidity might also be necessary for others that rely on you for support, such as children, grandchildren, or in some cases, one's parents.

Perhaps you own a family business that might find itself in a cash crunch if you should become incapacitated or die. The business may need liquidity to keep employees around and not look for other employment, or to pay for a replacement key employee.

Liquidity is necessary for those that are highly leveraged and have large loans, such as mortgages, car payments, or other investment loans. In these instances it is very important to have liquid assets available to keep up with the obligations under the notes, so that loved ones aren't burdened with major decisions as to what assets might need to be sold to keep the notes afloat.

If you have an estate that is taxable, hopefully, you have enough liquid assets to pay any estate or inheritance taxes that might be due. If you have a large retirement account, your estate may also need liquidity so that the retirement account balances don't have to be withdrawn earlier than what otherwise may be necessary. If retirement account amounts are necessary to pay funeral expenses or estate taxes, for example, extra amounts have to be withdrawn just to cover the income taxes imposed on the retirement account withdrawal. It can become a vicious circle.

Investors in real estate should beware of liquidity problems, especially during these times of low market value for real estate. Several years ago, before the market collapse, I had a client who was heavily invested in real estate. When he died, the estate was forced to sell many parcels just to pay estate taxes and other administrative expenses. The problem was, real estate takes a while to market, contract and close. Today that's an even bigger problem. You don't want your loved ones to be in a position where they have to "fire sale" assets in these situations.

One answer to liquidity problems is to purchase a life insurance policy within an irrevocable life insurance trust. The life insurance trust beneficiaries should mirror those in your other documents, so that the money paid on the insurance claim can be used for those taxes and expenses that would normally have to be borne by the estate and its beneficiaries.

There are other solutions available for those that feel they may have a liquidity problem. This is an issue that is not often addressed. If you believe that you might have a liquidity issue in your estate, ask your attorney and financial advisor what steps are right for you.

When To Throw It Away

My father-in-law, Ronald, is a pack rat. He and my mother-in-law can't park their cars in the garage of their condominium because of all his stuff cluttering it up. There are old transistor radios, televisions (the black and white variety), kitchen appliances and a host of other things that you couldn't sell on eBay if you tried.

"What's this?" I asked picking up a large plastic bottle off a folding table overflowing with all sorts of junk.

"Vitamins!" Ronald replied, "I got those on sale at Eckerd's!"

"Eckerd's hasn't been around in how many years?!" I asked, examining the faded label on the old bottle. "These expired in 1994! Why don't you throw them away?" I said tossing them into the garbage can. From the look on my father-in-law's face, I could tell he wasn't happy with me.

Which leads me to this topic—when to throw away old estate planning documents? Often when I update clients' documents they ask me which of their old documents they should get rid of.

Let's address ancillary documents first. Generally speaking, you can get rid of most old durable powers of attorney, health care surrogates and living wills if they have been updated. The one thing that you have to be careful about in this group is the durable power of attorney. Generally speaking, it's okay to get rid of old durable powers of attorney. Where this general rule doesn't apply—and you need to take other action—is when one of three things has happened: 1) the power holder has a copy of it; 2) it has been used; or 3) a copy of the power of attorney is on file with a bank or financial institution.

If any of those three things are true, then you should have your attorney go through the legal steps necessary to actually revoke the power of attorney. Florida law provides step-by-step instructions that must be followed to properly revoke an old durable power of attorney, including sending notice to the power holder as well as to the proper offices of any financial institution where it has been used. Failure to legally revoke an old durable power of attorney could result in its continued use by the power holder—and unintended and possibly adverse consequences.

Next let's talk about wills. When you update your will, you might update it by adding an amendment to it, called a "codicil," or you may revoke the old will in the new one and create a whole new will. When you amend your will with a codicil, you should retain the old one, since it (or parts of it) remains valid. When you update a will by restating it in its entirety and revoking the old one, then it is usually okay to throw out the old one.

The only reason you may wish to keep an old will (or a copy of it) when it has been restated in its entirety is when you want to show a history of some act, such as disinheriting a certain friend or relative.

If you have a revocable living trust, you usually want to retain the old trusts, even if they have been restated in their entirety. This is due to the fact that new trusts usually build on old ones. As an example, let's say that I have a trust dated January 1, 1996. I restate that trust in its entirety on July 1, 2011. I want to keep the old trust because it has a provision in it that allowed me to amend it, and usually the new trust keeps the date of the old trust so that I don't have to re-title all of the assets that have been transferred to it. So if the IRS or a financial institution needs to see the old trust to make sure that the new one amending it is valid, it's a good idea to have that old trust around for that proof.

When you're like my father-in-law, who likes to keep things, then this column is of little use to you. But if you are like me and like to clean out useless clutter from your life—then you should ask your attorney which documents you can safely dispose of.

And, by the way, if you would like an old blender that won't work, give me a call. I can get you a great deal on one.

Should The Guardian For Your Children Also Serve As Estate Administrator?

The Michael Jackson estate provides good material to apply to everyday planning situations. We have learned that Jackson's 79-year-old mother, Katherine, who is now the legal guardian of his children, has petitioned the California Probate Court to replace the special administrators of his estate, music executive John McLain and attorney John Branca.

This raises an important question. Who is best suited to run the "business" of an estate administration? Should the guardian of the children—who presumably has the most at stake—be put in charge of the estate administration, or, are there more compelling reasons to name someone else to fill this role?

I would suggest that the person who is named as the guardian of the minor children should generally be separate from the person or parties who are the administrators of the estate. First, you are looking for completely different qualities in the types of people that you name to fill those roles. Second, the guardian of the minor children usually has their hands full just raising the children and may not have the time necessary to run the business and legal affairs of an estate. Third, the person who is guardian may also have a conflict of interest in filling the role of trustee.

Let me explain these three points, using the Michael Jackson estate as an example, and then applying the concepts to an ordinary citizen's estate.

It's apparent that in filling the role of guardian you want someone who will be devoted to your minor children. They obviously need to be good caregivers, who have the energy it takes to raise children. With each passing generation it seems that the task of raising children is getting more and more difficult. In Michael Jackson's case—the celebrity factor alone presents numerous challenges and concerns.

With the average citizen you still need to be cognizant that your minor children's lives will be uprooted—they may change schools, where they live, where they worship—their whole world is turned upside down. The person you name as guardian needs to fill an important role as the steady hand in a tumultuous time.

Contrast this with running the estate administration. These tasks are filled with day-to-day complexities. Making investment and business decisions is commonplace when a young family man or woman dies. The estate administrators' tasks include maximizing the value of the estate, including the income that will be needed to support minor children into adulthood or beyond.

In the Michael Jackson case, it's evident to me that a 79-year-old mother who is serving as the guardian of the children has enough on her hands, and that the creation and management of a music, merchandising and licensing empire should be spearheaded by someone other than her. She may have vast experience in those areas, but as stated, she already has her hands full.

In the ordinary citizen's case, if you own a business or a professional practice, time is of the essence. You will need an experienced hand or two to maximize the sales value of that business or practice, or it will likely all be lost in short order. Key employees must be retained to ensure they don't flock to competitors or become competitors. Their nerves must be calmed that they won't be out of a job. Customers and clients need assurances that their matters will be taken care of.

Finally, I would suggest that there is an inherent conflict of interest when the guardian of the minor children serves as a sole trustee over the estate administration. When you separate the functions of administrator from guardian, you are in essence putting checks and balances in to ensure that the estate assets and income aren't improperly used. Since the beneficiaries of the estate are minors, it is vitally important that they are not put into a position to be taken advantage of, either intentionally or unintentionally.

Let me leave you with this example to illustrate the point. Assume that the guardian, upon being told that she has the responsibility of raising three minor children, says that she needs a new home to have the space necessary for the new additions in her life. Should she take the estate funds to buy that new house?

The correct answer is that she should not. While she certainly can charge the estate a reasonable rent during the time that she is raising the kids, and should be reimbursed for all normal and necessary expenses, she should not take money to build or buy a bigger house. The house is in her name, not the children's name. Taking a big chunk of cash to add on to a home or to buy a bigger one, with the equity in the home going to her ultimately, is not a proper use of the estate funds.

When the guardian is also the administrator, there is no check and balance to discuss these issues and to arrive at something that is fair both for the guardian and for the children.

When you think about naming guardians and trustees/administrators, keep the Michael Jackson saga in the back of your mind. It is providing good lessons for us all.

The Dangers Of Spreading It All Out

" Claire" was a client of mine who used to spread out her money over several different banks. She chased the best interest rates for her Certificates of Deposit investments. In the end, she owned several CDs spread out in a number of different institutions. She said that in so doing she "killed two birds with one stone" by taking advantage of the higher teaser interest rates as well as maximizing her use of the FDIC insurance limits should any one bank fail.

She also had a number of different brokerage accounts. When Claire passed away, she had statements from Fidelity, Vanguard, Merrill Lynch, UBS and Charles Schwab. Claire had once voiced her concern that she didn't want to lose her investments by putting them all into one firm.

When Claire died her estate was a bloody mess.

It took several months simply to marshal her assets so that her successor trustee could decide which assets should be sold, which retained and how much of a balance she had between cash and investments inside of her portfolio. It took her trustee a very long time to consolidate her assets into a couple of accounts so that her affairs could be put in proper order to pay her taxes and administrative expenses and ultimately be distributed to her beneficiaries.

So now I'm going to debunk some of the most common reasons that the Claries of the world may give for spreading their assets over too many accounts:

"I don't want to put all of my eggs in one basket." While it is true that diversifying one's portfolio is wise, that doesn't necessarily

mean having many different custodians. Consider the possibility that Claire's UBS broker doesn't know what investments Claire owns in her Charles Schwab account. Both of those accounts together may own some of the same stocks, resulting in Claire having a combined portfolio that isn't balanced to her needs and risk tolerance.

"I'm afraid that if the bank goes under then I'll lose my Certificates of Deposit unless I have them spread out over several institutions." Here one must understand the FDIC (Federal Deposit Insurance Corporation) rules when you deposit money at a FDIC insured banking institution. If the account is in your individual name, the FDIC currently insures up to $250,000. But if you have the account in the name of your revocable living trust and that trust has up to five unique beneficiaries (regardless of the relative percentage each is to be distributed), then the account is insured up to $1,250,000 (or $250,000 per "unique beneficiary"). If you have a trust with more than five unique beneficiaries, then additional coverage is available, but the beneficiaries' percentage interests must be equal. Therefore, if you title the bank deposit accounts into a qualifying trust that meets the FDIC unique beneficiary requirements, you may have quite a bit more coverage than you thought that you otherwise had at one bank.

"If I put all of my investments into one brokerage account, and if that firm goes under, then I will have lost my entire investment portfolio." Bernie Madoff did more to frighten individual investors than any stock market crash could do. Here you have to understand the SPIC (Securities Investor Protection Act). Assuming that your brokerage institution is an SPIC member, then if it fails, you have to understand if it is doing so subject to a SPIC liquidation or to a Chapter 7 bankruptcy proceeding. In

SPIC liquidation, the goal of the SIPA trustee is to return to the customers the securities in their accounts, often through a transfer of the accounts to a financially healthy brokerage firm. When that isn't possible, the SIPA trustee has the authority to purchase securities to replace any that were missing, tapping into the SIPC's reserve fund when necessary to cover the acquisition cost. The SIPC reserve funds are available to satisfy the remaining claims of each customer up to $500,000, including a maximum of $100,000 on claims for cash. Under Chapter 7, all of the brokerage customers receive a pro-rata share of the proceeds from the sale of the securities, not from the securities themselves. So a Chapter 7 bankruptcy could be very harmful to a firm's clients, although these have been extremely rare occurrences. The key here is to ensure that the brokerage firm you are dealing with is an SIPC member.

The risks of spreading your portfolio out into too many financial institutions are just as real as the reasons to spread those risks out. The best bet is to ask questions and to choose a select few institutions that you feel are safe and trustworthy.

Acting In Concert

D id you ever wonder where the phrase "acting in concert" comes from? It may have originated from the Old Italian word "concerto" meaning "agreement, harmony," which sounds very nice. You would hope that two people who have to decide things together would do so collegially and with mutual consensus on the issues.

But the phrase may also have originated from Vulgar Latin "concertare" meaning "to settle by argument, debate, or to separate"—decide by fighting. This definition suggests an adversarial process to reaching agreement.

Which brings me to this estate planning topic—how many cooks should you have in the kitchen when creating your estate planning documents? Normally, when a husband and a wife have a will or a trust, they name each other as personal representatives (executors), successor trustees or agents under a durable power of attorney or health care surrogate documents.

Who should succeed the surviving spouse when making all of these decisions is where all of the real fun begins.

Many times parents will name their children to act as their successors. They might name two adult children to make their legal, tax, financial and health care decisions together. They might name them in successive order, but in several instances they might want two or more adult children to act together. They expect the children to "act in concert."

This then begs the question—do both of the designated children have to agree in order to carry out business? Under Florida law the general answer to that question is "yes."

And here's where it gets interesting. What happens if the two parties named in the legal documents can't stand one another? One says the sky is blue and the other disagrees. There's no shame in the fact that we have raised children who don't see eye to eye; that seems to be common among many siblings for whatever reason.

But when you are entrusting your legal, financial and health care decisions to those who you love, but who may not necessarily get along, what should you do? One choice is to clearly name the children in successive order. Indicate who is to act first, then second, then third.

The idea of putting two cooks in the kitchen at the same time isn't always a bad one, however. One child might be good with financial aspects but might be impulsive. Another child might temper the impulsiveness of the first. So even if they butt heads on occasion, naming two very different siblings to act together might actually lead to better decisions.

When choosing two or more individuals to serve together in these roles, you should first communicate with all of them what to expect. Tell them that they'll be working together. Set expectations. You might tell them that while you expect them to debate certain decisions and not see eye to eye on all matters, you are choosing them both because you appreciate and value their different perspective on things. This kind of a conversation might help them see their differences in a new light and be more open to one another's viewpoints.

If, however, you suspect that the bad blood between them may lead to stalemates, then it is a wise idea to impose a third party "tie-breaker." You might name a close friend, relative or advisor to fill this role only when necessary. The legal documents can be drawn to anticipate these issues and provide for a means to resolve them.

One type of document is a bit problematic—your Durable Power of Attorney. Under Florida law, you cannot create a "springing" Durable Power of Attorney, meaning that it is only effective if the person holding the one before it can't act. The Durable Power of Attorney document is valid the minute that you put pen to paper and sign it. Therefore, when you have more than one Durable Power of Attorney, you usually have multiple individuals, all with current authority.

One solution is not to give individual Durable Power of Attorneys, but rather name multiple individuals in one document. While this avoids the multiple individual powers problem mentioned above, it also creates a situation where the incapacity of one of the agents named in the document renders the entire document useless. So that is usually not a recommended course of action.

The bottom line is to carefully consider those that you are naming in positions of authority within your legal documents, and to communicate what you have done and your expectations for when they must act for you. And then hope for the best!

It Depends!

A potential client called to ask a question that he claimed was "simple." After a ten-minute dissertation outlining a very complicated fact pattern, all I could say was, "It depends."

He wasn't very thrilled with my answer, and I can understand why. It would seem that lawyers sell more "Depends" than Walgreens and CVS combined!

And that leads me to this topic, which is why so much of what you put into an estate plan depends upon your particular facts, and how everyone's different fact pattern when applied against the same law results in different outcomes.

What do I mean by this? Take, for example, two couples, both of whom have a net worth of $4 million. Both of those couples are Florida residents, in their first marriage and have two children with four grandchildren. Let's even throw in that both couples share the same recreational interests and socialize on the weekends.

The first couple's assets consist of a Florida home, a northern lake front cottage residence, and some stocks, bonds and mutual funds. The second couple's assets are composed largely from a family business and 401(k) plan.

Even though the couples share the same marital history, the same number of children and grandchildren, and may even socialize together on the weekends, the first couple's estate plan should look very different than the second couple's estate plan. This is due to a variety of factors. Even though they have the same net worth and the federal income, estate and gift tax laws are not different for both couples, the effect that those same laws have on the different types of assets that the couples own usually will result in a different estate plan.

State laws that apply have different results as well. Some states have estate and inheritance taxes while Florida does not. When one owns real estate in a state that has such taxes, then one's estate plan may be drafted with the anticipation of minimizing or deferring those state taxes.

And it's not just about taxes. The couple that owns the family business might be restrained from certain types of planning avenues due to internal corporate agreements, leases, vendor agreements, employment agreements and the like. All of these should be considered when fashioning a proper estate plan.

So when the couples go out to dinner together and compare notes on what their estate planning attorneys are recommending, they are likely to discover that one says something very different than the other. This doesn't mean that one is wrong and the other right. The attorneys are probably giving good advice, based upon the factual circumstances (and differences) between the couples.

It's not very often that you find two couples with the so much in common. Throw into the mix different degrees of net worth, different medical histories and problems, second marriage situations, children from different marriages, children with varying degrees of need and ability, different estate planning objectives, charitable intent (or lack thereof), and the list goes on—it's pretty easy to see why two couples who share the same amount of wealth may have vastly different estate plans.

How do you begin to understand what you might need? In my office we use a Client Organizer. You can find it on our web site, www.sbshlaw.com. Click on "Estate Planning" in the left menu bar, then scroll down to where the client organizers are mentioned. You'll find that we ask a lot of detailed questions. These questions lead us to understand what issues your plan might address.

We ask all of our new clients to complete an organizer. Sometimes we meet resistance, as the new client doesn't understand why we're asking them to complete the detailed list. But as you can see from the few paragraphs above, if we don't know what the particular issues are for any given client, we can't give proper advice.

Do you know what's it like when you visit your estate planning attorney but refuse to tell him anything about you? It's like going to the doctor and saying, "Doctor, it hurts!"

The doctor asks, "Where does it hurt?"

And then you reply "Guess!"

Your factual situation and your goals is what should drive your estate plan. If you haven't spent enough time talking about your unique set of circumstances with your estate planning counsel, then you may not have a plan that is right for your situation.

Next time you're out to dinner with friends and they try to tell you that what they've done is what you should do with your planning, pause and reflect on how different we all are, and how those differences add up when putting together something as unique as a personal estate plan.

Five Dangers Of Holding Assets And Property As Tenants By The Entireties

From time to time, a client will visit with me convinced that he or she has protected their assets from the claims of creditors by placing all of their assets and properties in a joint tenancy known as "Tenants By The Entireties." This is a popular but limited form of asset protection that has its benefits—and traps.

First, let's review the three different forms of joint ownership. They are "Tenants in Common (TIC), Joint Tenants with Rights of Survivorship (JWROS) and, as mentioned above, Tenancy By The Entireties (TBE). Tenants in Common is an undivided interest of joint ownership. This means that each party has the right to alienate, or transfer the ownership of, her or his ownership interest. This can be done by deed, will, or other conveyance. When one joint owner dies, their interest is subject to probate.

In contrast, owning assets or property jointly with rights of survivorship avoids the probate process, but is similar to TIC in that either party can individually alienate or transfer his interest. When this happens the asset is owned as TIC.

Individuals owning assets or property as tenants by the entireties cannot alienate or transfer without the consent and signature of the other.

Now that you understand the different forms of joint ownership, let's review the benefits of TBE. Holding assets as TBE has certain advantages for married couples. When one spouse dies, the surviving spouse owns all the assets without the need for probate. Creditors of only one spouse cannot reach the assets, as both husband and wife must be liable for a creditor to successfully attack the assets.

But there are traps for the unwary when relying on TBE for asset protection purposes. Allow me to present to you the top five— with a special thank you to my colleague attorney, Phillip B. Rarick in Miami, Florida for his help in putting these together:

1. **You must be married.** TBE is only available to those in a legally recognized marriage. In Florida, this rules out same sex unions as well as common law marriages. Even if a couple who is not legally married titles assets or property as tenants by the entireties, they will not be afforded the asset protections enumerated under the law.

2. **Assets held jointly before marriage** do not automatically become TBE upon becoming married. To achieve TBE status, the assets must be re-titled from one of the spouses to them jointly as tenants by the entireties after the marriage.

3. **TBE assets can be attacked when both spouses are liable.** If a creditor has a judgment against both spouses, then the creditor can reach TBE assets. This can happen when one spouse causes a terrible car accident when both spouses own the car involved in the accident. Further, if one spouse dies or the marriage ends in the middle of a creditor problem, the creditor will be able to attack the TBE property.

4. **The account must be created properly or the protection is lost.** When one spouse owns a bank or brokerage account, for example, and simply adds the other spouse's name as TBE, it will not be considered

TBE property. There is a rule that TBE assets and property must be created with four "unities"—those of time, title, interest and possession. Therefore, the proper way to create a TBE account that is currently owned by only one spouse is to close the account and open a new account in both spouses' names as TBE.

5. **Joint with Rights of Survivorship is not TBE.** While Florida law presumes TBE ownership between a husband and wife when opening a bank account, if the bank officer checked a JWROS box on the account application then that will trump the TBE presumption and protections. Therefore, bank and brokerage signature cards should always be checked to assure TBE ownership and protections.

There are additional issues surrounding TBE property, particularly in second marriage situations where there is a nuptial agreement that defines Non-marital property that should not be subject to the other spouse in a divorce proceeding. Further, if your estate plan contemplates assets in one spouse's name or the other's (including ownership in a revocable trust), then it is important to consider the estate planning ramifications of any transfer of ownership.

As one can readily see, there are many considerations when opening up bank and brokerage accounts or titling real estate into joint name, and they are not to be taken lightly.

Liability Protection Is Also Important For Retirees

M any of my clients who are retired tell me that they want to simplify things. Their children have grown; their careers have wound down. Now that they're living off retirement savings, many start to look for expenses that can be cut back.

Since they have a fair amount of life savings and there are no more dependents, life insurance may not be as important as it once was. The thousands of dollars of annual premium payments may no longer be necessary or in the budget, so policies might be terminated or cashed in.

Professional and trade memberships aren't useful anymore, so they're discontinued. Business lunches aren't part of the daily routine. The country club membership up north isn't used much anymore, so it's discontinued in favor of the golf membership here in Florida.

Cars might be leased instead of bought. Eating out at restaurants might be curtailed.

Some money magazines even suggest cutting back on your homeowner's liability, automobile and umbrella liability policies. But that would be a big mistake.

Why?

The answer is simple. Because if you get into a car accident that is your fault, you might find yourself responsible for damages beyond the liability protection that you've cut back to under your car insurance policy. If the injured party sues you after the accident, and a judgment is entered against you, then the plaintiff could go after your life savings to make up the difference between what your automobile liability policy pays and the amount of the judgment.

Assume, for example, a terrible scenario where you are involved in an accident that severely injures someone, crippling them for life. The liability that you may be held responsible for could certainly be more than a $250,000 limit one finds on many automobile insurance policies. Medical costs, lost wages, pain and suffering, the loss of the injured person's ability to enjoy life, among all of the other damages, could be in the millions.

The same holds true for your homeowner's liability insurance. If someone is injured on your property and you are deemed to have been somehow negligent, then you could find yourself at the wrong end of a judgment and have to pay damages over the amount that your homeowner's liability insurance policy covers. A pool, for example, is considered under the law to be an "attractive nuisance." If a neighborhood toddler should wander onto your property and drown in the pool, you may be held negligently liable even though the child was not invited onto your property.

So even if you are retired, you remain subject to many of the same risks and liabilities that everyone else must guard against. Nevertheless, I've heard all sorts of excuses why retirees shouldn't purchase maximum liability protection. But to counter those, all you have to do is turn on the television. How many personal injury attorney ads do you see? And each one essentially asks the viewer, "Isn't there anyone we can sue for you?"

Liability insurance is so important not only for the amount of protection that it offers, but because it also pays for attorney fees to defend you in case you are simply accused of negligence. Even if it turns out that you are not negligent, the costs of defending a claim might take a big chunk out of your life savings if you don't have a policy that also serves to pay these expenses.

Then there's the mistake that some make with regard to their estate planning. Some wrongly assume that if they have placed all of their assets inside a revocable living trust, then they've protected the trust assets from liability. This isn't the case. In almost all revocable trusts the trust and its assets are legally yours, which means that you can do anything that you want with your trust assets. Because you have that much dominion and control over the assets, your judgment creditors can demand restitution from your trust assets.

So what should you do? The best practice is to increase the liability coverage on your home and car and then purchase—in addition to those policies—an "umbrella" policy. The "umbrella" policy covers liability up to its stated policy amount over and above the home and car policies.

A $2 million umbrella policy might cost a couple thousand dollars annually (or perhaps even less) and is a great investment to protect you and your hard-earned savings from the claims of a judgment creditor. Not only will this provide much needed coverage, it should also give you peace of mind.

If you value what you've worked so hard to accumulate over the course of your working career, consider making a visit to your liability insurance carrier to review whether your coverage adequately protects you.

Chapter Six

Family Dynamics

Wealth Preservation Lessons From Athletes

Despite earning more than $27 million in salary and millions more in endorsements, basketball superstar and cultural phenom, Dennis Rodman, appeared in court this past March because he was unable to pay $800,000 in past due child support. He claimed that he was broke.

Scottie Pippen, a teammate of Rodman's on the Chicago Bulls championship teams, found himself near bankruptcy just a few years after his retirement despite career earnings in excess of $110 million.

In May of last year, World Series superstar Curt Schilling announced that he had lost his entire $50 million baseball fortune on a failed video game company.

Professional boxer Mike Tyson earned and squandered an estimated $300 million net worth.

Seventy percent of NFL players are completely broke three years after leaving the game, despite an average annual salary of just under $2 million.

A common theme amongst all of these tales is that those who earned and lost enormous sums had no prior experience with monetary success. Like a lotto winner, they suddenly found themselves bathing in millions. Unable to manage their newfound fortunes, and unable to create a high-quality vision of their post-athletic careers, these athletes lost what took them a lifetime of training, sacrifice and hard work to achieve.

There are lessons to be learned for those planning estates—even for those of more modest means.

Traditional estate planning works to divide financial assets among family members without considering the other things that lead to the success that generated the wealth in the first place. Speaking as one inside the industry, estate planning professionals have become very adept at economically dividing up the money amongst the heirs with little regard to transferring the intangible wisdom, values, experience and relationship assets to future generations.

What appears to be the philosophy underlying traditional estate planning? *Beat the taxman and ultimately dump all you can on your heirs, regardless of their ability to handle sudden wealth.* As we've seen with the athlete examples, an heir to an estate can, in a few years, wipe out what took a lifetime to create. Moreover, dividing up the financial assets all too often ends up dividing the family.

This is more of a systemic problem within the industry comprised of attorneys, accountants and financial advisors than one associated with any one individual family's plan. I am now in the process of addressing this issue, and you'll read more about my findings in future columns. The problem as I see it is that it is not uncommon for estate planning professionals to focus on wealth transfer without a corresponding acknowledgement to the role of wealth responsibility.

And I am not condemning the hard work that the estate planning community does for its clients. The transfer of financial wealth while minimizing taxes is an important element that should be universally addressed. There are other components missing, however.

What is needed in addition to the traditional process is a program designed to document and transfer the family's other, more important assets, such as the family's values, experience, wisdom and relationships. For those of you who missed that column, I asked: What are the most important things that you would want to pass on to your family? Is it the financial assets, or instead, is it the wisdom, experiences and values that got you there?

I pointed to an entrepreneurial client who once confidently told me that if he suddenly lost everything, he could regain it all in a couple of years with the education, experience, knowledge, wisdom and relationships that he had built over the course of his lifetime. Those are the true assets that can best set the stage for successive generations' success.

So what kind of process needs to be put into place to achieve the transfer of these intangible family assets?

The way it happens is by transferring wealth through account-ability and leadership. Notice that I didn't say "management." Managers are typically hired by leaders to help run things, to keep things on track. Attorneys, accountants and financial advisors are good managers as long as the family has put into place a system of vision creation, accountability and leadership.

Leaders, in contrast, set the vision for the future. They define the parameters under which managers manage. When the family leader documents his or her own core values, defines the unique abilities that helped get him or her to their perch, and can transfer his or her accumulated wisdom to successive generations, the family is ready for the next step.

This often includes determining how the other family members can fit into perpetuating the family's success. And it's not usually achieved by the next generation simply becoming younger versions of the family leaders. Trying to create a "Mini-Me" too often results in family disharmony, tensions and failure.

Five Questions When Family Business Is A Large Portion Of Net Worth

What do you do when a significant portion of your net worth is wrapped up in a closely held business interest and one or more of your children are involved in that business? That's a loaded question that will have a different answer for each family. I thought that I'd give you the five biggest questions that each family should ask of their attorney and CPA when a family business is part of the estate planning equation.

1. **What's the true value of the business?** While many family businesses are portable to either the next generation or as a part of a sale to a third party, some businesses are dependent upon its owner and have little or no value if that owner were to retire or die. Some businesses may have succession value, but that value would be lost entirely unless a succession plan is considered and implemented.

2. **How do we leave the business to the next generation?** If there are likely candidates to take over the family business, it won't happen successfully without a plan. Will senior management accept the younger family member as their new boss or leave to work for a competitor or to create a new business? What incentives can be offered to key employees to keep them as a part of the team? How will the next generation be groomed? For gift tax and estate tax planning purposes, should transfers of business interests occur now or later?

3. **Will the current business owners still need income through retirement?** This is perhaps one of the stickiest

issues to confront. When transferring a family business for gift and estate tax purposes, the retention of an income interest may result in the entire value of the business being included in the transferor's estate for estate tax purposes, which can be disastrous. There are many avenues around this problem, however. Employment and consulting agreements, sale of business interests with installment notes and Grantor Retained Annuity Trusts are just a few of the methods that can be used to satisfy the need for income.

4. **What to do about the children who are not a part of the business?** Generally speaking, it is usually not a good idea to leave family business interests to children who are not actually working in the business. This only leads to resentment between the children who are working and those that are expecting dividends for their shares. Consequently, there are two entirely different ways of thinking about leaving a family business to children. The first is that the children who are working the business are inheriting a "job" and therefore should get a share of the non-business assets. The second is that the children who are working the business are receiving the most valuable asset and the non-working children should therefore get a larger share of the non-business assets. There is no right or wrong answer to this dilemma.

5. **What legal agreements need to be put into place to secure the future vision?** A will is probably not enough when considering all of the elements that need to be put into place to wrap up a family business succession plan into a tidy package. Shareholder or partnership, employment, consulting and trust agreements will likely all need

to be considered. Only after the first four questions are answered will the family have a better idea of what legal means are necessary to ensure a smooth transition at the lowest possible tax cost.

Each of the above questions will open other, more detailed questions. My thought in this section was to give a broad overview. The type of entity involved, such as "S" Corporation, LLC, partnership or the like will also drive what issues need to be resolved to have a successful plan put into place.

Once that plan is agreed upon, it's wise to review and to update it at least every two years or so. Laws change, goals change, people's vision of their own future changes. Finally, consider talking to your family about your plans. Parents often assume things that may or may not be true about their children's hopes, dreams and expectations.

We Never Even Played Catch

Several years ago, an elderly client died. His four middle-aged children gathered in my conference room to discuss the trust administration. The deceased was a real "go-getter," having led an entrepreneurial, hard-charging lifestyle. It didn't come without drawbacks, for he had experienced three failed marriages and some other issues that I would soon discover.

While I reviewed the trust and the process that the family would follow to liquidate his holdings, file the proper notices, clear any creditors that might be out there and file tax returns, I noticed that the deceased's youngest son was staring out the window, apparently disinterested in the conversation. I just assumed that the emotion of losing a parent consumed his attention.

While a daughter was asking about the logistics of moving some valuable artwork across the country to an auctioneer, the youngest son suddenly piped up.

"We never even played catch," this now forty-something man said, tears welling in his eyes.

I'll never forget that day. My kids were much younger then, and when I arrived home after work that night I hugged them tight and suggested that we all take a dive in the pool after dinner—which is not something that I do a whole lot of. We splashed and played "Marco Polo," while my wife sat in a lounge chair shaking her head at my apparent craziness.

Life's funny in a way. Most of us feel the strain of constant responsibilities to our spouse, children and other loved ones. We feel the need to work, provide for our families, and make sure the children get a proper upbringing and education.

But sometimes we get lost in the details, forgetting the big picture. Like carving out a moment or two to watch a beautiful sunset, taking a stroll on the beach, or just playing catch.

Many island residents enjoy having their families visit over the winter and spring seasons. I imagine that with those up north suffering through one of the coldest winters since 1978, we'll be seeing more of our family and friends booking flights to our sunny spot in Florida this year. While it can sometimes be difficult with adult children and grandchildren making our daily lives a little more hectic, remember that it will only be for a few days.

So take a bike ride. Enjoy a sunset. Rent a kayak. Grill up some hamburgers while uncorking your favorite wine.

You'll be happy you did.

It's Not The Money Or Property They Fight Over

I was very close to my great grandmother, whom I called "Bubby." A framed picture in my home includes her image along with an 1890 silver dollar. She told me that her father handed her a silver dollar bearing the year of her birth when she arrived in America. She hadn't seen him in many years, as he had to save for her passage. Until my Bubby's death in 1976 we celebrated our birthdays together, as ours were only one day apart on the calendar.

When she died that silver dollar was invaluable to me. I was only 12 years old, but I dearly wanted it to remember her by. My sister, incidentally, has our Bubby's soup spoon framed in a box. It hangs proudly in my sister's dining room.

So you might find it interesting that in my twenty years of practicing estate planning law I rarely encounter siblings who fight over a deceased parent's money or property. Generally speaking, the very few disputes I've refereed between siblings involved tangible personal property items like rings, watches, jewelry and other items just like coins and soup spoons.

Don't underestimate the sentimental value of an item that's been handed down over the generations from father to son or from mother to daughter. If you have more than one son, you may not want to assume that the eldest will treasure granddad's watch. Mothers of daughters and even granddaughters often own a certain string of pearls, a diamond broche or a bracelet that has sentimental value to one or more family members.

So if you own such items that you would like to see passed down to a certain child or grandchild, the first course of business is to find out whether he or she wants it. It doesn't have to be the main topic of conversation during a visit or phone call, but at some opportune moment it makes sense to confirm the intended recipient is willing.

Don't take "let's not talk about this now" as an answer, either. Many adult children don't want to sound as if they are awaiting your imminent demise. An appropriate response might be, "I intend to hold onto my (insert item name here) for quite some time. I just want to make sure that if I leave it to you that this is something you would treasure as I have. Or perhaps there's something else that you find more valuable sentimentally."

Be careful here. I've had some occasions where more than one child proclaims that he was "promised" an item by their father or mother. If you don't intend to promise that certain item, but are merely talking about it, make that clear.

Once you've decided who is to receive these tangible personal property items, then it is time to make a list. Florida law actually gives us an easy mechanism to make a list of our tangible personal property outside of our will or trust, and to easily amend it without having to visit your attorney.

So long as our will or trust mentions the list properly under the Florida statute, (this would be the job of you working with your estate planning attorney) then you may create a list and it need only be signed and dated. The list does not have to be witnessed. If you should choose to update the list, sign and date it again. I suggest providing a copy of the current list to your estate planning attorney so that he may retain a current copy in your file.

One other note of caution—if you give an item away during your lifetime, remove the item from your list. Also, if you intend for the value of the gift to be deducted from the total value of what that beneficiary receives from your estate or trust, then you should mention this to your attorney to ensure he includes appropriate language within your will or trust documents.

What happens if you don't have such a list? Then it is typically up to your personal representative and/or trustee to decide who is to receive which tangible personal property items, or which ones should be sold or auctioned. This is where the disputes may arise. The child with the unfortunate task of deciding the fate of sentimental items might find themselves in the unfortunate position of wanting something, but it might look like self-dealing if they take it when another beneficiary also expresses a desire to acquire that same item.

Creating such a list can mean more than leaving thousands of dollars to your loved ones. Although my Bubby didn't have much in the form of monetary wealth when she died, she left me a real treasure, one that can never be replaced.

Son Using Father's Trust For Son's Personal Advantage

When you're named as a trustee to a trust, especially a trust in which you are also a beneficiary, you are subjecting yourself to several legal responsibilities of which you need to be keenly aware. The foremost of those responsibilities is the potential conflict of interest that you may have in conducting any aspect of trust business.

Suppose, for example, that Son is the trustee of Father's trust, as Father has become incompetent. Son was named as the successor trustee. Father went so far as to tell his estate attorney that he named Son to fill that role because of Son's business acumen. When Father dies, Son and Daughter are the beneficiaries of the trust.

Assume further that Son is a real estate developer working on a project that needs a cash infusion. The project could result in millions of dollars in profits, but it could also go bust. Son is the confident sort who never expects one of his ventures to fail. Upon examination, the trustee powers contained in the trust document include the power to invest in stocks, bonds, mutual funds, real estate and business ventures.

So is that enough for Son to take Dad's trust assets and invest in the venture? Does it matter if Son invests Father's trust as an equity partner—buying shares in the venture—or if Son loans money from Father's trust, effectively making it a creditor of the venture?

What should Son do? Or should Son just keep Father's trust's existing asset mix?

It's not such a simple question, right or wrong. Son was correct by first examining the trust instrument to determine if he even had the power to act as trustee to make such an investment. But the power alone is not enough.

Assume, for example, that Son intends to invest $750,000 of Father's trust into the real estate venture. If the total value of Father's trust approximates $1.5 million, then Son would be investing an unusually large percentage of the whole into a risky venture. This would probably fall outside of the "prudent investor rules" that Son should follow as trustee.

The "prudent investor rules" (Chapter 518 of the Florida Statutes) indicate that a Trustee should act reasonably given the risk tolerance of the beneficiaries, the investment portfolio mix and the goals of the trust. To take such a large amount of Father's trust to put into a risky real estate venture would likely fall outside of the prudent investor rules.

Assume, instead, that Father's Trust is worth $5 million and that Father made his money in real estate ventures before turning the family business over to Son. Now it would appear that a $750,000 venture may not fall so blatantly outside of the prudent investor statutes.

But what if Daughter is uncomfortable with the decision to so invest? Could that change our conclusion? As trustee, Son not only has a duty to Father to ensure that the trust is properly used for Father's benefit for the rest of his life, but Son also has a duty to the remainder beneficiaries, including Daughter. Daughter's risk tolerance should also be considered when making trust and investment decisions.

In addition to the prudent investor rules, Son has the obligation to account to all "qualified beneficiaries" of the Trust. In my example, Son, himself, and Daughter are "qualified beneficiaries" even though they are not vested—meaning that their interest in the trust property is not certain until Father's death. The accounting not only must report the income, capital gains, losses and expenses of the trust, but must also report material transactions. The material transaction would likely include the real estate venture.

What if Daughter objects to the transaction? Can she block it? Since Son is the trustee, he is the one who decides where to invest the trust assets. If Daughter has enough lead time, she could conceivably file a Court action to stop the investment. Usually, however, the trustee has already made the investment. In this case, if the deal doesn't work out then Son would likely have personal liability to Daughter should she sue based on breach of fiduciary responsibilities.

Finally, let's take the worst-case scenario where Son simply takes Father's trust money for his own use and never reports it to Daughter. When a beneficiary suspects that the Trustee is using the Trust property and assets for his own use and not for the express purposes of the trust, the proper course of action is to file an action to remove the trustee.

From time to time, I'll receive a call from a beneficiary of a trust complaining that they don't have enough information to even determine whether their suspicions of improper activity are taking place. In these instances the beneficiary should demand an accounting, as is their right under Florida law and most other state's laws. The accounting should indicate whether the beneficiary's suspicions are true or not. If true, then the next steps of removing the trustee and seeking retribution payments back to the trust would be appropriate.

One can now see how important the selection of a trustee is. Don't take this choice lightly, as a high degree of wisdom, integrity and judgment is constantly necessary when making daily decisions.

Co-Signing Loans For Children And Grandchildren

" Ed" telephoned me recently with a problem. "Craig" he said, "I have a bank coming after me for $200,000. Does my revocable trust offer me any protection?"

I was surprised to hear that Ed was in financial trouble. While everyone has suffered under the recent economic troubles, the last time I spoke to Ed, he and his wife were on solid footing.

As it turns out, it wasn't Ed who caused the bank problem. I learned that Ed's son, "Bruce," purchased a home five years ago, when Bruce was employed. In order to help Bruce qualify for the mortgage, Ed cosigned the mortgage note.

You can guess what happened. Bruce lost his job. Bruce then fell behind with his mortgage payments. The home was foreclosed. Since the value of the home has decreased significantly, the bank's subsequent sale of the home following the foreclosure was for an amount less than the outstanding balance of the mortgage. The bank then obtained a deficiency judgment against both Bruce and Ed.

Since Bruce has no assets, the bank is seeking recourse from Ed. The first I learned of this mess was Ed's call to me asking whether his revocable trust somehow protects him against the bank. I advised Ed that his revocable trust assets are deemed to be his, and are not a protected asset. Since Ed can freely spend and consume his trust assets, they are not protected against creditors. Ed's credit rating could also be adversely affected by these problems.

This issue points to a real problem that is unfortunately becoming more common. Before co-signing notes for your children or grandchildren, you should consider the worst-case scenario and whether that scenario could be financially devastating.

In addition to the monetary losses Ed may have incurred, there could be gift tax repercussions to the guarantee Ed signed. While an old Tax Court case held that an agreement to guarantee the payments of another's debts does not constitute a completed gift for purposes of the gift tax rules, the IRS position has in the past been that when a person guarantees the payment of another's debts, the guarantor transfers a valuable property interest, and therefore a completed gift has occurred.

A controversial 1991 Private Letter Ruling, for example, held that a guarantee is a completed gift, although no guidance was provided suggesting what the value of such a guarantee might be. The IRS cited a Supreme Court decision, *Dickman v. Comr.,* a 1984 case that held a parent's agreement to guarantee payment of loans conferred a valuable economic benefit to the child, as without the guarantee, the child may not have obtained the loan or would have had to pay a higher interest rate.

This controversial ruling has since been withdrawn without IRS comment. However, the IRS may maintain the position that if the child defaults on the loan and the parent repays amounts under the terms of the guarantee, additional gifts are made to the extent that the parent is not reimbursed by the child.

In Ed's case this would constitute additional heartache. Not only may he be required to step in to cure the deficiency on the mortgage foreclosure, he may also lose some of his lifetime gift tax exemption.

The bottom line is that one should tread cautiously when cosigning or guaranteeing family obligations.

Meaningful Last Words

At a recent meeting, "Harry" complained to me while reading over his estate planning documents. "These seem so...cold, so....'legal'..." he said slowly, searching for the right words. "I understand that these documents have to use this legal language so that my estate gets the benefits of the law, but I'm having a hard time knowing that these will be my last words that I communicate to my family."

I understood Harry completely. Who wants their last words to read "I instruct my trustee to distribute a fraction of my estate, the numerator of which is comprised of the largest amount that would not be taxable...blah blah blah?"

I am sure that no one wants that.

I'm going to propose that you consider an alternative. This alternative can be made into a very meaningful and fun exercise.

What I'm referring to is to leave a separate letter—apart from your will—for each of your most important loved ones.

This letter shouldn't be about "who gets what" from your estate—that's for your will and trust. Besides, you don't want to inadvertently say anything that might contradict what's in your legal documents that could lead to beneficiary disputes.

Instead, what I'm talking about here is for you to create something really special. Too often we don't share our true emotions with those closest to us. We often tell our spouses that we love them, but we don't tell them why we love them. We might tell our children that we are proud of them, but we don't tell them why we are proud of them. We may truly admire something about a lifelong friend, but we are often afraid to open up and tell them what we've admired about them—or even that we harbored admiration to begin with.

How great would it be if we shared all of those thoughts with those closest to us? So I propose that you do just that. Write a letter and tell your loved ones how much they've meant to you. Then have that letter kept with your will, to be opened concurrently.

I thought that I'd suggest a few basic thoughts for those who might not be comfortable in putting words on paper:

Keep it Positive: When you are writing a letter that you don't intend for a loved one to receive until after you have departed this earth, it's a good idea to keep it positive. Everyone is subject to valid criticisms for our faults and unfulfilled expectations. Don't use this letter as a means to review those. These are your last words. Don't you want to leave them with a smile? But do be sincere. Don't heap praise where praise really isn't believable. Everyone has positive qualities. Talk about those here.

Write Separate Letters: Don't combine everything into one letter. Write one for your spouse. Another to each child or other loved one. That way your letter can be very personal for that particular person.

Open a Spousal Letter with How You Fell in Love: You might open a letter to your spouse recalling the first time that you met, and how you knew that you were in love. Talk about the qualities that she or he possessed and how those qualities grew better over time.

Recall Your Child's Early Years: For your children you might open a letter about their early years—how much you cherished having them in your life. There may have been certain traits, characteristics or events that foreshadowed later successes they achieved. Talk about those, and how you noticed them.

Tell Them Why: Don't be shy about telling your loved ones the "whys." Why you are so in love. Why you are so proud. Why you smile when you think about them. With kids it might even be fun to tell them why you wanted to have kids in the first place, and how different it was raising them as opposed to what you expected before you ever had kids.

Review Fun Family Times or Accomplishments: Every relationship has its ups and downs. Many of the ups can be chronicled as happening during a certain event—a vacation, a sporting event, a holiday gathering. While everyone might have already grown tired of hearing the same stories around the dinner table over and over, you might be able to provide a twist; relay why that story meant so much to you and how it demonstrates your loved one's special qualities.

Regrets: Generally speaking it's not a good idea to create a list of regrets. But you might have some that would have a positive spin. "I regret that I didn't tell you this earlier, and hope that by telling you this now, you'll know how much you meant to me," for example. You may regret certain incidents and want to apologize for them. If this is the case, do your best to keep it concise while not trying to place blame or guilt on your loved one.

Your Hopes and Dreams: Talk about your hopes and dreams for your loved one—particularly if they are young. If they aren't young anymore, you can talk about how proud you are of their accomplishments. Maybe they've raised great kids of their own.

Perhaps they've overcome a lot of obstacles and you've noticed how far they've come. That's great stuff. Let them know it.

Wind it Up: Make sure that you leave them with a warm statement. I saw one letter where a father told each of his children that he wanted them to know that he believed in an afterlife, and although his children may no longer be able to touch him or hear him, they could talk to him and he would be there to listen. He told them that he trusted their judgment, and he hoped that they would live the rest of their life with confidence that everything happens for a reason. It struck me as a powerful confirmation of his love, devotion and admiration.

I hope that this helps to provide the start of an outline if you should feel this important to do for your loved ones. I'm working on a letter for my wife and for each of my children, which I intend to update as the years go by. I'm hopeful that these writings will mean more to them than anything material that I leave behind.

Troublesome Choices With Special Needs Beneficiaries

Gary and Tina have two children, including one adult daughter, Samantha, who is on disability and Medicaid. When Gary and Tina discuss their will, they wonder if Samantha should be disinherited. Instead, Gary and Tina would, at their deaths, leave their entire estate to their son, Jerry, with instructions to take care of his sister.

That's one way to deal with the problem. Of course, giving all of their estate to Jerry may pose certain problems. What would happen, for example, if Jerry got sick or died before Samantha? If Jerry died and his will left everything to his wife or children, would they be as willing to take care of Samantha?

Another alternative would be to leave amounts in a trust for Samantha, since she is unable to manage her own financial affairs. Gary and Tina have to be careful when going down this road. Government benefit programs such as Medicaid have very strict asset and income limitations. The beneficial interest that Gary and Tina leave to Samantha would likely disqualify her from the receiving any further government benefits. In other words, upon the death of the survivor of Gary and Tina, Samantha would no longer qualify for the government benefits she received up to this point. This is true despite provisions of the trust that make any distributions to Samantha discretionary.

There is, however, another alternative that Gary and Tina could build into their estate planning documents. Upon the death of the survivor, their will could contain a testamentary trust known as a "Special Needs Trust" or it is sometimes referred to as a "Supplemental Needs Trust."

The idea behind a "Special Needs Trust" is that it would serve to supplement what the government benefits provide, but it will not disqualify the beneficiary from receipt of the benefits. The Special Needs Trust accomplishes this by mandating an independent trustee to make distribution decisions, and the authorized distributions under the terms of the document are only for those things that the government won't pay for but that do not disqualify the beneficiary.

Examples of permissible payments and distributions usually include medical and dental expenses, training and education, rehabilitation, travel to visit relatives, payments necessary for private residential care rooms (as opposed to doubles that the government may only pay for), payments for care managers, food and clothing and such other life necessaries.

Federal and state government agencies continue to limit the use of Special Needs Trusts in an effort to disqualify anyone that may have access to assets and income from receiving government welfare and disability benefits. Therefore, the use of a Special Needs Trust that works today may in the future disqualify the beneficiary. Because the Special Needs Trust doesn't actually get funded until the death of the survivor of Gary and Tina in my example, it might be a good idea for their attorney to insert "Trust Protector" language inside of the document to allow for posthumous changes that might be necessary to comply with ever-changing laws.

Yet another alternative is to forgo the government benefits entirely. For those wealthy enough to leave amounts that would allow their special needs beneficiary adequate assets and income to live out their lives in reasonable comfort, wills and trusts might be drafted anticipating that when the inheritance occurs the beneficiary will come off of the government aid entirely. From that point forward, rather than providing a "Special Needs Trust" that could only pay for limited expenses, a "General Needs Trust" that is broader in scope could apply.

Assuming that Gary and Tina choose to build a Special Needs Trust inside of their estate planning documents, they should be careful about assets that their will or revocable trust does not govern. If Samantha is named as a beneficiary to an IRA account, annuity or life insurance policy, she would likely be disqualified from receiving the government benefits. While there is a way to route those types of assets and accounts through a Special Needs Trust, there are adverse income tax consequences that may apply.

Gary and Tina have much to ponder. No choice is "right" or "wrong." Each family ultimately decides what is best, considering their individual facts and circumstances.

Spoiling The Grandkids

When my wife and I have a cross word with one of our daughters, it isn't uncommon for them to secretly get on their cell phones to dial Grandma from the privacy of their bedroom to complain. They get to vent about what rotten parents Patti and I have become and how we are being so unfair or otherwise overly demanding of them.

Imagine asking your daughter to pick up that wet towel off of the floor of her room for the hundredth time. How unreasonable!

But having caring and loving grandparents is good. It balances out the family dynamic. Grandparents tend to provide a broader, calmer perspective. They're not in the heat of the battle, and they've been through those battles before.

So it's interesting for me as an estate planning attorney to see how, in their estate plans, grandparents treat their grandchildren. A predominant school of thought is to leave everything to the children and let them take care of the grandchildren. Sometimes, however, the grandparents want to include the grandchildren directly in the estate plans.

And here's where it gets interesting. Suppose that son, Robert, has two children and the other son, Richard, has three. So if Grandpa leaves each grandchild $10,000, then Robert's side of the family receives an extra $20,000 of bequests, while Richard's side of the family receives $30,000. So is that unfair?

It's all how you look at it. If you are trying to treat Robert and Richard equally, you could argue that Richard is getting more. But is he really? My experience with these issues is that grandparents tend to change their perspective on treating grandchildren "equally" over time. Allow me to explain.

While the grandchildren are young (from birth through high school or college age), the grandparents tend to think of the grandchildren as extensions of their children. In other words, Richard's children should only get $6,667 each while Robert's children each get $10,000 so that both sides (Robert and Richard) are treated equally—a total of $20,000 to each "side" of the grandchildren.

As the grandchildren exit college, however, the grandparents tend to think of them as their own individual unit with no difference as to whether they are offspring of one son or the other. In other words, as the grandchildren enter young adulthood, anecdotally, I would tell you that in my experience the $10,000 bequest to each grandchild doesn't seem to bother Grandma and Grandpa as much. They think of their grandchildren more as independent young adults and less as extensions of one side of the family or the other.

It gets trickier when there are stepchildren involved. Blended families are much more common today than they were a generation or so ago. And in many cases, the step-grandparents have a close relationship with their step-grandchildren. Here, the grandparents have to make a decision whether the step-grandchildren should receive anything at all—or if they do, whether they receive the same amount as the biological grand-children.

Complicating matters further is that many don't understand how the law works. When you leave amounts to a child *per stirpes,* and if that child predeceases you, then unless you have a specific provision to the contrary, that deceased child's stepchildren do not receive amounts from your estate. If, on the other hand, your child has legally adopted the step-grandchildren, then they are no longer step-relations. Adopted grandchildren are treated under the law the same as biological grandchildren.

You can decide to treat step-grandchildren (who have not been adopted) the same as biological grandchildren by so stating in your will or trust. But you actually have to make an express statement in your estate planning documents to have them treated that way.

Often grandparents don't know what they should do about step-grandchildren. Should they be treated the same as biological grandchildren? Should they be treated half as well? Should they not be mentioned at all? Will their child be offended if their stepchildren are not provided for the same way as the biological grandchildren are treated?

There are no right or wrong answers. Each family is different. The relationship between the grandparents, the parents and the grandchildren will usually dictate how this all plays out. I usually encourage my clients to talk to their children to get their feelings on these matters. Ultimately, it is the decision of the client what they want to put into their will or trust. The best way to approach these issues is to look into their own hearts to decide what's best for them and their families.

Because ultimately, how you decide to treat your family— blended family and all—in your estate plan is how you feel about those who are close to you. Whether you have a large estate or a more modest estate, it really doesn't matter.

What matters most are the relationships that you enjoy through the years. Because I know that when my kids feel upset with Patti and me, our parents feel warm and special that our kids want comfort from them.

And all of that means more than anything a will or trust can say.

Moochers

Moochers. It seems that almost every family has one. We work real hard to raise our children, send them away to college and we hope they then go on to lead productive lives. But then many families have one grown child who always seems to need a handout.

"Can I borrow some money? I'm behind in my mortgage payments."

"My old car needs thousands of dollars of repairs. Maybe you can just buy me a new reliable one."

"Junior really needs braces and I can't afford them."

"I can't make ends meet."

In today's hard economic times a certain amount of money problems is understandable. But then there are the adult children who just seem to go from one tragedy to the next. As parents, our inclination is to bail them out. We don't want to see our children suffer. But by continuing to keep the moocher child on the dole, are we not enabling them to continue improper behavior? Won't this all end badly?

Constantly bailing out our needy adult children eventually leads to bigger problems between family members. I can't relate to you how many times I've seen this with various clients and their families. Mom and Dad might be making gifts to Son to keep him economically viable. The other children resent it for a variety of reasons. The responsible adult children view their brother as taking advantage of their parents' goodwill.

The bad feelings grow over many years.

Suddenly one of the parents is deceased, and the other parent becomes disabled. Usually one of the responsible children is named as trustee and also has a durable power of attorney. Then all of the you-know-what hits the fan when the moocher child asks the responsible child for a handout from Mom's trust.

"I'm not giving you any more money from Mom's trust! You've taken enough over the years!" Responsible Child asserts.

"What am I supposed to do? Declare bankruptcy?" Moocher Child answers. "I'm just going to go to Mom and ask her to tell you to give me the money."

I've seen clients suffer their own financial problems because they couldn't say "no" to one of their adult children's money requests. But for those who have adequate resources, the question then becomes, "Is it proper to keep helping an adult child?"

There's no good answer or outcome to this scenario. That's why when families are supporting an adult child, they should probably build provisions into their trust that say whether or not the adult child should continue to receive gifts after Mom or Dad become incapacitated and someone else is handling their economic affairs. Another good idea is to consider adding a statement in the will or the trust that lifetime gifts should count against the adult child's inheritance, so when the estate is one day divided up, the children who were responsible will end up with more of the estate in an attempt to even out what occurred over the years.

But this usually delays the inevitable. Eventually, the moocher child will run out of sources of funds, either because the gifts stop once the parent becomes incapacitated, or after his parents' deaths when the equalization of the estate leaves the moocher child with an inadequate amount of money to survive on for very long.

This problem is compounded when you consider our increased longevity. If the moocher child is in his late sixties or even seventies before his parents pass on, he is often unemployable at that point. Perhaps he has physical or other disabilities that make most jobs out of reach. Many employers won't consider hiring someone at those ages as well.

Finally, there's the question as to whether an adult spendthrift child should handle his or her own inheritance once Mom and Dad are both deceased.

Just know that if you have a moocher child who you know that you shouldn't continue enabling, but you can't stand the thought of cutting them off, you might be making his future situation a whole lot worse by continuing to make the gifts.

Does Leaving Everything To Children Avoid Charges Of Parental Favoritism?

The bible is replete with stories describing ill consequences when a parent favors one child over another. Jacob's deception of his father, Isaac, in order to receive the blessings of the first born, even though Jacob's twin brother, Esau, was entitled, happens to be one of the most famous. A related biblical story is regarding Jacob's favoring his son, Joseph; giving Joseph a multi-colored coat angered Joseph's brothers, who sold him into Egyptian slavery.

Sibling rivalry, especially to inure inheritance rights from their parents, therefore appears to go back to the beginnings of recorded time. It's been my experience that parents struggle with how to treat their children fairly when deciding how to divide up their assets and possessions. Most of the time, parents will favor dividing everything equally in an effort to not show any favoritism and to curry goodwill between their children.

But does this strategy always work? What about the case where one of the siblings took care of an infirm parent for years? She may expect some kind of monetary reward in the estate plan, and may feel hurt if the parent fails to account for the extra effort. Yet if the parent does reward the dutiful child with a disproportionate share, her siblings may protest.

"It was her choice to take care of Mom, and it doesn't make up for a lifetime of being part of family in which everything was always equal," they may say.

Paradoxically, the sibling who remains close to the parent often does not feel she is the favored child. A parent may take for granted the devoted daughter who visits her in the nursing home every day. Then, on the rare occasion when her brother walks in, the overjoyed mom announces, "Oh my son is here! He is so kind to visit me!" The daughter might hope that such imbalance will be corrected in her inheritance, although typical patterns of family interaction tend to persist, even at the end of life.

What about the situation where one child needs the money and the other doesn't? The parent might decide to leave all or a significant portion of the estate to the needy child, potentially causing ill will between them.

"I know that 'John' needed the money more than I did," 'Lou' once complained to me, "but he ALWAYS needed the money. Mom and Dad continually bailed him out of one financial disaster to the next. I NEVER asked for a dime. And now, here at the end, look what they did."

Valid feelings, certainly.

I've also seen the other end of the spectrum. "Listen," 'Sheila' explained to me while deciding what to put into her will, "I've given Bobby so much money over the years that it wouldn't be fair to give him more in my will. Everything should instead go to Susan and Edna. Let's leave Bobby out of the will."

Very often wills are used not only as a means of conferring favor, some have used them as a means to measure a child's performance in accordance with the parents' standards. "Everything was fine until you married that girl," for example.

Sometimes—because neither the parents nor children ever wanted to broach uncomfortable subjects—it's only when the will is read that son or daughter discovers that one or both parents harbored such unspoken resentments.

Also, many adult children interpret the will as a kind of final report card. "Did I grade an A or an F?" they might wonder. Putting a younger sibling in charge as being the personal representative (executor) may send a message to the older siblings that they didn't measure up. Nevertheless, it's important to name the most responsible one as the executor, as I've written about before.

There's obviously a lot of emotional baggage to consider when making an estate plan. As we've learned over the millennium, there are no 'right' or 'wrong' answers. Only those that best fit you and your family.

Is This A Business Or Family Transaction?

"Howard" died, survived by his three sons, "Ken," "Vincent" and "Jim." Knowing that his three sons didn't see eye to eye, Howard had named his brother, "Bill" as the trustee of his trust and the executor of his estate, hoping that Bill would provide a calming effect among the family. As it turns out, there were some big problems in the estate.

Dealing with the death of a loved one brings out a lot of emotion. Especially when that loved one is your parent. Sometimes—in the thick of such a stressful and troubling time—unresolved conflicts between siblings make the estate administration that much more difficult. And in this particular family, the problems were boiling to the surface following Howard's death.

Howard had mortgaged his Florida home in order to pay for a townhouse in Vermont for Jim, where Jim lived and worked—when he had a job. Jim was not the most fiscally responsible son, having had numerous financial problems in the past. Because of Jim's financial problems, Howard titled the Vermont townhouse in another son's name (Vincent).

Jim had failed to pay the property taxes on the townhouse, which not only threatened Vincent's ownership of it (unless Vincent decided to pay for the taxes on a unit that he didn't reside in and which he didn't want or need) but also threatened Vincent's credit rating.

When it came time to settle the administration, Vincent didn't want to own the townhouse that Jim was living in, but the family couldn't title it into Jim's name because of Jim's financial problems. Further, the loan against the Florida home adversely affected all three of the son's inheritances. Vincent and Ken resented Jim because the mortgage against the Florida home was such that when it was sold there would be little or no equity left to split among the three of them.

Ken complained to Bill, making demands that Jim should just pay the balance of the mortgage and take the Vermont townhouse, leaving the Florida home to be sold, with the net proceeds divided amongst the three. Bill explained that Jim couldn't possibly qualify for a mortgage given his financial condition, and even so, the value of that mortgage would exceed the value of the townhouse due to the real estate market crash. Someone with good credit wouldn't get that loan anyway.

Vincent threatened to kick Jim out on the street, saying that since he was actually the owner of the townhouse, he had the right to do that. The family was fractured.

When a family is confronted with issues like this, they often turn to an attorney, asking what everyone's legal rights and responsibilities are. Bill found himself distraught dealing with these volatile and emotional issues. "I never expected my role to be so hard," he confided.

I would suggest that in this situation, before the legalities are addressed, a bigger issue needs to be resolved. The question that I would pose to each of the three sons is this: "What is your ultimate goal here?"

And by that I don't mean that one son ends up with more money, or another son has to pay the mortgage.

What I really mean to say is this: "Is the settlement of your father's estate a family transaction or is all of this strictly business between the three of you?"

If settling the estate is a family transaction, then the ultimate goal is to retain some sense of family harmony while at the same time trying to achieve as fair of an outcome as possible to all parties. If, however, it's strictly business, then each individual needs to have their own lawyer push hard to represent their individual legal rights in an attempt to achieve the best economic outcome for themselves.

It's either an "all for one and one for all"—or, "looking out for number one."

At the end of the day, whether or not a son will inherit more money from his father's estate may not matter. What's the true cost of that transaction if brothers never speak to one another again, or if an uncle doesn't know his nieces and nephews because the families are fractured?

The best solution, for example, might be to pool all the resources to get out of debt and to carry the Florida property until the economy recovers. Another solution might be to sell everything for what the family can get, pay off the debt and hope for the best. In either scenario, the sons all might end up with a lot less than they originally thought they'd inherit.

In a situation like Howard's, the family has to realize that the sum of its parts—working together—has a much better chance of a favorable outcome then all of the sons fighting individually for what's legally theirs.

Do You Have A Legal Right To Know?

One of the most common questions bouncing around on-line legal advice forums and that I hear quite frequently from "cold calls" coming into my office goes something like this: "My Mom named my sister as her trustee. I think that Sis is taking all of Mom's money. When I ask Sis what's going on, she won't tell me anything. Do I have a legal right to the information?"

The answer is that "it depends." I joke around that attorneys sell more depends than Walgreens and CVS combined! But with most questions, like this one—the answer really does depend on the relevant facts of each and every situation. So in some situations Brother may have a right to know what Sis is up to, while in others he may not.

To illustrate my point, let's first make the assumption that Mom is still alive. In this case, Brother probably doesn't have any legal right to information about Mom's trust and Mom's assets. Mom named Sis as trustee, or perhaps as a successor trustee in the event of Mom's incapacity. Mom has a right to keep her affairs private. If she has named Sis as the trustee, then she trusts Sis to act appropriately and to act in Mom's best interests.

With no oversight it is entirely possible that Sis is stealing Mom blind. And revocable trusts, by and large, don't have any oversight. A benefit to revocable trusts is that they are private and outside of the court system. That same benefit might also be called a potential detriment. Because there is no oversight on the trustee's activities, she might be doing things that she ought not to be doing. That's why it is so important for Mom to carefully consider who she should name as her trustee. It's extremely difficult for Brother to legally gather information during Mom's life under this set of facts.

It's not until Brother actually becomes a beneficiary of the trust does Brother have access to the trust information. Brother is not technically a beneficiary of the trust until Mom dies, assuming that Mom has named Brother as a beneficiary.

In Florida law, there is a defined term known as a "Qualified Beneficiary." At the time of Mom's death, Brother (assuming he's named in the document) becomes a "Qualified Beneficiary" of Mom's trust. As a Qualified Beneficiary he has rights to receive a copy of the trust document, as well as an inventory and accounting of trust assets and income. He can also request an accounting from the time that Sis became trustee of the trust—that may have occurred during Mom's lifetime.

Is there a way that Brother can legally access the trust information during Mom's life? Under certain circumstances he might have such rights. If Brother is named as a co-trustee with Sis, then he has every right to all of the information. If Brother suspects wrongdoing on Sis' part and has a Durable Power of Attorney, Brother may also have the ability to access the information. As a Durable Power of Attorney holder, Brother might be able to gather the information based on the fact that he is also Mom's fiduciary and has an obligation to make sure that her affairs are properly tended to. It's entirely likely that Brother would have to go to Court to force Sis to disclose the information. That might be time consuming and expensive.

Brother's attorney's fees might be paid by the trust if it can be shown that the legal action was necessary to prevent Sis from wrongfully taking trust assets, or that Brother's attorney's work in any way benefited the trust or Mom.

Let's examine more closely Sis' fiduciary duty to act in Mom's best interests while Sis is trustee for Mom. What this means is, if there is a choice between doing something that benefits Mom or doing something that might benefit Sis down the line, Sis is supposed to disregard her own interests and act solely in the best interests of Mom.

A good example of this is whether Sis is spending Mom's money for the best care available, or whether she is getting second-rate care in order to preserve more of the estate for herself in the event of Mom's death. If Mom's assets can afford a single room in the assisted living facility but Sis doubles Mom up to save money, it might be argued that Sis wasn't acting in Mom's best interests.

Similarly, if Sis is making gifts to herself from Mom's assets without regard to Mom's wishes, this could also be evidence of Sis not acting in a fiduciary capacity.

As you might imagine, these types of allegations are hard to prove. There are always two sides to every coin. What may appear on its face to be improper conduct may eventually appear to have a valid purpose behind it.

In order to avoid these types of conflicts, Mom might consider naming co-trustees. There was probably a good reason that Mom named Sis and not Brother as trustee. Assuming that Mom doesn't want to name Brother, she could name a bank, trust company or even a trusted professional, such as Mom's CPA, to serve as a co-trustee. Whenever there is an independent third party acting and looking over the shoulder of the family trustee, the likelihood of malfeasance is greatly minimized.

In any event, when considering your duties as trustee for another, you should always ask yourself whether, if what you are doing is brought to light, someone might accuse you of acting improperly. It's a fine line sometimes.

Renting Your Home From Your Kids

A common estate planning technique that is used to transfer residences from one generation to the next while at the same time minimizing the consumption of your gift and estate tax exemptions is to use a "Qualified Personal Residence Trust" (QPRT). But when the QPRT expires and the residence is transferred to the children, you need to be careful or this estate planning strategy may fail.

Allow me first to review how a QPRT works. Assume you own a residence that is currently worth $750,000 and that you are 72 years old. You want to transfer the residence to your children without consuming $750,000 of your gift tax exemption. So you create a QPRT, where you retain the right to live in the residence for a period of your choosing, and then at the end of the term of the QPRT, the home is transferred to your children.

Because you retain the right to reside in the residence for a period of seven years, the gift that you are making to your children is a "remainder interest" in the home seven years from now. So the value of the gift is the future interest of this $750,000 asset seven years from now. The value is an actuarial determination based upon your age, current interest rates and the value of the residence transferred.

In my example, a $750,000 residence put into a 7 year QPRT by a 72 year old under current interest rates results in a gift of approximately $468,000 (as opposed to a $750,000 gift).

The longer the period of time that you choose to retain the right to reside in the residence, the lower the amount of the gift. If the children have to wait ten years until the residence becomes theirs, the actuarial value of the gift is only $356,000. So it makes sense to stretch out the term of the QPRT as long as you feel is necessary and reasonable.

But here's the rub: you have to survive the term of the QPRT for the tax savings to be realized. So the longer the QPRT term you establish, the greater risk that you have in not surviving the term.

Here's another problem that a lot of people who have done QPRTs run into, and that's the fact that the children own the residence at the end of the term. If you continue to reside in the home as if nothing had happened, then the IRS will disregard the QPRT when you die. The residence will still be included in your estate for estate tax purposes.

You can still use the residence—but you must rent it. And you can't rent it for a dollar or some other nominal amount. You must pay fair market value for the time that you spend in the residence. The IRS has successfully defeated QPRTs where, even for a short period after the termination of the QPRT, the parents did not rent the property from the children for fair value.

This becomes an even stickier issue when you are dealing with Florida homestead residences. So long as the residence is in the QPRT for its term, it should continue to qualify for the Save Our Homes property tax assessment caps and for the homestead exemptions. But once the QPRT terminates and the home is distributed to the children, it loses that status—unless the lease that the parents entered into meets certain statutory criteria. So if you own a homestead residence that is in a QPRT, you might want to discuss what strategies you could employ to maintain the beneficial property tax treatment.

Another issue that may arise is if one of the QPRT beneficiaries becomes incapacitated, dies or has creditor problems that may cloud the title to the property. Here, many of those issues can be avoided by naming a trust as the beneficiary to the QPRT rather than the children individually. This strategy, however, must be thought out and implemented at the inception of the QPRT, since these instruments are all irrevocable.

If you have a residence in a QPRT, it would make sense to discuss these issues with your attorney prior to the termination of the trust.

CRAIG R. HERSCH

Same-Sex Couples Estate Planning

L ast year brought several favorable developments for same-sex couples in the tax and estate planning arenas. First, in June, the Supreme Court ruled in the *Windsor* case that same-sex couples were entitled to the same federal estate tax benefits that a traditional married couple enjoys. In *Windsor,* the surviving spouse and executor of a same-sex union sued the IRS for recovery of taxes paid that would not have been by a traditional married couple by way of the marital deduction.

The surviving spouse claimed that the Defense of Marriage Act (DOMA) that outlaws same-sex unions and therefore leads to the denial of the estate tax marital deduction was unconstitutional. While the Supreme Court did not rule specifically on the direct issue, it did rule in a split (5-4) decision that when individual states recognize same-sex marriages, the federal government cannot deny benefits to surviving spouses, including legal and tax benefits. That decision led to the surviving spouse in the *Windsor* union receiving the same federal tax benefits that a traditional married spouse would have received, and therefore, the estate tax paid was refunded.

The Justice Department decided not to contest the constitutionality of the Supreme Court's decision. Shortly thereafter, the IRS issued a Revenue Ruling (2013-17) that responded to the Supreme Court's opinion in *Windsor*, ruling that same-sex couples who are legally married in states or foreign countries that recognize the validity of their marriages will be treated as married for all federal tax purposes, even if they live in a state or other jurisdiction that does not recognize same-sex marriages. Specifically, the IRS raised and answered the following three questions:

1. Do "spouse," "husband and wife," "husband," and "wife," include lawfully married persons of the same sex? Here the IRS answered "Yes."

2. Is this true if the jurisdiction in which the couple is currently domiciled, unlike the jurisdiction in which the marriage was established, does not recognize same-sex marriages? Again, the IRS answered the question as "Yes"; in other words, if a same-sex couple was legally married in Massachusetts—that does recognize same-sex marriages—but subsequently moves to Florida—that does not, the couple will still receive the benefits of being considered married for federal legal and tax purposes.

3. Is this true of registered domestic partnerships, civil unions, and similarly recognized formal relationships? Here the IRS answered the question "No." The same-sex couple must be legally married in a state or country that recognizes same-sex marriages in order to be considered married.

When the revenue ruling was released, Secretary of the Treasury, Jacob Lew said, "Today's ruling provides certainty and clear, coherent tax filing guidance for all legally married same-sex couples nationwide. It provides access to benefits, responsibilities and protections under federal tax law that all Americans deserve. This ruling also assures legally married same-sex couples that they can move freely throughout the country knowing that their federal filing status will not change."

These pronouncements and rulings provide many federal income and estate tax benefits for same-sex married couples. As mentioned in the *Windsor* case, the estate tax marital deduction is available to same-sex couples, as is portability of unused spouse estate exemption, the filing of joint income tax returns, tax free gift transfers between spouses, gift splitting so that the spouses can double the amount of tax-free gifts to other loved ones and a variety of other benefits.

There are also downsides for same-sex married couples under the tax laws. The "marriage penalty" that serves to tax two-income earning married couples at a higher rate than if they were both single now applies to same-sex married couples. The maximum mortgage interest deduction is limited to $1.1 million of debt among a married couple as opposed to $2.2 million to a non-married couple.

Participants in certain employee benefit plans subject to the ERISA laws will be required to obtain the spouse's written consent before designating anyone other than the spouse (such as a trust) as beneficiary of certain benefit plans. Losses are generally not allowed for transfers between spouses as well.

Although these new rules did much to clarify the income tax filing status for same-sex couples at the federal level, same-sex couples in non-recognition states will have to deal with their income tax filing status at the state level. Even if the state is a conformity state (that is, the state income tax return follows the federal return with certain specified adjustments), many non-recognition states have announced that same-sex couples must file separate state tax returns. This may require a same-sex couple that files a joint federal return to prepare pro forma federal returns with filing status as separate before they can prepare their state tax returns. The non-recognition states that follow this approach include Arizona, Idaho, Kansas, Louisiana, Michigan, North Carolina, North Dakota, Ohio, Oklahoma, Utah, Virginia, and Wisconsin.

There will also be will construction issues in non-recognition states. For example, if a will governed by the law of Virginia (a non-recognition state) grants a New York beneficiary the power to appoint trust assets at death to the beneficiary's spouse and the New York beneficiary has entered into a recognized same-sex marriage, can the New York beneficiary exercise the power in favor of the same-sex spouse? Other construction issues may arise in dealing with the discretionary power to distribute principal to a spouse where the will or trust instrument is governed by the law of a non-recognition state and the beneficiary has a same-sex spouse.

Same-sex spouses who entered into prenuptial or postnuptial marital agreements have often addressed how the fact that they did not qualify for various income tax benefits and other benefits affects their property rights vis-à-vis each other. Those agreements should now be reviewed, and future marital property agreements should be structured in light of these new laws.

There's definitely a lot to consider. Those who are in same-sex marriages should take the time to review their planning to make sure that it is up to date with all of these changes.

Chapter Seven

Tax Planning

You Can't Take it With You But You Can Leave it Behind

There's the old adage that when one dies, "you can't take it with you," so you might as well use up whatever it is before you go. But the estate tax law included in the 2012 American Taxpayer Relief Act (ATRA) allows you to leave your estate exemptions behind for your spouse.

In other words, under the 2012 estate tax law each of us has a $5.25 million exemption. This is generally good news, since a married couple together can shield $10.5 million of combined assets from estate tax! (*Since writing this article, in 2014 the federal estate tax exemption increased from $5.25 million amount* *to a whopping $5.34 million! This means that a married couple can shield a combined $10.68 million from federal estate tax.*)

Unlike prior years when you had to divide your assets between the husband's name and the wife's name in order to use up both of their estate tax exemptions, there is something called "portability" built into the law. While portability has been around since 2010, no one knew whether it would be made more permanent. Now we have that answer.

At least for now.

How does portability work? Let's look at an example where the husband dies and his estate only has $2 million. The remainder of his $5.25 million exemption ($3.25 million) isn't lost as long as the surviving spouse files a timely federal estate tax return. Instead, his unused exemption transfers over to her column.

If a timely federal estate tax return is not filed, however, then the husband's exemption is forever lost. You might then call the already inappropriately named American Taxpayer Relief Act (whom exactly does it relieve, I would like to know) the Estate Tax Return Preparer Relief Act, because it is now important to file estate tax returns on estates that may not rise to the level of being taxable in order to preserve the exemption.

So in my example above, provided surviving wife files an estate tax return for husband, her exemption is now $8.5 million (her 5.25 million plus his unused $3.25 million). Unless she remarries. Then she loses her exemption. Unless she gifts his exemption amount away before she remarries. In which case she can use his exemption and perhaps her new spouse's unused exemption, provided she survives him, too!

Should we not therefore call this new law "The Black Widow(er) Relief Act"?

A reasonable question to ask with the portability of estate tax exemptions is whether the new law does away with the traditional notion of dividing assets between husband and wife.

Maybe, but it's not so clear. Why would I say that? What would be the reason to divide the assets equitably?

One reason is the generation skipping tax exemption. While the estate tax exemption is portable, the generation skipping tax exemption is not. Consider the clients who wish to bequeath their assets in trust for their children and avoid estate tax inclusion in their children's estates. It doesn't make sense to avoid taxation in parents' estates only to have those same assets taxed when the children die.

In order to maximize intergenerational planning, you still generally want to divide assets between husband and wife, because the generation skipping tax exemptions only work if the assets are divided.

There may be other reasons to divide assets between husband and wife. If you want to protect assets for your spouse from their creditors or from their future divorcing spouses, then dividing assets makes sense. For those that have to worry about the state death tax because they either reside in a state that still has a lower death tax exemption, or who own real property in a state that has a death tax, dividing the assets might be necessary.

It also makes sense to divide assets when you have second marriage situations with children from prior marriages, and you want to ensure that your children receive the assets and amounts that you intended.

This new world of portability offers many planning opportunities. There's going to be a lot more creativity in estate planning now that the shackles of federal estate taxation are looser. Imagining a flexible trust that benefits a variety of beneficiaries—from a surviving spouse, to educating grandchildren, to making charitable bequests—is going to be a lot easier now that the exemption amount is higher.

The danger really remains, however, for those that are lured into complacency and who fail to plan, thinking that the main reason to do the planning is no longer a concern. The new income tax laws, particularly those surrounding the Medicare Surtax, are also going to become a larger concern.

It just keeps getting more interesting, doesn't it?

Reverse Estate Plan To Eliminate Capital Gains

Estate taxes will not concern as many families now that the federal estate tax exemption amount has increased to $5.34 million. The increase in the marginal estate tax brackets, coupled with the Medicare Surtax result in income tax planning becoming more important inside of many family's estate plans.

I recently attended the Heckerling Estate Planning Conference, a one-week high-level continuing education course designed for trust and estate attorneys, CPAs and trust officers. Top academics and lecturers impart wisdom on the 5,000 attendees from around the country on how to help families plan their estates to minimize taxes and achieve the family's goals.

During one of the sessions, an interesting idea surfaced related to the elimination of capital gains by "reversing" the normal estate plan. Instead of leaving assets down the generational line, this strategy actually moves assets from a younger generation member to a parent or other older generation family member.

In order to understand the strategy, one must first understand the "step up" in tax cost basis concept. If I purchase a stock at $1/share and later sell that stock for $10/share during my lifetime, I recognize a $9 capital gain and pay taxes on that capital gain. If, however, I die with that stock in my estate and it is worth $10/share, generally speaking, my beneficiaries receive a "step up" in tax cost basis equal to that asset's date of death value.

So in my example, if I die with stock worth $10/share and leave it in my will to my children, and if my children were to sell the stock at $10/share shortly after my death, then they would not recognize the capital gain that I would have recognized had I sold the stock the day before I died.

Normally individuals' estate plans leave assets to their spouses, children and grandchildren—not to their parents, who have a shorter life expectancy. But consider a strategy where an individual has an asset worth $1 million that has a tax cost basis of zero. If he were to sell the asset, then he would recognize a capital gain equal to $1 million and pay 23.8% in federal capital gains taxes totaling $238,000.

Assume in my above example that the owner of the $1 million asset is a wealthy middle-aged child who has a poorer parent. Provided that the family members can work together, there is an opportunity to eliminate the capital gains tax.

Suppose, for example, that the child transfers the asset into a trust for his parent that pays the income to his poorer parent for the parent's lifetime. The trust contains something known as a "general power of appointment" that allows the parent to direct the disposition of the asset, but if the parent doesn't so direct, at the parent's death, the asset continues on in a generation skipping tax exempt trust to the child and that child's descendants who originally gifted the asset to the parent.

If parent survives the transfer of the asset by at least one year, then on the parent's death the asset would receive a step up in tax cost basis to its current fair market value of $1 million. If the parent dies after the one-year period, leaving the asset back to the child in trust, and the trustee sells the asset, then the original capital gain could be eliminated.

There are issues that must be dealt with for the strategy to be successful. The trust must be drafted in such a way so as to avoid the IRS claiming that the whole transaction is a fraud to evade taxes, so the parent should not be so restricted that he must leave the asset back to the child who made the gift. Along those same lines, if the parent isn't restricted, then the child may lose the asset in a gift to his or her siblings. These types of issues can be mitigated in several ways. The wealthy child could, as just one example, purchase an assignment of interest from his or her siblings of any assets that parent might leave them from this particular trust.

Another danger is if the poorer parent has any creditors who could have an interest in the assets of the poor parent's estate. Again, these types of issues must be considered and planned for.

This is just one example. With the increase of both the federal gift and estate tax exemptions, a multi-generational family that shares common goals can work to save estate, gift and income taxes in a number of different ways.

Step Up To Minimize Taxable Gains

A lot of people get confused by capital gains and income taxes in estates. One basic concept that I will cover here includes the "step up" in tax cost basis that wipes away capital gains when we leave assets to our loved ones at our deaths through our will or revocable trust.

Say that I purchased a share of Coca Cola stock many years ago at $1/share. Now suppose it is $11/share. If I sell that stock today, then I realize the $10 capital gain and pay tax on it. If I apply a 20% capital gains tax rate with a 3.8 percent Medicare Surtax (some call this the ObamaCare tax), then I may pay as much as $2.38 out of my $10 gain to Uncle Sam. If it is short-term capital gain, then I may lose as much as $5, especially if I live in a state that imposes state income taxes.

If I give the share of stock away during my lifetime to my daughter, she takes it at the same tax cost basis that I have in it ($1) and would recognize the same capital gain that I would pay if she sells it, even if she sells it after my death.

But if, instead, I hold on to the share of stock and bequeath it to her in my will or trust, after my death she receives a step up in tax cost basis equal to the fair market value at the time of my death. So in my example, if I die when it is worth $11/share and she inherits it then sells it after my death, she recognizes no capital gain. No capital gain is much better than paying a capital gain rate between 23.8% and 50%.

The new estate tax laws that allow everyone a $5.25 million federal estate tax exemption provide planning opportunities to minimize the tax, including those who have joint revocable living trusts. A married couple can together shield $10.5 million of assets from federal estate tax.

The trick is now to set up one's estate plan to minimize income taxes, since the tax rates are increasing at both state and federal levels.

First, a word of caution. The applicable IRS Code Section (1014) denies step up in tax cost basis to assets transferred to decedents within one year of death. As an example, assume that Daniel is on his deathbed. His wife, Doris, transfers $4 million of appreciated stock into his name in the months before his death. Here, the applicable IRS Code Section serves to deny his spouse the step up in tax cost basis when Daniel's will leaves the stock back to Doris.

This is clear if Daniel's will or trust leaves the assets directly back to Doris. But some argue that if, instead, the assets are left in trust back to Doris, then a full step up in tax cost basis should be enjoyed.

Alan Gassman, a tax attorney colleague of mine in Clearwater, Florida, agrees with the opinion that when a joint revocable living trust is included completely in the estate of the first decedent spouse, a full step up in tax cost basis should be achieved when the trust continues under what is known as an ascertainable standard—this is the "health education, maintenance and support" limitations found in many trusts.

He reads the applicable Code Sections to say that if Dan and Doris create a revocable living trust and fund it together in such a way as to include all of the assets in Dan's estate when he dies, and if the trust then continues for Doris, granting her income rights and principal invasion rights for her health, maintenance and support, then all of the assets inside of the trust should receive a step up in tax cost basis at Dan's death.

This is contrary to the official IRS position, but appears consistent with the language under the statute. With the increase in federal estate tax exemption amounts, trusts could conceivably be drafted to take advantage of this opportunity. The family would have to be willing to live with the risk of challenging the IRS position, but there may be a lot to gain and little to lose.

With top marginal tax rates (including state income taxes) on short-term capital gains approaching 43 - 50%, estate planning to minimize income taxes is going to become more important. There are other issues surrounding trust income and the tax rates, so careful planning with qualified professionals should be considered before acting.

How Much For My Image?

Next to the newspaper column that I write for our local newspaper is my portrait photo that was taken a few years ago. I'm certainly not famous, although I recently dined at Gramma Dots where someone recognized me as the guy who writes the column. They told me that they appreciate the information I give, so I was flattered.

So when I die and leave behind estate planning books that I've written and a pile of my old columns, how much do you suppose the accountants would report as the value of those things? How about my likeness? If my estate licensed my likeness, what would the value be for federal estate tax purposes?

My guess is that my estate would value that with a big fat zero.

Amazingly, that value of zero would only be $2,105 less than what Michael Jackson's estate reported as the value of *his* likeness. Never mind that Michael Jackson's likeness is currently licensed to sell T-shirts, music, and is seen on television commercials, among other things. The IRS disagreed with his estate's valuation, pegging its estimate of Mr. Jackson's likeness at $434 million. The estate tax difference on those estimates approximates $170 million.

How about the value of the rights to various compositions that Mr. Jackson owned at the time of his death? He owned the license rights of many of his own recordings, but also to some Beatles hits, including "Yesterday," "Sgt. Pepper's Lonely Heart Club Band" and "Get Back." Jackson's estate valued those recordings at zero. The IRS says they're worth $469 million.

The difference between what Michael Jackson's estate estimates as the federal estate tax that it owes and what the IRS says that it owes is greater than $500 million. The IRS estimates Jackson's estate to be valued at $1.125 billion, which sharply contrasts with the $7 million valuation his executors say he was worth.

In addition to assessing the extra tax, the IRS also imposed 20 percent penalties and interest for what they claim to be a gross underreporting.

These issues highlight the problems in valuing assets for estate tax purposes. While Michael Jackson's case is extreme, these same issues apply to many of us. At one end of the valuation spectrum, you have marketable securities. Since these are listed on a stock exchange and can be sold on a moment's notice, everyone can agree on the value of publicly traded stocks, bonds and most mutual funds.

Real estate valuations are somewhere in the middle of the "difficult to value" spectrum. Appraisers can use the selling price of "comparable" properties—but no two properties are exactly the same. Whether or not the real estate produces rental income makes the valuation of it that much more problematic, as there are many different components involved. The value of the land must be considered, along with the value of the buildings and improvements, as well as the leases. A lease with a tenant that is going to expire in a year would not be as valuable as a 10-year lease. Leases signed by local tenants who are experiencing financial problems aren't as valuable as regional or national tenants with strong balance sheets.

Family business interests tilt towards the more difficult end of the valuation spectrum. What would the value of the business be if the patriarch/matriarch wasn't involved anymore? Is that an important factor? Depends on the business. What is the business' going concern value? What is the value of the business' underlying assets, such as real estate and inventory?

Sometimes it makes estate planning sense to take hard-to-value assets (real estate, for example) and transform those assets into even more difficult to value interests. A common example includes real estate assets that are transferred into a family partnership. In so doing, a business valuation specialist may use "discounts" when valuing the underlying property for purposes of the gift, thereby reducing the value of the taxable estate for estate tax purposes.

The IRS is not fond of these discounts but will consent to those that are not overly aggressive. Suppose, for example, that father owns commercial real estate valued at $5 million. By contributing that real estate into a family partnership, the value of the minority shares gifted or otherwise transferred to family members usually enjoy a discount associated with their lack of control and lack of marketability. After all, who would pay full value for a 10% interest in a partnership that doesn't have a ready market, where the shares are restricted by agreement and where one doesn't have the ability to control?

When planning one's estate these factors should play into the discussion, and the plan can be adjusted to reflect the opportunities associated with difficult to value assets.

The Middle Aged Uncle And Aunt Table

My wife's 98-year-old grandmother recently passed away. Mollie Leber was a wonderful, kind, generous and extremely smart woman who was born in Poland. Mollie immigrated to the United States when she was a little girl after her father first arrived here and secured passage for her and her mother. She would later marry and work with her husband in a dry goods business on the lower east side of Manhattan, which they later moved to Brooklyn. She raised two children, had five grandchildren and had ten great grandchildren at the time of her death.

She was the prototypical family matriarch. "GG" as we called her (for Great-Grandma), lived here in Florida the last twenty-five years or so to be close to her family. There was a hole in our hearts this Passover when GG was missing this year from the gathering around the Sedar table.

Time marches on, though. They say everything goes from generation to generation. As one generation leaves us with memories, the next generation must step up and serve as the new leaders.

But with that said, when we're talking about estate planning, the use of the term "generation skipping" sometimes brings misunderstanding. So I thought that I'd write about a topic that might help you understand what "generation skipping" typically refers to in your estate plan.

In order to understand generation skipping, you must first understand how the United States federal estate and gift tax system works. We all know that if our estates exceed our available exemption from estate tax at the time of our deaths, then an estate tax will be levied. The government wants this to happen as each generation of the family dies off. When grandpa dies his estate pays taxes; when son dies then his estate pays taxes, and when grandson dies then his estate pays taxes.

Estate planning attorneys came up with a bright idea several decades ago. If we put all of the assets into a trust that continues on for each generation, then legally each generation can be called a beneficiary but is not an owner! Therefore, the estate tax shouldn't apply as each generation dies off.

Congress caught on to this loophole in 1976 and created an additional tax called the Generation Skipping Transfer Tax (GSTT). What this tax does is impose another tax (in addition to the estate tax) at the estate tax's highest marginal rate on transfers (either lifetime or at death) that skip a generation. Amounts in trust from father to son to grandson that are designed to "skip" son's estate for estate tax purposes are said to be subject to a "generation skipping transfer tax." So if I have $1 that is subject to both estate and generation skipping taxes, as much as 78 cents of that dollar could be consumed by tax.

But Congress did give us all an exemption from the GSTT. Today that exemption mirrors the estate tax exemption of $5.34 million as of 2014. So Granddad can create a $5 million trust that continues on for the lifetime of son and is not included in son's estate for estate tax purposes, then can go on to grandson without tax.

Contrast this with an outright bequest to son that would end up being taxed in son's estate when son dies.

Good estate planning attorneys will typically counsel their clients to retain assets in trust for successive generations to utilize the generation skipping transfer tax exemption. This doesn't necessarily mean that the client is "skipping" his or her children in favor of his or her grandchildren. Instead, amounts are held in trust for the children and continue on to the grandchildren in an effort to minimize estate taxes as each generation dies off.

Clients can even name their children as the trustees of the trust that the children are also beneficiaries of. In other words, using your generation skipping transfer tax exemption does not always mean that you have to use a bank or trust company as a trustee. Naming a child as trustee who is also a beneficiary, however, does require special provisions to be embedded inside of the trust to avoid having the value of the trust taxed in the child's estate when he or she dies.

The generations move on quickly, don't they? Patti and I attended one of her young cousin's weddings not too long ago, and we were seated at the table with Patti's brothers and their wives and some of her other cousins who were also about our age. I looked around the room and said to my wife, "Do you realize which table we are at?"

She looked at me quizzically, "What do you mean?"

I pointed at some of the other tables. "Look, over there are the young married couples who all have young children, and over there are the singles—the friends of the bride and the groom—who are all flirting with one another, and over there are all of the grandparents!"

"So?" Patti asked.

"We're at the middle-aged uncle and aunt table!" I exclaimed. "Somehow we've graduated from the young married table to the table with all of the middle-aged parents who have teenage and college age children! When did that all happen?"

Patti kissed me on the cheek and laughed at me. "It happens sooner than we all like to realize," she said.

How To Maximize The Inheritance

D id you know that with the exact same assets and the exact same beneficiaries, your estate plan may pay out significantly different amounts to your beneficiaries? In other words, the structure of your estate plan can make all the difference in the world to how much Uncle Sam gets as opposed to how much your beneficiaries receive. Consider this illustration:

A single client desired to give amounts to his two daughters and to charity. The client wants the charity to receive the remainder of a $1.5 million trust upon the tenth anniversary of his date of death, with the daughters receiving income during those ten years. The client owns a $1.5 million IRA with another $2.5 million of other investments that are owned outside of any qualified retirement plan. Client also owns a life insurance policy with a death benefit of $350,000 and a current cash surrender value of $120,000. Aside from the trust that is to be distributed to charity, the client wants everything else to go to his daughters.

Client's prior planners carved out a $1.5 million bequest in his revocable trust that provides income to his daughters for ten years and then pays the remainder to the charity. His revocable trust is primarily funded with his $2.5 million investment account. Client's life insurance policy designates his daughters as primary beneficiaries as does client's IRA account. Assume that client passes away and his unused federal estate tax exemption equals $3.5 million (the current 2009 exemption amount).

In this scenario the daughters receive the income from the trust that designates charity as the ultimate beneficiary, but the trust as drafted does not qualify for the federal estate tax charitable deduction. Because client's total estate exceeds the $3.5 million threshold, his estate must pay federal estate tax in the approximate amount of $360,000.

Assuming that the trust for the charity earns and pays 6% income to the daughters annually, they realize $900,000 of gross income from the trust. Upon the daughter's death, the trust distributes a net $1.5 million to the educational institution. The daughters receive the life insurance proceeds of $350,000 outright, but withdraw the entire amount from the IRA in the year following their father's death, resulting in the payment of approximately $750,000 combined federal and state income tax.

Under the prior plan, the net to client's daughters would therefore approximate $2 million and the net to the charity approximates $1.5 million. Uncle Sam became a beneficiary to the tune of $360,000 in the form of estate tax. These amounts do not reflect the "time value of money"—the effect of waiting for the income stream on the trust to mature.

Let's assume that client restructures his plan as follows: Rather than the charity receiving net amounts from client's after-tax assets, the IRA now names a 6% Charitable Remainder Trust for a ten-year term payable to daughters, with the remainder distributed to charity. At client's death, the charitable remainder trust provides his estate an estate tax charitable deduction in the approximate amount of $700,000. Client's insurance was placed into an irrevocable life insurance trust, with daughters as the beneficiaries. Assume that client survives the three-year inclusion period of the trust.

Under this new plan, there is no federal estate tax due since the use of the charitable remainder trust combined with using the IRA to fund client's charitable intent. The combination of the charitable and insurance trusts brings client's gross estate below the taxable level. Uncle Sam is no longer a beneficiary. The use of the IRA to fund the charitable intent also results in less income tax dollars being paid to Uncle Sam.

Daughters therefore receive income of $900,000 (before income tax) from the charitable trust for the ten years, $2.5 million of after tax assets from the estate, and $350,000 of life insurance proceeds for a total of $3.75 million. The net to charity remains at $1.5 million. Uncle Sam, you may recall is now excluded as a beneficiary for estate tax purposes. Like the prior example, the above amounts do not reflect the time value of money received over the course of the ten-year charitable trust.

Comparing the two plans, the daughters make out significantly better under the revised scenario—*$1.75 million better*. We had the exact same assets as before, and the exact same beneficiaries as before. We just structured the plan differently, taking into account tools that reduce estate and income tax exposure.

This example clearly demonstrates that how you structure your estate plan does—and it will often—make a difference to your beneficiaries, sometimes to the tune of several hundred thousand dollars or more.

The IRA Conundrum

Estate planning with Individual Retirement Accounts, 401(k)s, pension and profit sharing plans and other similar investments can pose some real problems. For purposes of this section, I'm going to lump all of these types of accounts together and call them "IRA accounts," although each different type of retirement account does have its own planning issues.

I'm going to try to frame the issues that those who have any degree of their net worth tied up in IRA accounts should be aware of. Briefly, those issues include the economic and tax ramifications of leaving the accounts to our loved ones, the restrictions of how we can leave those accounts, and how easy it is for one of our beneficiaries to make a big mistake when they inherit our IRA account.

I'm going to leave Roth IRA accounts out of the discussion, since Roth IRAs are an entirely different animal with their own sets of issues. I'll leave that discussion for another time.

In order to understand the issues for traditional IRAs and similar accounts, it's a good idea to review the economic and tax significance of our IRA accounts. Most of us achieved an income tax deduction when we contributed sums to our IRA. Moreover, our accounts grow tax deferred until we begin making withdrawals. When we withdraw amounts, however, we recognize them as ordinary income on our tax returns and pay income tax.

Our tax laws require us to begin withdrawals from our IRA accounts upon attaining age 70½, whether we need the money or not. These are mandated "minimum distributions."

When we die, a whole set of other rules take effect, and these rules are different depending upon whether we die before we reach 70½ or after, as well as who we name as our beneficiary.

These rules may be temporarily suspended if we leave our IRA outright to our spouse, since he or she is the only beneficiary who may "roll over" our IRA into his or her own IRA account. When this happens, the inherited IRA account assets are treated the same as if our spouse owned the IRA all along.

But there's a trap for the unwary here. In second marriage situations, those that name their spouse as the primary beneficiary, and our children from a prior marriage as the alternate beneficiary, sometimes assume that when our spouse dies then our children will always receive the IRA. This isn't necessarily the case.

When our spouse "rolls over" the IRA into his or her own IRA account, then he or she can designate whomever he or she wants as their primary beneficiary. Even if they name the children of their deceased spouse as the primary beneficiary, the children may not inherit the whole account. Why? This is due to a number of reasons.

First, the spouse may live long enough to withdraw all of the monies for his or her own use. Second, the spouse may remarry and the new spouse may have legal rights to all or a portion of the IRA account.

There are additional issues when our children inherit our IRA account directly. Remember that our spouse is the only person who can roll over our IRA balance. Children cannot roll over our IRA into their own IRA account. Instead, the account becomes an "Inherited IRA."

Our children must begin to take minimum distributions even if they are not yet 70½. These distributions are based on a different table than the one that the original account owner bases his or her withdrawals on. Sometimes our children get bad advice and withdraw the entire IRA balance at once. This leads to an enormous income tax liability, since they are taxed on the income just as we would have been had we withdrawn the monies.

Under Florida law, our IRAs are generally protected from the reach of our creditors. Not true for the beneficiaries of our IRA accounts. In order to protect the inherited IRA accounts from the reach of creditors, predators and divorcing spouses of their own, a special type of trust must be built that would serve as the beneficiary for our child.

But that trust must be built in such a way as to qualify the child for deferred minimum distributions for the rest of his or her life. If the trust is not properly drafted, then there is a good chance that the entire balance of the IRA will become taxable upon our deaths, or that our beneficiaries will otherwise have to withdraw the IRA based upon an older beneficiary's life expectancy.

These are just a few of the complexities when considering an estate plan for someone who has IRA balances. Before you complete your IRA beneficiary designation, it's usually a good idea to discuss these issues with your estate planning attorney.

Income Statement vs. Balance Sheet

A client recently asked me, "Will my children be taxed on their inheritance?" This particular client did not have assets in her estate that would be valued at more than $5.34 million, the current federal estate tax exemption. Since she was also a Florida resident, her estate would not be subject to any state inheritance or death taxes.

"No," I told her, "except the IRA account money will be taxed to them as income when they withdraw it, just as you are taxed as you take distributions from that account."

"But what about the house?"

"No. Not taxable."

"The certificates of deposit?"

"No."

"My regular investment account?"

"No. The distribution of those assets are not taxed as income."

"Yes, but are they taxed as an inheritance?" she asked.

That's when the core of her misunderstanding dawned on me. And I believe that many others harbor the same misunderstanding. Most of us deal with the tax on our income every year when we file our Form 1040s. That tax is computed on our net taxable income, which is calculated as the difference between our gross income and our allowable tax deductions and credits.

Gross income includes earnings from employment, profits from our businesses, dividends, interest, traditional IRA and 401(k) distributions and the like. Deductions include payments for our home mortgage interest, charitable contributions and medical expenses, for example. The tax that we pay on our income is therefore a tax on our personal *income statements*.

Estate and inheritance taxes, in contrast, are a tax on our *balance sheet* at the time of our deaths. Our balance sheet does not describe our net income; rather, it describes our net worth—our assets less our liabilities.

Our net worth is calculated by subtracting our liabilities—mortgages, credit card balances, etc.—from the date of death value of our assets, including our homes, real estate, business interests, partnerships, investment and savings accounts, retirement plans, annuities and life insurance.

When determining the estate tax, our net worth—our taxable estate—is first calculated. Our taxable estate equals the difference between our date of death net worth and allowable estate tax deductions. Examples of allowable estate tax deductions include qualifying distributions to our spouse and charities as well as estate administrative expenses such as legal, accounting and trustee fees.

The final amount of our taxable estate is then applied against our available estate tax exemption. The federal estate tax exemption for 2014 is $5.34 million. Any "taxable gifts" that we made during our lifetime (gifts that exceeded the annual exclusion amount, which was $10,000 in prior years, but has increased to $14,000) are deducted from our estate tax exemption to arrive at our available exemption at the time of our death.

If our taxable estate does not exceed the estate tax exemption, then no estate tax payment is due. So the distributions of our assets—our balance sheet items—are not taxable as income to our beneficiaries.

Note a couple of complexities I alluded to above. Retirement plans, such as Traditional IRAs, 401(k)s, pensions and profit sharing plans and annuities have a "double whammy" in that they appear both on the income statement, when the beneficiary takes distributions (and is therefore taxed on those distributions) and the balance sheet—as an element of our net worth, therefore making those assets subject to estate tax.

Another is life insurance. Generally speaking, beneficiaries do not pay income tax on the receipt of life insurance death benefits. Without advanced planning, however, the death benefit of our life insurance policies is an asset that appears on our net worth statement, therefore subjecting the death benefits to estate tax.

You might wonder about capital gain taxes. While the distribution of a house, for example, does not create an income tax event, will our beneficiary have to report a capital gain when they sell the home? Here one must understand the "step up in tax cost basis" that our beneficiaries receive when we die.

Because the estate tax is calculated on our "date of death" fair market values of our assets, our beneficiaries receive a new tax cost basis equal to that value. So if the home we leave our beneficiaries is worth $500,000 when we die, but we only paid $200,000 for it, if our beneficiaries sell the home shortly after our death at $500,000, capital gains tax will not apply.

There are exceptions to the "step up in basis" rule as well. Retirement accounts (IRAs, 401(k)s, etc.), annuities and other similar accounts that enjoyed income tax deferral during our lifetime do not enjoy a step-up in basis. Our beneficiaries pay income tax on the distributions.

I hope that this clears everything up for you! Don't get lost in all of the exceptions when trying to figure out whether your estate will be taxable. Just look at your net worth. Everything else is details that can be worked out with your advisors when you plan your estate.

Recipes Written In Russian—Formulas

L ast Sunday night I cooked dinner with my youngest daughter, Madison, who is in sixth grade. She found a recipe that she was interested in making, so we went together to the grocery store to buy all the ingredients. She dutifully diced the chicken, prepared the vegetables and mixed the spices. We seared it all in the wok and served it to her two older sisters—who are finicky eaters. They took some tentative tastes, then dug in! Chef Madi's dinner was a big hit!

The cookbook that Madi and I used was written in simple language that even a child could follow. Too bad that certain types of recipes that I commonly use in my law practice can't be written that way. In fact, if you ever read the recipes that I am referring to, you would think that they are written in Russian and not in English.

What in the world am I talking about? For those of you who have tax planning in your wills and trusts you'll find these recipes—which are referred to as "formula clauses"—right at the beginning of the part of the document that talks about what happens when you die.

These formula clauses are designed to divide your assets into separate baskets, usually into a marital trust and a bypass or credit shelter trust, so that your estate tax exemption is fully utilized at the time of your death. You can read these clauses over and over and probably not understand them. This is true no matter which estate planning attorney drafted the document. We don't draft these provisions to confuse our clients, although that might appear to be the goal.

The reason these provisions are so difficult to understand is due to the fact that we have to comply with many different provisions of the tax and trust code, as well as various IRS rulings and pronouncements. Words like "pecuniary amount" and "fractional formula relating to numerators and denominators" are used to direct the trustee.

But here's the funny thing about these formulas—they're not all the same and they're not forms. Just as some food recipes result in a beef dish, while others cook up a vegetarian meal, the formula clauses that are used in your estate planning documents should be tailored to the types of assets that you own, whether or not you are married, and how many generations of your family your trust is designed to benefit.

Certain types of formulas allow your executor or trustee to pick and choose which assets of yours should be held in the marital trust and which assets should be held in the credit shelter trust. Other types of formulas make the trustee allocate all of the different types of assets more or less proportionately amongst the marital trust and family trust. Each of these different formulas has a distinct set of advantages and disadvantages—with differing income and estate tax results.

So how do you pick these formulas? In most cases you won't. Your estate planning attorney will do it for you. If you have the curiosity—and if you really want to impress your attorney—ask him why he chose the formula that he did. If he can't give you a straight answer on this, then he might not understand the differences himself, and you might need more of a specialist!

But here's something that you should know in any event, and that's this: These formula clauses often change over time. The tax laws change, which usually necessitate a change in your formula clause. Along the same line, when the types of assets that you own change, then it's important for your formula clause to change. If you happen to be a surviving spouse, and you are leaving amounts to your children and grandchildren, then that's yet another reason for your formula clause to change.

What happens if you have an out-of-date formula? It's kind of like having stale ingredients for your recipe. The meal's not going to turn out so well. Chances are you're going to have to trash it and go to a restaurant, spending a lot of money on a meal that you never intended to.

So if your will or trust has sat locked up in your safe deposit box for a couple of years, it's time to review your will and trust's recipe. Believe me when I say that in so doing your family will be glad you did—whether they appreciate it or not!

The New Estate Planning Paradigm

Gone—hopefully for good—are the days when many of us worried that the federal estate tax would consume half of our hard-earned wealth when we died. The federal estate tax exemption amount currently is $5.34 million, allowing a married couple to together shield $10.68 million, and those amounts are tied to inflation, meaning that they will increase in the coming years.

Even so, the new estate planning paradigm will be to minimize income taxes. Without proper planning, those taxes could consume half of the income that our estates and trusts generate for our loved ones after we die.

This is largely due to the higher income tax rates (that began in 2013) imposed on estates and irrevocable trusts, along with the 3.8% Medicare surtax imposed on net investment income. Adding those two taxes together, the highest marginal federal income tax rate balloons to 43.4%. For beneficiaries who live in a state that imposes a state income tax, the highest combined federal and state tax bracket could exceed 50%.

Capital gains will also be taxed at higher rates after we die, as the Medicare surtax could push those rates up to 23.8% before any state income taxes are imposed.

What's so scary about all of this is that once an estate or irrevocable trust's income exceeds the whopping sum of $12,150 it is in the highest marginal income tax bracket.

There are proactive steps that one can take to minimize these taxes. Because of the shift in these laws, the standard estate plan that, upon death, creates a credit shelter trust and a marital trust may become a relic of the past for those whose net worth is below the estate tax thresholds. Instead, several new concepts will leap to the forefront when considering how to structure one's estate plan.

This isn't to say that trust planning is dead—quite the contrary. Trust planning remains necessary to ensure proper distribution to our loved ones, keeping our assets within our bloodlines, divorce protection, planning for disability or incompetence, preventing beneficiary disputes, business succession planning and a host of other benefits.

What's likely to happen is that attorneys will work with their clients to redesign their trusts to meet the challenges of this rising income tax environment. One opportunity, for example, is to take greater advantage of the "step up" in tax cost basis at death. If I bought a share of stock at $1, but at my death it is worth $10, then my beneficiaries inherit the stock at the $10 amount when I leave it to them.

The problem is that when I leave the stock in a "credit shelter" or "bypass" trust to my spouse, as most estate plans do (to the extent that my assets are worth less than the estate tax exemption amount, they are usually first funded into the credit shelter/bypass trust to consume my exemption), then my spouse receives the step up in basis at my death, but our children miss out on the step up when she dies. This is because the credit shelter/bypass trust is designed to exclude those assets from her estate for federal estate tax purposes. Consequently, in the "standard" estate planning scenario, you only get one step-up at the first spouse's death on that spouse's assets.

But there are ways to achieve the step up in tax cost basis at **both spouses' deaths,** meaning that our estate plans can be fashioned to leave our spouse with no capital gains inherent in our assets and do the same for our children when the surviving spouse dies. This could save more than 23.4% (or higher for beneficiaries who live in states with state income taxes)!

The reason that these opportunities exist is due to another new twist in the law called "portability." Under the old law, if my estate plan didn't create the credit shelter/bypass trust at my death, then I would have lost the use of my federal exemption forever. This is one of the reasons why attorneys were so diligent in dividing assets up between spouses and creating separate trusts.

Portability allows us to not be concerned with estate tax inclusion so long as the combined net worth of both spouses is less than their combined federal exemption. In other words, we don't lose the first deceased spouse's exemption even if we don't create the credit shelter/bypass trust.

Therefore, I can construct my plan in such a way as to protect and ensure that my assets will benefit my surviving spouse for the rest of her life, protect them for our children and keep those assets out of the hands of any new spouse she might remarry, while at the same time minimizing capital gains taxes. I can also construct the income distribution provisions to ensure that the income is taxed at my beneficiary's marginal tax rate, which is likely to be lower than that of the trust.

As always, the estate planning arena has changed significantly.

Estate Planning Issues On Conversion From Traditional To Roth IRA

I previously wrote a column covering the unique ability that we all have to convert traditional IRAs into Roth IRAs, providing a timeline that you can follow when working with your advisors.

I'm now going to review for you some of the estate planning issues that are affected should you choose to convert a traditional IRA into a Roth IRA. While the question whether to convert is typically a financially driven decision, once that decision is made you should meet with your estate planning attorney to make sure that the converted Roth IRA fits properly into your estate plan.

Asset Protection
In Florida IRAs are generally considered to be asset protected by statute. Roth IRAs, however, appear to fall outside of the scope of the statutory definition of what is protected. Federal laws also limit asset protection to Roth IRAs. Before converting to a Roth, if you are in a high-risk occupation, or should you be involved in an activity or in a lawsuit that merits a close look at what assets are protected, you should meet with your estate planning counsel.

Beneficiary Designation Forms
Upon converting to a Roth IRA, your beneficiary designation forms should be reviewed to ensure that they coordinate with your overall estate plan. The preparation of proper beneficiary designations is critical to ensure that each separate share for your beneficiaries allows for the maximum opportunity to achieve tax-deferred growth.

IRA Trusts
Because of the additional investment of paying upfront taxes on on the conversion to a Roth IRA, most clients will be well

advised to take the additional step of leaving the Roth IRA into a special protected trust as opposed to outright to their children. An IRA left outright to a beneficiary has limited asset protection in most jurisdictions, while a trust can serve to protect the beneficiary against predators, creditors and divorcing spouses.

Estate Tax Exemption and GST Planning

Roth IRAs are generally the best types of assets to leave in continued trusts for your children and grandchildren because of their special income tax free nature.

Estate Tax Apportionment Issues

Estate tax apportionment deals with what assets and what shares of your estate pay any estate tax that might become due at the time of your death. Since state death tax exemptions are often different from federal death tax exemptions, this becomes an even larger issue for those that either live or own property in a jurisdiction that has a state death tax.

Charitable Planning

For those that incorporate charitable planning into their estate plans, the income tax ramifications from the conversion of a traditional IRA into a Roth IRA merit another close look at how the charitable intent is satisfied.

These are just a few of the estate planning issues that merit attention when converting a traditional IRA into a Roth IRA. So be sure to include your attorney in the discussion with your CPA and financial planner when deciding to convert a traditional IRA into a Roth IRA.

The Challenge Of Annuities With Trust Planning

For the past several years, investors have experienced low yields both in bonds and in dividend-declaring stocks. For those who mainly rely upon their investment income for retirement needs, it has been a tough environment. Financial firms have responded with a variety of annuity products that are designed to provide much needed income. Some annuities even promise growth features that are either guaranteed or tied to the stock market, or have quasi-insurance, like features that pay out a death benefit.

While these annuity products may fit the present needs of their investors, caution is advised when naming trusts as the beneficiary of the annuity following the primary annuitant's death.

One may want his or her trust to be named as the beneficiary of the annuity for a variety of reasons, including second marriage situations where the investor wants his or her spouse to enjoy the income but eventually wants the equity that is left after the spouse dies to go to their children. Other investors don't want their children to inherit a fixed sum of money and would rather have them receive it as the same income stream that they had. Sometimes a beneficiary has qualified for Medicaid or another government program, so leaving assets to a Special Needs Trust is necessary so as not to disqualify the recipient from that government program.

Annuities, however, have built in income imbedded within them. Like IRAs, 401(k)s, and pension and profit sharing plans, when distributions are made from an annuity, some portion of it is usually taxable income. This is not a problem when the annuity is being distributed to an individual.

When an annuity names a trust, however, there may be significant income tax problems upon the death of the original annuitant. Trusts are not considered people and are therefore treated differently under most annuity contracts, even if the trust has individual beneficiaries. Some annuities require all of the remainder of the balance to be distributed outright to a trust upon the death of the original annuitant, for example.

When this happens, the trust recognizes the taxable income. But if the trust calls for its "income" to be distributed to the beneficiary, this does not necessarily mean that all of the taxable income that was distributed to the trust will "flow through" to the beneficiary of the trust.

This is because the annuity itself is the "corpus" or the "principal" of the trust. So under the trust statutes, the taxable income that is distributed to the trust is considered its corpus and is accumulated. Only the earnings on that corpus is considered the income.

Under the federal tax law, trusts are subject to a compressed income tax rate schedule. In other words, the highest marginal income tax rate (39.6% presently) occurs once the trust accumulates as little as $14,000 of taxable income. Moreover, the Medicare Surtax (aka ObamaCare) applies at another 3.8%. So the accumulated income could be subject to a 43.4% marginal income tax rate on the annuity that terminates to the trust upon the death of the annuitant. If the trust is established in a state that has a state income tax, even more could be lost to taxes.

Moreover, every annuity contract is different. Some annuity contracts will look through the trust to pay out to the trust beneficiary, as long as such a payout complies with the trust terms. Other annuity contracts require a fixed payout over a term certain number of years.

For the reasons that I mention, annuities are known as "wasting assets" under Florida's principal and income statutes. In other words, they pay out and are diminished over time. They are also called "income with respect to a decedent" (IRD) items under the federal tax law, as they have built in income that is going to be taxed to something (a trust) or someone (a direct beneficiary) upon the death of the original annuitant.

Sometimes annuities are owned inside of an individual's IRA. When this occurs, the provisions of the annuity contract that apply upon the death of the annuitant are very important to consider.

So when you own annuities, and particularly when annuities make up a significant portion of your net worth, it is important to let your estate planning attorney know if you own significant annuities and to ask your financial advisor to provide your estate planning attorney a synopsis of the contractual rights and obligations that your annuities offer and require.

ObamaCare Medicare Surtax Affects Estates & Trusts

With the significant increase to the federal estate tax exemption, many individuals feel that estate planning isn't as important as it used to be. Regular readers of this column know that isn't true for many non-tax reasons. Here, however, I'm going to review a very significant federal income tax surcharge that affects estates and trusts beginning with 2013.

Most of you are aware that the Affordable Care Act (a/k/a ObamaCare) imposes a 3.8 percent Medicare surtax on most forms of unearned income when taxpayers have net investment income or modified adjusted gross income above certain amounts. ($250,000 married filing jointly; $125,000 for married filing separately; $200,000 on all others).

The surtax may also affect estates and irrevocable trusts that have Net Investment Income above a very low amount—$11,950. So if Dad dies with a trust that benefits Mom, and that trust earns interest, dividends and capital gains totaling $80,000 that are accumulated inside of the trust and are not distributed to Mom, then Dad's trust could owe a Medicare surtax of $2,586.00 in addition to all of the income and capital gains taxes that it normally would pay. Moreover, the interest and dividends would be taxed at the highest ordinary income tax bracket (now 39.6%) and the capital gains tax rate in this example would also be at the highest federal marginal rate (now 20 percent).

The Medicare surtax may be minimized or even legally eliminated with proper planning both inside of your estate plan and in how your plan is administered following your death. Moreover, the income tax rates on the interest and dividends as well as the capital gains tax rates could be reduced with proper planning.

The first item to consider is that the $11,950 threshold on Net Investment Income applies to estates and irrevocable trusts. It does not apply to revocable living trusts. If you established a revocable living trust, then the income earned by the trust is taxed to you as if the trust doesn't exist. There is no difference between having a revocable trust and not having one from an income tax perspective during your lifetime. It is tax neutral. If a revocable living trust will benefit you and your family, then the Medicare surtax should not affect your decision as to whether you should establish a new trust or retain an existing trust.

When you die, however, your estate is either created through your will, and/or may become a "testamentary trust" (which means a trust that forms after your death) for the benefit of your spouse or children. Estates under wills and testamentary trusts are by definition irrevocable. You may have also established a lifetime irrevocable trust. All are negatively affected by the low Medicare surtax threshold.

There are planning options available, however. When estates and irrevocable trusts distribute all of the Net Investment Income to the beneficiaries, then the surtax would apply to the beneficiaries' tax schedules and not to the estate and trust schedules. By applying the individual thresholds mentioned in the second paragraph above there might not even be a Medicare surtax due, and the income and capital gains tax rates may also be drastically reduced.

But it is not always feasible to have the estate or trust distribute all of the income and capital gains to the beneficiaries. A spousal trust may have been created to protect the surviving spouse's inheritance, minimize estate taxes when he or she dies, or to preserve the trust for the children in second marriage situations. An irrevocable trust for the children may have been created to protect the children's inheritance from divorcing spouses, creditors or predators. Assuming that these non-tax reasons exist for the creation of the irrevocable trust to begin with, then one can't just assume that the best course of action would be to make interest, dividend and capital gains distributions out of the trust to avoid the Medicare surtax. There, one would be letting the tax tail wag the proverbial dog.

There are alternatives available. The trust could be drafted in such a way as to give the trustee (who may also be the beneficiary) discretion to recharacterize capital gains and income and make distributions to minimize the potential tax bite. The trust could also be drafted to classify the beneficiary's interests as "grantor" interests under the Internal Revenue Code. What this means is that the collapsed $11,950 trust rate schedule would not apply to the trust shares benefitting the spouse or children. Instead, the more favorable individual tax rate schedules would apply.

Needless to say, the ObamaCare surtax along with the higher income tax rates imposed will require clients and their advisors to review their estate planning. There isn't a blanket answer to everyone's plan that fixes the problem. Each individual's plan and goals need to be considered to arrive at the right solution for his or her unique situation.

What the New Health Care Reform Law Means To Your Estate

Previously, I wrote how taxes under the new Health Care Reform Act (HCRA)—otherwise known as ObamaCare—affect many. I'm now going to describe how the new health care law imposes harsh taxes on irrevocable trusts and estates of deceased persons. You may recall that I wrote that the HCRA imposes a 3.8% surtax on modified adjusted gross income (MAGI) above $200,000 for individuals, or $250,000 for married couples.

For irrevocable trusts and estates, the trust income tax rate schedule is "compressed." Once irrevocable trusts and estates reach MAGI of only $12,000 (in 2013), then the surtax is imposed. But this surtax may be mitigated or even avoided with proper planning.

You may wonder why there is such a large discrepancy between individual tax rates and those imposed on estates and irrevocable trusts. This is because the tax code favors trusts that do not accumulate income. When an irrevocable trust or an estate distributes all of its annual income to its beneficiaries, then the trust does not generally pay any income tax (or surtax). Instead, the income is added to the income of the beneficiary to whom it was distributed. The beneficiary "picks up" the income on his or her own income tax return.

If the beneficiary who receives a distribution from an estate, or irrevocable trust does not have MAGI above the thresholds, then no surtax would be imposed.

But when irrevocable trusts and estates accumulate income as opposed to distributing that income, then the irrevocable trust or estate reports that income as taxable and will generally pay income tax. That is where the HCRA surtax of 3.8% kicks in when the income that accumulated exceeds $12,000.

Assume that Mike, an unmarried beneficiary of an irrevocable trust, is scheduled to receive a distribution in spring of 2015. If the distribution occurs in 2014, then it doesn't matter what Mike's MAGI is, there will be no surtax, since the surtax isn't imposed until next year.

If the distribution occurs in 2015, however, and if Mike's income exceeds $200,000, then the distribution will also create an additional surtax. Here, the trustee should consider accelerating the distribution this year (2014) or use the 65-day rule that allows a trust to treat a distribution of income that occurs in the first 65 days of 2015 to have occurred in 2014.

Assume instead that in 2015 Mike's income is far less than $200,000, but instead the trust accumulates the income it earns rather than distributing it to Mike. Assume further that the trust income accumulated exceeds $12,000. Here, there would be a surtax that could have been avoided had the income been distributed to Mike.

Many trustees desire growth inside of the trusts they manage. So how do they accomplish this without being hit with a crippling 3.8% drag on their investment return? Here, a little foresight can work to everyone's advantage. Tax-exempt bonds and tax-deferred annuities are two examples of investments that avoid the surtax while earning income. Unrealized gains are also not taxed until realized. So a growth strategy might be employed.

Estates of deceased persons who own "S corporation stock" have special issues as well. You may already know that when a small business owner incorporates and files a "Subchapter S" election with the IRS, then the corporation does not pay any income tax at the corporate level. Instead, all of the corporation's income is "passed through" to its owner, who pays the income tax on his or her tax return. Without an S election, income earned by the corporation would be double taxed—once when earned by the corporation as income and then again when distributed as a dividend to its owner.

When an owner of an S corporation dies, however, there are special elections that the estate must make to continue the pass through treatment of the income rather than incurring tax at two levels.

But there's a problem. Generally speaking, an irrevocable trust created from an estate of a deceased person will not qualify as a valid shareholder and will disqualify an S corporation from "pass through" tax treatment unless a Qualified Subchapter S Trust (QSST) election is made within a certain time period after the death of the S corporation owner.

When that election is made becomes important for purposes of the surtax. Remember that individuals have higher thresholds before the imposition of the ObamaCare surtax ($200,000 or $250,000 versus $14,000). Until the QSST election is made, however, the estate recognizes the income, thereby increasing the likelihood and amount of surtax. Once the QSST election is made, the income is treated as the beneficiary's and not the estate or trusts. Consequently, the QSST election should be made as soon as possible.

There are many other ObamaCare effects on irrevocable trusts and estates. But I do want to take a moment here to distinguish between revocable trusts and irrevocable trusts. Many of you who have revocable living trusts should not worry. While the grantor (owner) of the trust is alive, revocable living trusts are not treated the same way as irrevocable trusts and estates, because a revocable living trust is not a separate taxpayer apart from its grantor (owner).

The bottom line is this—if you are a trustee or a beneficiary of an estate or an irrevocable trust, you may want to discuss the effects of the ObamaCare surtax with your legal, tax and financial advisors well before the end of this year.

Chapter Eight

Incapacity

Jahi McMath Brings Up Questions About Living Wills

Those following the news have likely heard about the 13-year-old San Francisco girl, Jahi McMath, who has been declared brain dead following complications arising out of surgery to remove her tonsils and adenoids. Apparently, the surgery was prescribed to treat sleep apnea. During the surgery she experienced massive blood loss, leading to brain damage and a heart attack from which she has not recovered.

After a court-appointed neurologist declared the young girl brain dead, the Children's Hospital Oakland wanted to remove her from life support. Jahi's parents fought in court to continue the life support and won the rights to move her to an assisted living facility that is willing to keep Jahi on life support.

This tragic case begs the question as to the point in time when life no longer exists. In blogs and newspaper articles, bioethicists argue whether Jahi will ever recover, as well as the ethics behind both keeping Jahi on life support or removing her. One can only imagine the heartache that this young girl's parents must be experiencing.

Because this young girl is a minor, she could not have signed a legal document such as a living will, which would indicate her choices in the event of these terrible circumstances. But those of you who are adults reading this have that choice, so in this column I'm going to review how a living will would work with an adult who has signed one in this circumstance. Since we're here in Florida, I'll be applying Florida law.

Living wills aren't foolproof, but they do provide your direction in the event of an end-stage life support issue. Even with a living will, questions remain as to when the preconditions are satisfied that would result in the termination of life support.

Through living wills, Florida law enables individuals who are in a terminal condition, end-stage condition, or in a persistent vegetative state to direct life prolonging procedures to be discontinued, as long as two physicians have determined that there is "no reasonable medical probability of one's recovery from said condition, and where the medical procedures would only serve to prolong artificially the process of dying." Once those factors have been determined, the administration of medication or the performance of medical procedures deemed necessary to provide comfort, care or to alleviate pain may continue.

The problem rests in the subjective nature of the determination itself. "Terminal condition" is defined under the statute as a condition caused by injury, disease or illness from which there is no reasonable medical probability of recovery and which, without treatment, can be expected to cause death.

"End-stage condition" means, under the statute, "an irreversible condition that is caused by injury, disease or illness which has resulted in progressively severe and permanent deterioration, and which, to a reasonable degree of medical probability, treatment of the condition would be ineffective."

"Persistent vegetative state" means "a permanent and irreversible condition of unconsciousness in which there is the absence of voluntary action or cognitive behavior of any kind, or an inability to communicate or interact purposefully with the environment."

Reasonable people could certainly disagree as to when any of the above conditions are satisfied. Florida law provides that the surrogate named in the living will has legal standing to prevent a doctor or hospital from carrying out the living will where the surrogate differs with the opinions of the physicians. In such event, a legal process is set forth under the law that must be followed. So who you name to act on your behalf is important. They should know what you would want in various circumstances.

As medical science advances, the decisions related to carrying out end-stage heroics becomes more difficult. Because of this, it is now more important than ever to have a valid living will in place that outlines what every individual would want to happen. While we all must take a leap of faith that those making the determination whether we have met the preconditions are making accurate judgment calls, the alternative is not any better.

Most state laws, including Florida's, provides for a legal process where there is no living will. In such case, extrinsic evidence, such as discussions that have occurred regarding these issues, may be admitted into evidence before a court. This is what happened in the Terri Schiavo case. In that case Mrs. Schiavo's husband and parents fought it out in court whether her life support should be continued or removed.

Thankfully, most of the time a living will is not necessary for most people. Nevertheless, the occasional news event reminds us that having an up-to-date living will is essential.

When Does The Living Will Apply?

Many are familiar with the "living will," which is otherwise known as the "right to die" legal document. Not to be confused with living trusts, which govern the disposition of our assets, living wills state what life prolonging procedures you want discontinued in the event that the procedures won't save your life, but instead, would only prolong the process of dying.

So, if you were to sign a living will that said to discontinue mechanical breathing, do not engage in cardiopulmonary resuscitation, or to remove food and water tubes, then the doctors and hospitals are supposed to allow you to die naturally, but they can and should (according to most living will documents) "provide comfort, care and alleviate pain."

Anecdotally, many clients become reluctant to initial the provisions that say to discontinue life-prolonging procedures. "What if I have a heart attack right now?" they ask. "If I say that I don't want CPR then will they not try to revive me?"

I explain to them that even if they had a cardiac event the moment after they sign the living will, the document doesn't yet apply. Under the statute, when determining whether a patient meets the preconditions necessary to follow the direction in the living will, two physicians must agree that the patient suffers from an imminently terminal end stage condition, or is in a persistent vegetative state from which he or she will not recover.

It's best explained by example. Assume that Marvin signs a living will that says not to resuscitate him, to remove him from mechanical breathing machines and to remove the food and water tubes should he be judged to meet the statutory preconditions.

Then suppose that immediately after signing his living will, Marvin has a heart attack and falls to the floor.

Should the paramedics revive him? Of course! Two physicians have not yet stated that Marvin has met the preconditions, in that they have not determined that Marvin has reached an end stage/terminal condition or persistent vegetative state with no hope of recovery. So even though Marvin has signed a living will that says not to perform CPR, the paramedics should and will perform whatever lifesaving treatments at their disposal.

Next, assume that upon arrival in the hospital, Marvin is hooked up to machines that keep his heart pumping and his lungs breathing. He has no brain waves. After a few days, the doctors determine that Marvin has reached the statutory precondition. He is not considered someone who will recover, and he is likely to remain in a persistent vegetative state for as long as the machines keep him going. So now we turn to his living will. Marvin has said that he doesn't want any more heroics if the life prolonging procedures will not lead to his recovery but instead are only serving to prolong the process of dying.

In consultation with Marvin's health care surrogate (often his wife or other family member), the doctors remove Marvin from life support. Now let's assume that a small portion of his brain actually keeps his heart beating and lungs breathing but the doctors and his family all believe and know that Marvin will remain in this persistent vegetative state forever—or at least as long as he remains on food and water tubes. We now look to Marvin's living will to see if he wants those removed.

If he directed their removal, then those can also be removed. Some individuals hesitate to remove the water tube for fear of a painful death. I've had doctors tell me two different sides of that story. Some say that if your kidneys have shut down then the introduction of water might be painful to the patient. Others have said that patients in this condition are usually administered morphine, which deadens all pain.

Making these decisions on a living will document can be very difficult. But it is much better to have a living will in place that says ahead of time how you wish to be treated, then to have a Terri Schiavo situation. You may recall that she was in a comatose state for years, and her husband and parents fought it out in court to determine what her wishes were. She never completed a living will. Had she, then she probably would not have made national news nor would she have been the subject of Congressional debate.

So, while living wills pose tough questions, it is better to deal with them while you are competent and fine than having your family wrestle with them should you find yourself in a dire medical condition.

Is Your Living Will Akin To A Death Panel?

'm following the nation's health care debates with great interest, as I assume most of you are as well. As a partner in a small law firm, I'm keenly aware of how costly it is to provide health insurance to our own families and to our employees, yet I know how important having adequate health coverage is. Like most employers, we can't go on shouldering thirty percent annual health insurance premium increases year after year, and that's probably one of the many reasons health reform has been such a hot political topic.

President Barack Obama presented his plan that would presumably introduce the concept of a government provider that would compete with private insurers. Apparently, his theory states that a government provider would create competition against private insurers, resulting in lower health care costs.

I'm personally skeptical of the government's ability to manage a national health plan that would result in lower costs, and I point to Medicare and Medicaid as historical examples. Present forecasts predict that current tax revenue will not support Medicare and Medicaid into the next generation without significant tax increases, benefit cutbacks, or both.

While I'm not smart enough to know all of the right answers, when I hear about state law barriers that prohibit insurance firms from crossing state lines, or all of the myriad of rules that differ from state to state that result in practical limitations on private insurers from competing in certain markets, I wonder whether there are other answers besides having the federal government fill the role as our nation's primary health care insurer for those of us who are working or school age.

But that's for others to ponder.

I want to now consider one of the juicy topics that's actually lead to fisticuffs in town hall meetings. The background is that as a nation it's been reported that we spend a significant percentage of our health care dollars on the very last weeks of life. These dollars often do not lead to any more quality of life for the patient.

The worry (whether real or imagined, I can't tell) is that under a government sponsored program, there will be "death panels" that will determine whether dollars should be spent on a patient's terminal condition—kind of like the Roman spectators giving a thumbs up or thumbs down at the end of gladiator matches. It's a chilling thought to wonder whether a diseased Lance Armstrong would have survived such a tribunal back when his prognosis looked bleakest. Would we now have the seven-time Tour Champion raising millions of dollars for cancer research or would he have been relegated to his deathbed before he was able to achieve such greatness?

And that's precisely the worry that many express while signing living will documents. You may already know that living wills are the documents that allow you to declare ahead of time whether you would want life prolonging medical procedures withheld in the event it was determined by two physicians and your health care surrogate that you are in an end stage terminal condition, or a persistent vegetative state, with no hope of recovery.

The Terri Schiavo case just up the road in Pinellas County highlighted what might happen if one doesn't have a living will and ends up in such a condition. Nevertheless, I have had several clients express concern that the living will essentially gives the doctors the ability to form one's own "death panel." If the doctors proclaim that there is no hope of recovery, then the life support is terminated.

I don't believe that to be the case. In my twenty years of practicing estate planning law, I can't recall an instance where a client's family has telephoned me with the worry that the doctor or hospital is going to turn off the life support against the family's consent. While you might point to Terri Schiavo's parents as a prime example, remember that she didn't have a signed living will document, which lead to the controversy over her care.

When my wife's great uncle died a few years ago, the family sat by his side and held his hand when the life support ended. By then he was comatose, while a morphine drip was administered to alleviate any pain. Everyone agreed that the heart and lung machines weren't going to bring him back. While it was a sad time for the family, we all realized that life isn't infinite.

These are weighty decisions. It's interesting to watch our society struggle with life and death concerns, and with how our resources are allocated accordingly. As citizens I believe we have a duty to let our elected officials understand our thoughts and concerns.

My Mom's In ICU And I Think She Needs An Estate Plan

Several times a year, I receive a telephone call that goes something like this: "Hello, my friend gave me your name and I really need your help," the caller says.

"What can I do for you?" I begin.

"My mother needs a Will...and a Durable Power of Attorney. And while I'm thinking of it, she should also have a Health Care Proxy."

"So, it sounds like your mother needs a complete estate plan. Does she have any of those documents now?"

Sometimes the answer is "No." Other times the answer is "Well, her documents were done 20 years ago and they're not really relevant anymore."

So, my next question is, "When would she like to come in to visit with me?"

And here's the answer that I never want to hear: "Well, that's the problem...Mom's in the Intensive Care Unit at Health Park. She suffered a massive heart attack, and we don't know how much longer she'll be with us."

"Oh my! I'm sorry to hear that. Is she competent to discuss her estate plan with an attorney? Is she on any medications that might alter her state of mind?"

There's usually a long pause on the line before caller says, "Well, she does have lucid moments when she knows that we're in the room with her."

I feel sorry for people who get trapped in this type of a situation, but honestly it falls under the category of "too little, too late." Procrastination is never a desirable trait, especially when considering something as important as creating the legal documents necessary to take care of yourself in the event of a health problem or distributing your assets to your loved ones at your death.

While not one of us likes to consider the possibilities of our decline in health or even our own demise, these are realities of life that will happen to all of us. It's not a matter of "if" these sorts of things will happen, but instead it is a matter of "when" they will happen.

The hospital ICU ward is not the ideal place to make these types of decisions. A major problem when working with a client who has recently been traumatized with a major health event is in determining whether they are legally competent to sign anything.

In order to make a will, for example, one must be able to understand the extent and scope of one's assets and how those assets are to be distributed under the terms of the will. It sounds like a low standard, but someone who is on morphine or other pain medications probably lacks capacity, at least until they recover somewhat. And for those who suffer strokes or other brain issues, they may never recover to the point of having capacity.

Undue influence is another concern. When a patient is surrounded by certain loved ones when making a will, there is the chance that others who were not present and who may not benefit (or benefit as much as someone else does) under the will can claim that the patient was unduly influenced, and therefore, the will should be overturned. The law may actually favor the challenger as it presumes undue influence in these types of situations.

Another problem is that not all estate plans are equal. The client may need a will or they may need a trust. That depends on a variety of factors including the types and amounts of assets that they own. When you create a will or a trust there are many sub-issues that should be carefully thought through, including who is going to serve as your personal representative, trustee, agent under a durable power of attorney and health care proxy. Distribution issues must be considered and beneficiary forms conformed to the estate plan, as well as life insurance, estate tax and income tax planning issues to name a few.

Sometimes one can successfully navigate these issues while in the hospital, or even under hospice care. It's likely going to cost a lot more in professional fees since everything is on a rush basis and the attorney and his team are going to have to travel to the hospital to review documents and obtain signatures.

In short, dealing with this scenario is a nightmare for the patient and for his family.

Do yourself a favor; make sure that you don't find yourself in this situation. If you or a loved one has procrastinated completing your estate plan, hopefully this will "scare you straight" into getting it started.

When You Pose A Financial Danger To Yourself

I once received a call from an elderly (90s-plus) client's son, "Craig, we have a problem," he began.

"What's that?" I asked.

"Well, I just flew in from Michigan and when I arrived at Dad's condo, I noticed a large stack of mail that hasn't been opened. So I asked him if it was okay that I went through it."

"Go on," I said.

"Aside from a bunch of unpaid bills and junk mail, I found some bank statements that he had never opened or reconciled. So I asked him if it was okay for me to open those. When I did, I found that he had written a $10,000 check to Maria."

"Who is Maria?" I asked.

"His housekeeper!" Son responded. "And the check was clearly in his handwriting. When I showed him the check, he had no recollection of ever writing the check or giving her that amount of money."

"Oh my!" I said. "I think it's time that we remove Dad from being his own trustee of his trust."

"Certainly," Son said. "But this isn't the worst of it. Not only did he give Maria $10,000, he also bought her a new car!"

"How did you discover this?" I asked.

"I found another check to a local car dealer. And he doesn't remember anything at all about that either. So what are the steps that we need to take?"

I reviewed the provisions of Dad's trust with Son, describing how Son has the power to remove Dad from remaining in the office as trustee of his own trust. This would change who controlled the brokerage and financial accounts. It's a pretty big deal, akin to taking the keys away from someone who shouldn't be driving an automobile any longer.

To make sure that this was the proper course of action, Son took Dad to a neurologist who reported what we suspected. Dad had some form of dementia, perhaps Alzheimer's. So taking the financial "keys" away from Dad was the right thing to do.

While none of us ever wants to consider the day that we should no longer handle our financial affairs, it is imperative that our estate planning documents contain provisions that allow for a clean transition to someone that we trust to make these decisions for us. This is where revocable trusts really shine over wills and durable powers of attorney.

In a trust, the original grantor of the trust (Dad) acts as his own trustee until he should no longer act. When it comes time to change trustees, there is a clear and definite succession of management.

A Durable Power Of Attorney, in contrast, is the primary legal document used when there is no revocable living trust. But placing Son's name on an account as the "attorney-in-fact" (that's the name we use for the person to whom the powers are delegated under the durable power of attorney) does not necessarily remove Dad's name from the account or prohibit Dad from writing checks on the account.

Furthermore, Durable Powers of Attorney are harder to implement with banks and brokerage firms. This is because the financial institutions are concerned about their own liability when a person purporting to use a Durable Power Of Attorney attempts to place their name as a signor on various accounts. The financial institutions generally do not have the same concern with trusts, since the account is titled in the name of the trustee of the trust, and the trust document itself contains the line of succession of trustees. The bank's liability is much more limited in that succession.

Finally, it is important to note how someone is to be removed as a trustee in his or her own trust. Many years ago, I used to draft a provision that a physician's statement is necessary to remove the original grantor from acting as his or her own trustee. What I have found is that many physicians are reluctant to sign a statement that removes their patient from acting as their own trustee for a variety of reasons, including the physician's own liability and the HIPPA laws.

So I usually recommend that a client name one or more of their trusted relatives, friends or advisors to sit on a "disability panel" that serves the same purpose if the client's physician won't sign a trustee removal document.

These issues are never easy to consider or talk about. Luckily, in Dad's case we were able to recover most of the money he gave away, and the dealer took back the car with a full refund. But his experience is a lesson that we should all consider when implementing our estate plans.

Major Changes Under Duress Not A Good Idea

I t's not uncommon to panic under extreme pressure. And there's no pressure like when a loved one is very sick or near death. There's a temptation to "tie up loose ends" and to direct your financial advisors and attorneys to make "last minute adjustments" before it's too late.

Resist that temptation, especially if you've recently updated your planning.

I've seen families make irrational decisions that can be attributed to a lack of understanding about their estate plan. In many married couples' estate plans, for example, there are two trusts, one for the husband and one for the wife. The reason that two trusts exist is to take advantage of both spouse's estate tax exemptions.

Sometimes there is a misperception that when one spouse dies then that spouse's trust will be distributed to the surviving spouse. But that's usually not what really happens. In most cases, the decedent spouse's trust continues on as a separate trust for the surviving spouse's benefit for the rest of his or her life. Often, the surviving spouse will become the trustee of the decedent spouse's trust as well.

The reason that the decedent spouse's trust is not distributed outright may have something to do with protecting the assets for the spouse or for future generations. Under the prior law it could have defeated the estate tax planning that was put into place.

By making a distribution outright to the surviving spouse, then all of the estate would be taxed when he or she dies. So that is why the husband/wife trusts are typically held for the surviving spouse rather than being distributed outright to him or her.

Not understanding this fact, panicked families will collapse the trust before the sick spouse dies and put everything in the well spouse's name. As I pointed out in the preceding paragraph, doing this will likely defeat the estate tax planning and balancing of assets that was put into place to take advantage of the tax exemptions.

Other times families will reposition assets between the trusts just before the sick spouse dies. This can also lead to problems related to capital gains taxes. Normally, when a person dies holding appreciated assets, the assets receive a "step up" in tax cost basis equal to the date of death value. If I purchased Coca Cola Company stock at $1/share and when I died it was worth $10/share, then my beneficiaries will normally inherit the stock at the step-up value of $10/share. If they sold it shortly after my death for $10/share, then the capital gains tax that would have been realized had I sold the stock the day before my death disappears.

But if the family tries to transfer appreciated assets into a dying person's name in an effort to receive the step-up in tax cost basis, they will have an unpleasant surprise. The tax law anticipates people trying to take advantage, so there's a rule that disallows step-up if the asset was transferred within one year of death. So making last minute changes here could actually do harm to the family.

Should a family therefore not worry about last minute planning if a loved one is gravely ill? Certainly if that person's documents haven't been updated in quite some time it makes sense to review them with competent counsel. But the family would be wise to carefully think through any choices that they have, and consider the time it would normally take to implement those choices successfully. If the health and mental stability of the sick person isn't expected to hold out for long, then it makes sense to "triage" the strategies in such a way as to take care of the most important things first.

Another important thought in late-stage planning includes the fact that any significant changes might be subject to challenge. If a sick person suddenly disinherits someone in favor of another family member, undue influence and competency issues might arise.

If this is a possibility, the family might want to ask attending physicians for statements regarding the sick person's competency, carefully document all of the medications that are being administered (with an eye towards whether any might affect decision making) and take steps to ensure that the sick person visits alone with counsel rather than having family members who might be or become beneficiaries present at the meetings.

Dealing with the loss of a loved one is almost always stressful. No one wants to compound the stress by having to deal with legal, tax and financial issues at the end of life. The best way to avoid that problem is to take care of things well ahead of time. But if you or a loved one find yourself in this situation, be very careful that you don't cause more harm than you solve.

Comfort In, Dump Out: How Not To Say The Wrong Thing

Susan Silk, a clinical psychologist, recently wrote an interesting piece for the *Los Angeles Times*, explaining how not to say the wrong thing when interacting with those who are suffering from terminal illnesses or who have just lost a loved one. Recovering from breast cancer surgery, Dr. Silk told those concerned about her that she wasn't up to receiving visitors.

Imagine her shock and hurt when a colleague said to her, "This isn't just about you."

"It's not?" Dr. Silk wondered. "My breast cancer is not about me, it's about you?"

Dr. Silk described another incident when a friend named Katie had a brain aneurysm. Katie was in intensive care for a long time, finally being transferred to a step-down unit. No longer covered with tubes and lines and monitors, Katie remained in rough shape. That's when one of Katie's friends visited but then stepped into the hall with Katie's husband, Pat. "I wasn't prepared for this," the visitor told Katie's husband. "I don't know if I can handle it."

While the visitor clearly was moved by Katie's condition, what she said wasn't appropriate. And it was wrong in the same way Dr. Silk's colleague's remark was wrong about her cancer being "not only about you."

Dr. Silk has since developed a simple technique to help people avoid this mistake. It works for all kinds of crises: medical, legal, financial, romantic, even existential. She calls it the Ring Theory.

Draw a circle. This is the center ring. In it put the name of the person at the center of the current trauma. For Katie's aneurysm, that's Katie. Now draw a larger circle around the first one. In that ring put the name of the person next closest to the trauma. In the case of Katie's aneurysm, that was Katie's husband, Pat. Repeat the process as many times as you need to. In each larger ring put the next closest people. Parents and children before more distant relatives. Intimate friends in smaller rings, less intimate friends in larger ones. When you are done you have a "Kvetching Order."

Here are the rules. The person in the center ring can say anything she wants to anyone, anywhere. She can kvetch and complain and whine and moan and curse the heavens and say, "Life is unfair" and "Why me?" That's the one payoff for being in the center ring.

Everyone else can say those things too, but only to people in larger rings.

When you are talking to a person in a ring smaller than yours, someone closer to the center of the crisis, the goal is to help. Listening is often more helpful than talking. But if you're going to open your mouth, ask yourself if what you are about to say is likely to provide comfort and support. If it isn't, don't say it. Don't, for example, give advice. People who are suffering from trauma don't need advice. They need comfort and support. So say, "I'm sorry" or "This must really be hard for you" or "Can I bring you a pot roast?" Don't say, "You should hear what happened to me" or "Here's what I would do if I were you." And don't say, "This is really bringing me down."

If you want to scream or cry or complain, if you want to tell someone how shocked you are or how icky you feel, or whine about how it reminds you of all the terrible things that have happened to you lately, that's fine. It's a perfectly normal response. Just do it to someone in a bigger ring.

Comfort IN, dump OUT.

There was nothing wrong with Katie's friend saying she was not prepared for how horrible Katie looked, or even that she didn't think she could handle it. The mistake was that she said those things to Pat. She dumped IN.

Complaining to someone in a smaller ring than yours doesn't do either of you any good. On the other hand, being supportive to her principal caregiver may be the best thing you can do for the patient.

Most of us know this. Almost nobody would complain to the patient about how rotten she looks. Almost no one would say that looking at her makes them think of the fragility of life and their own closeness to death. In other words, we know enough not to dump into the center ring. Ring Theory merely expands that intuition and makes it more concrete: Don't just avoid dumping into the center ring; avoid dumping into any ring smaller than your own.

Remember, you can say whatever you want if you just wait until you're talking to someone in a larger ring than yours. Unfortunately, we all get our turn in the center of the ring. Until that happens, this Kvetching Order may be a useful guide when comforting those closer than you are to the ones who are in the center of the ring.

Bank Accounts And Elderly Abuse—Closer To Home Than You Might Believe

From time to time I get calls from an adult child of one of my clients, accusing a sibling of stealing money from their common parent. Sometimes the accusations are baseless, as the accused child may be doing nothing more than withdrawing funds to take care of their mother or father, and the sibling has no idea how much medical and nursing care costs.

But sometimes the accusations have some merit. The difficulty lies in what to do about it when it happens. As it turns out, Florida law defines abuse of the elderly and imposes harsh terms for those that partake in this activity.

So please allow me to pose a scenario in asking whether abuse of an elderly person has occurred:

Assume that Dad is only 60 years old, but despite his relatively young age he suffers from some form of cognitive impairment. Son, who is Dad's only child and sole beneficiary under Dad's will, is also a joint owner with rights of survivorship on Dad's brokerage account. The brokerage account assets approximating $400,000 consist solely of Dad's savings, as Son has not contributed any amounts to it.

Five years ago Dad placed the account in joint name with Son in an effort to avoid probate at Dad's death and for convenience purposes should Son need to assist Dad in writing checks and paying bills. During the five-year period, Dad didn't make a transfer of any amounts to Son other than to pay Dad's share of their living expenses.

Dad has a full bevy of estate planning documents, and has gone so far as to name Son as his agent under a valid Durable Power of Attorney.

Dad is subsequently adjudicated incompetent in a guardianship court. Shortly thereafter, Son has Dad write a check out of the brokerage account transferring $100,000 to Son personally, who then deposits the money in Son's own personal account.

Is this elder abuse?

There is a strong argument that Son has committed a first degree felony under Florida law, specifically §825.103(2)(a). Florida law punishes individuals who stand in a position of trust or confidence with the elderly person when they exploit the elderly. "Exploiting" under the law includes knowingly obtaining or using an elderly person's funds, assets or property with the intent to temporarily or permanently deprive the elderly person of the use, benefit or possession of them.

The statute defines an individual as standing in a position of trust or confidence as a person who is a parent, spouse, adult child or other relative by blood or marriage, is a joint tenant with the elderly person on an asset, has a legal or fiduciary relationship to the elderly person (such as holding a durable power of attorney or acting as trustee of a trust), is a caregiver or otherwise is entrusted with the elderly person's funds, assets or property.

So even though Dad has named Son as his agent under a Durable Power of Attorney, coupled with the facts that Son is also a joint owner on the brokerage account and is Dad's sole beneficiary under his will, it would appear under the statute that when Son stuck the $100,000 check under Dad's nose after Dad had been adjudicated incompetent that Son committed a very serious crime.

The fact that Son had been in a position of authority over Dad actually worsens Son's case, not betters it. The law imposes the burden on those who have that trust. And even though Dad is only 60 years old, the law defines "elderly" as anyone over sixty, or if one is disabled and over 18, they could also be protected under the statute.

Unfortunately, elderly abuse is common here in Florida. It would appear that a vast majority of cases go unreported, as many involve family members who are reluctant to press charges against one another.

Nevertheless, elderly abuse is serious business. The punishment for elderly abuse under the statute includes restitution and imprisonment, depending upon the degree and severity of the abuse.

Financial abuse is not the only type covered under the law. Abuse can also include lewd or lascivious acts committed upon or in the presence of an elderly person, and the infliction of physical or psychological injury, including acts or omissions that might lead to such injuries.

If you believe that an elderly person has been abused, or if you want additional information about elderly abuse, you can call the Florida Department of Elder Affairs at 1-800-96-ABUSE or by visiting their website at http://elderaffairs.state.fl.us/doea/report_abuse.php.

Power of Attorney Abuses

You might be surprised to learn that the moment you sign a Durable Power of Attorney, your named agent has the immediate authority to sign checks, deeds and other legal documents as if they were you. In other words, you don't have to be incapacitated before the Durable Power of Attorney is active.

"But I don't want them to be able to act for me unless I can't act for myself," I've heard on more than one occasion. A power of attorney that isn't valid unless a precondition exists would be known as a "springing" power of attorney. In other words, it doesn't "spring" into action unless the precondition named in the document (such as the grantor's incapacity) occurs.

For many years Florida law did not authorize "springing" powers of attorney. Then, in 1996, the power of attorney statute was changed to authorize springing powers. Even though the law authorized them, springing powers of attorney weren't practical and were very difficult to use.

You may wonder why they weren't practical. The reason is that banks and other financial institutions were rightly concerned about their liability when honoring a springing power of attorney. Allow me to explain by example.

Suppose that "David" signed a springing durable power of attorney that authorized his son "Mark" to act as his agent if David becomes incapacitated—but only if David becomes incapacitated. David later suffers a stroke, so Mark presents the power of attorney to David's banking institution, expecting to be able to write checks on David's accounts to help his father write checks and pay bills.

Except that the bank won't accept the springing power of attorney. "How do we know that David is really incapacitated?" they ask Mark.

The bank is rightfully concerned that if they allow Mark to write checks, and if David later alleges that he was never incapacitated and that Mark's checks were therefore fraudulent, the bank would have a tough time defending their liability. At a minimum, the bank is going to want proof from a doctor that David is incapacitated—probably in the form of a signed and notarized affidavit from David's physician.

Mark then contacts his father's physician to get such a statement. Here, we might expect the physician to be afraid to sign something like that for his own liability. What if he signs such a statement and Mark writes checks on David's account to pay for an expensive vacation for Mark and his family? Might David one day sue the physician?

You can see where this is headed. Even though springing powers of attorney were legal, they weren't practical. This is now a moot point anyway, since a new Florida law now forbids the use of springing powers of attorney.

You might guess which groups lobbied to abolish them. Banks and brokerage houses led the charge to forever ban their use in Florida—mostly for liability reasons, as I explained above.

Consequently, Florida law now provides that when one signs a power of attorney, it is immediately active, whether or not the grantor of the power is incapacitated. One therefore needs to be extremely careful when selecting a person to act as your power of attorney agent. If you are afraid, for any reason, that the person you named might one day abuse their authority, then you should not name them.

It is always a good idea to discuss your expectations and wishes with whomever you plan to name in this important document—*before* you sign it. First of all, that person is going to have a lot of responsibility in the event of your incapacity. They may be responsible to write your checks, pay your bills, balance your accounts, manage your investments and file your tax returns among other things. It's not so much an honor to be named in a durable power of attorney document, as it is an immense responsibility.

Some decide to name two people. In this case, remember that each person will have an immediate right to act on your behalf. The danger in having two people is if they disagree on a course of action then you might have a stalemate—or worse—conflicting directions to your advisors. It's usually a good idea to select just one person to act for you at a time.

You might also wonder what happens if someone abuses their authority under a durable power of attorney. While the agent must act in a fiduciary capacity, the recourse would be to sue them for acting negligently. If they are judgment-proof (usually because they have no assets to collect against if they were to lose such a lawsuit), then the filing of the lawsuit itself would likely result in throwing good money after bad.

The bottom line: be very selective when deciding who your durable power of attorney document names to act for you. And if you happen to have a document created under the old law, now is the time to meet with your attorney to update your documents.

The Four Powers Absent In Your Durable Power Of Attorney

What can be more boring than your Durable Power of Attorney document? Most of the time it's considered a form where you name someone who would have the authority, in essence, to legally bind you by signing a document for you. You might be surprised to learn that the Durable Power of Attorney is a very important legal document, and that many of them don't contain powers that are absolutely essential in the modern world of estate planning.

I'm going to describe four powers that you might want to have your estate planning attorney include in your Durable Power of Attorney, if those powers aren't there yet.

The first power is the power to make gifts on your behalf. We all know that in 2014, we can make $14,000 tax-free gifts to anyone that we want. We can also make unlimited gifts for medical expenses so long as the payments are made directly to the medical care provider, as well as unlimited gifts for educational expenses so long as the payments are made directly to the educational institution.

In the event of your incapacity, however, the person holding your Durable Power of Attorney cannot legally make the tax-free gifts unless they specifically have the power to make those gifts imbedded in the document. The IRS does not consider a gift made under a Durable Power of Attorney which does not specifically mention the power to make gifts to be tax-free.

A general power to do "anything that I can do myself" or words to that effect is not specific enough in the IRS' eyes. You might believe that this is not an important power because you don't commonly make gifts to your family. But this power may be more important that you think.

Consider a situation where you need long term care and you don't have enough money to support yourself for the rest of your life. Or you might find yourself in a situation where your long term care costs may financially ruin your family, leaving your spouse or other loved ones destitute. In this situation, the person holding your Durable Power of Attorney may need to transfer assets out of your name so that you can qualify for Medicaid. Here the power to make a transfer in the form of a gift is vitally important.

The second power is to establish and fund trusts. In a situation where you are incompetent but you need the person holding the Durable Power of Attorney to qualify you for Medicaid, as I described in the last paragraph, not only must the holder of your Durable Power of Attorney need to have the ability to make transfers of your assets, but they also may need the power to create and fund trusts. Trust planning may be integral to qualifying for long-term care benefits or to minimize taxes. Unless the Durable Power of Attorney specifically includes such powers, chances are the governmental agencies dealing with the issues will not consider it to be sufficient for the holder of your Durable Power of Attorney to create and fund your plan legally.

A third power concerns IRA and other retirement account benefits. After you are age 70½, the IRS mandates that you withdraw a minimum distribution from your account annually. You may already have the minimum distribution automatically deposited into your checking account. But if there is a medical or other emergency requiring greater access to the IRA account, your Durable Power of Attorney better give the power holder the ability to withdraw funds from the account or to change your minimum required distribution.

Finally, especially if you are financially supporting someone else, it might be important for your Durable Power of Attorney to contain not only provisions for your own financial care, but that it authorizes distributions to those who you support. A common example of this is when you financially support an aging parent or other relative. If you should fall ill, the person holding your Durable Power of Attorney should be expressly authorized to use your financial accounts to continue to support those that you have always supported and who may need your support.

The bottom line is that you should not think of your Durable Power of Attorney as a form document. Read through it, and if there are any powers that should be there that are not, visit with your estate planning attorney to make sure that those powers are drafted into the document.

The Problem With Successors Named In A Durable Power Of Attorney

A Durable Power of Attorney (DPOA) is an important document that everyone should have as a part of his or her estate planning portfolio. Generally speaking, the grantor of a Durable Power of Attorney names someone who can legally act for the grantor in any number of ways. The person who is granted the power to act is known as the "attorney-in-fact" or "agent." For simplicity's sake, I'm going to refer to the grantee of the power as the "agent."

The DPOA may allow the agent to write checks to pay bills, sign deeds, complete beneficiary designations, enter into and/or enforce contracts, open accounts, close accounts, and direct investments, among other things.

DPOAs cease upon the grantor's death. In other words, they are no longer effective. The "Durable" in the name "Durable Power of Attorney" means that the powers survive the grantor's *incapacity.* A General Power of Attorney, in contrast, would cease if the grantor should become incapacitated such as through dementia or Alzheimer's disease. Most estate plans use the DPOA since the thought is that the power holder would only act if the grantor of the power couldn't.

Under Florida law, one can name an agent under a DPOA, and then if that agent is unable or unwilling to serve, another agent can be named as an alternate. It might look something like this: "I hereby name my wife, Patti, as my Attorney-in-Fact, and if Patti is unable or unwilling to serve, then I name my daughter, Gabrielle, to so serve."

I almost always try to persuade my clients from naming successor DPOA agents in the same document.

Why? Even though they are legal under the relatively new Florida statute on point, successor DPOAs are very difficult to use from a practical standpoint.

Consider the fact that any bank, financial firm or broker who is acting under a DPOA is suspicious of the document from a liability standpoint. Consider the scenario where my daughter, Gabrielle, walks into my financial advisor's office holding the DPOA and says, "I need to transfer $20,000 out of my father's money market account today."

My financial advisor looks at the DPOA, worried that if it is not authentic he could be liable for following Gabi's direction. So he asks Gabi, "Why are you using the power? Can I call your dad to see if this is okay?"

"Dad's in the hospital and isn't able to talk. I need to write some checks to pay a bunch of his bills and that is why I am here," Gabi answers him.

My financial advisor then reads the DPOA, and points to the first line that says my wife Patti is the first power holder and not Gabi.

"It says here that your mother is the first power holder and that you can only act if she can't," he says.

"My mom is out of the country and can't take care of these things now," Gabi says.

"I'm sorry," my financial advisor says, "I have to be very careful, as I may have a lot of liability here if for some reason you aren't supposed to act," he says. "I'm going to have to give this to my firm's legal department to sort out."

Gabi, worried that she won't be able to pay my bills on time is frustrated. "How long will this take?" she asks.

"I don't know," my financial advisor replies.

From there the whole thing can become a circus. The attorney for the financial firm may say that they need written proof that Patti can't act or that she is unwilling to act. It can take days if not weeks to resolve.

So what's the alternative? What I normally suggest is that each person you wish to name as your agent under a DPOA have a separate DPOA document that just names them individually. While there is a possibility that if you have two different parties acting under a DPOA that they are in conflict with one another, I will tell you anecdotally from personal experience that I haven't seen much (if any) of that in my practice.

With that said, if you name more than one party as a DPOA in separate documents, it is wise to tell the individuals you are naming of the fact that each has a separate power, and that your expectation is for them to work together and to consult one another. Or if you prefer that one only act when the other couldn't, that would be a verbal arrangement.

Remember that anyone acting as an agent under a DPOA has a fiduciary duty to the grantor of the power. They should only be acting in the grantor's best interests. If you fear that someone you name won't do that, or won't work in conjunction with another as you would request, then I would say that you probably shouldn't be naming that person in such a powerful document to begin with.

Differences Between Durable Power Of Attorney And Guardianship

A client's son recently called me. I could tell by his voice that he was frustrated. "The document that you drafted isn't working. I went to the bank to put my name on mother's account so I could write her checks and pay her bills and they said that the document you drafted was faulty and they can't do it."

"Which document are you referring to?" I asked, perplexed at the situation.

"Her Pre-Need Guardian," client's son replied.

"That's the wrong document," I explained. "The document that you need to take to the bank to put your name on the account is titled "Durable Power of Attorney."

I realized then that many people don't understand the difference between a guardianship situation and one where a durable power of attorney can be used. The "Pre-Need Guardian" document names someone that you would want to be appointed in the event that you were declared incompetent in a guardianship proceeding.

A guardianship proceeding is a court process where someone petitions the court to declare you legally incompetent. Courts take these proceedings very seriously since the case can result in your losing rights to sign your name and transact business, vote, get married or perform any task for yourself. Instead, a guardian is appointed to act on your behalf.

The guardianship proceeding is deemed adversarial in nature. The person whose competency is being questioned must have an attorney independently representing his or her interests. Reaching the decision to go to court to declare a loved one incompetent can be gut wrenching since the process is public. Mental health experts examine the person and testify before a judge whether the petition to declare incompetency should be granted.

Once declared incompetent, the judge then appoints a "guardian" over the person (now called the "ward") and/or his or her property (assets). This is where the Pre-Need Guardian document may be helpful in that it declares who the ward would want to serve in that capacity. The court will give much consideration to the wishes of the ward, as the Pre-Need Guardian document would normally have been signed at a time before he or she became incompetent.

Once the guardianship is established, the guardian has a legal duty to provide an annual accounting to the court of how the ward's assets and income were invested and spent. A guardianship process is often time consuming and expensive.

The Durable Power of Attorney document, in contrast, does not require any court process. Here, the person granting the powers of attorney appoints an "Attorney-in-Fact" to act for them in all sorts of situations. "Attorney-in-Fact" does not usually mean your attorney-at-law, by the way. Usually the attorney-in-fact appointed in the document is a relative or trusted friend.

The attorney-in-fact can bring the Durable Power of Attorney document to the bank or brokerage firm to place his or her name on the accounts in order to sign checks and to pay bills or manage investments. The attorney-in-fact is not an owner of the account, however. Instead, the attorney-in-fact is a fiduciary—meaning that he or she is charged with the responsibility of acting on behalf of the person who granted them the power. The attorney-in-fact must act prudently and in the best interests of the grantor.

So if you have a Durable Power of Attorney when would it ever be necessary to go through a guardianship process? In rare circumstances it is necessary to go through a guardianship even when there are Durable Powers of Attorney available. Consider the situation when a person has Alzheimer's and they might get engaged to be married to a gold digger who is only interested in taking advantage of someone who may be mentally incapacitated.

Once married without a prenuptial agreement, the new spouse has several legal rights in the financial interests of the mentally incapacitated spouse, both in the event of divorce or death.

Here, the family may act to protect their loved one by having him or her declared legally incompetent. Once so declared, their loved one can't legally sign a marriage license, gift money from bank or brokerage accounts or deed properties to their new spouse. I've seen instances where a vulnerable person was coerced into transferring all sorts of assets to their new spouse, even though their son or daughter was acting as the attorney-in-fact under a Durable Power of Attorney document.

Just because a person has been declared to have dementia or Alzheimer's doesn't necessarily void any legal contract (including marriage) that they subsequently enter into. So there might be instances where a loved one turns to you for assistance under a Durable Power of Attorney, but may continue to transact separate business on their own. When there are such dangers, it might make sense to consider having your loved one legally adjudicated incompetent to protect them from themselves.

Does Your Dog Bite?

One of my all-time favorite movie scenes is from *The Pink Panther Strikes Again,* where Inspector Jacques Clouseau (played by legendary actor, Peter Sellers) inquires of the innkeeper, "Does your dog bite?"

While reaching to pet the animal, Clouseau is viciously attacked, causing him to yell in shock, "I thought you said that your dog does not bite!?"

"THAT is not my dog," The innkeeper calmly replies.

Despite seeing it hundreds of times, I still laugh at that scene. As most of you know, the plot of the Pink Panther movie series revolves around the heist of a famous large, pink-hued diamond and Clouseau's ensuing shenanigans pursuing the thieves.

But it's not so funny when mother or father loses precious jewelry or other valuables while in assisted living or nursing home care.

Anecdotally, the loss of keepsakes and valuables appears to happen quite frequently when a loved one is in the care of another, whether in their own residence or in an assisted living facility. Unfortunately, when valuables disappear, they are almost never recovered, and it's very hard to prove who may be responsible. Further, most assisted living facilities are not contractually liable for valuable items lost or stolen while one is in their care.

I'm not, by the way, accusing all health care workers of committing theft. I'm sure many such caretakers have been accused of taking items that were long ago lost, but faulty memories lead to false accusations. With that said, enough valuables have disappeared from the homes of those being cared for, or from the rooms in assisted living facilities, that residents should consider taking precautionary steps to avoid the heartache of losing an item near and dear to their hearts.

So let's review what steps you may want to consider before moving yourself or another loved one into a residence where others are readily present.

First, if one owns valuables that one doesn't often wear, consider storing them in a bank safety deposit box. The annual charges are well worth the investment to ensure that your valuables aren't prone to those who may have sticky fingers. When you have a safe deposit box, it is usually a good idea to have a trusted relative as a signor on the box, and for you to advise the bank location and box number that you have rented as well as where your key is stored.

Second, if you have already considered giving some or all of your valuables away to loved ones now (as opposed to bequeathing them in a will), you may get the added benefit of watching your loved ones enjoy the gifts. Here, you should consider getting appraisals and filing gift tax returns if you or your spouse is likely to have to file a federal estate tax return and the valuables given to any one beneficiary exceed the annual exclusion threshold of $14,000.

Third, if you don't already have riders covering the valuables on your homeowner's or renter's policy, speak to your insurance agent. Your agent will tell you what steps should be taken to guard against loss. Most of the time, however, it is not the financial loss that hurts when losing jewelry and other keepsakes; it is the emotional loss as well. To that end, if you decide to give jewelry that is already covered by an insurance rider, make sure that you remove the rider from the policy after the gift is completed.

I have known some who use modern surveillance equipment to record video of those who work in the home. While I don't believe that this is the best option, it could catch a thief red-handed, so to speak, and lead to the recovery of the item if discovered soon enough after the heist.

I believe that the takeaway from all of this is that those who are vulnerable should work to minimize the opportunity of those who might be interested in taking valuables by not having them around to begin with.

After all, most of us don't have a trusted manservant like Clouseau's Cato Fong—who would never steal anything. Instead, Cato would rather karate chop the inspector upon his arrival from home after a hard day's work.

So don't end up like Chief Inspector Dreyfus, who eventually ended up in the funny farm (pun intended!). When you or a loved one is in need of assisted living or nursing home care, don't forget to secure the valuables.

You Can Do Anything I Can Do Better

You may have noticed in the title of this article that my intentional play on words is from the famous duet from the Broadway musical, Annie Get Your Gun. Most of us are familiar with the song that originally set the stage for the sharpshooting contest between Annie Oakley and Frank Butler.

The estate planning tie in, of course, is to a Durable Power of Attorney document in which you name someone who can "do anything" for you. The purpose behind the Durable Power of Attorney is to have a "back up" person who can act for you in the event that you are unable or unavailable to act.

The trick in these documents is to grant the specific power to the person named in the document (your "agent") so that they can write checks, manage your investments, enforce your contracts, sign deeds and do just about anything that you can do. Since we don't know exactly what actions someone may have to do for us if we become incapacitated, many Durable Power of Attorney documents are quite lengthy, as they contain numerous paragraphs about all sorts of powers.

Sometimes clients will bemoan the length of the document. "Why do we need to be so detailed?" they ask. "Can't we just say that the person I'm naming can just do anything that I can do?"

I have seen, in fact, some Durable Power of Attorney documents that are rather brief. They might only be one page and say something like this: "I grant my agent the maximum power under law to perform any act on my behalf that I could do personally."

So if your son walks into the bank to transact business on your behalf and presents a Durable Power of Attorney document that you signed, which contains only this broad language, is the document considered enough? Is it legal for the bank to honor the document and allow your son to conduct your banking business for you?

The answer to my question is a resounding "No." The Florida statute on point says, "an agent may only exercise authority specifically granted to the agent in the power of attorney and any authority reasonably necessary to give effect to that express grant of specific authority. General provisions in a power of attorney which do not identify the specific authority granted, such as provisions purporting to give the agent the authority to do all acts that the principal can do, are not express grants of specific authority and do not grant any authority to the agent."

So in my example, the bank cannot honor a one page Durable Power of Attorney that grants your son the right to transact any business that you might transact, where the document does not also grant the specific authority to transact banking business such as depositing or withdrawing funds and writing checks.

In fact, the most recent version of the Florida Durable Power of Attorney statute mandates not only that it specifically mentions the powers that you want your agent to possess, but goes on to require you to initial next to certain powers for them to be effective.

Examples of such powers that must be properly initialed include the ability to create trusts, fund assets into your trust, sign beneficiary designations and help with certain estate and life care planning matters.

It is likely that the Durable Power of Attorney forms you find in the office supply store or on the internet are insufficient to grant those that you love and trust to conduct your legal business for you. If you become mentally incapacitated and haven't already put into place a valid Durable Power of Attorney document that meets the statutory requirements, your loved ones might otherwise have to seek a guardianship in order to conduct your legal, business and financial affairs. This can be quite time consuming and expensive.

Some people become quite concerned with the thought of granting such broad powers to another. These are valid concerns. You should never grant powers to someone that you don't trust. If you don't believe that the agent you name in a Durable Power of Attorney document will not have your best interest first and foremost in his or her mind when acting, you should not grant them a power to begin with.

And that's not to say that family members who don't always see eye to eye shouldn't give each other Durable Powers. The main issue is whether they'll act in each other's best interest. Which leads me to wonder whether Annie Oakley would have given her sharpshooting rival Frank Butler her Durable Power of Attorney? You may recall the musical ends with Annie having won lots of money that saved the Buffalo Bill Wild West show and that she also ends up marrying Frank Butler.

I guess it takes an estate planning attorney to ponder such things.

Chapter Nine

Gifting

They'll Never Find Out About That Gift

get a kick out of those commercials, "What happens in Vegas stays in Vegas!"

Yeah. Right.

That goes against the age-old wisdom that when more than one person knows about something it's no longer a secret. Which brings me to this estate planning topic—reporting gifts that you make on gift tax returns.

Many individuals make taxable transfers and never report them. "How will the IRS ever find out about it?" many say to me when

I inquire as to prior gifts. Before I broach that subject, allow me to provide some background into gifts and taxes.

The gift and estate tax are really one tax. When we make lifetime transfers, they may be subject to the gift tax. What is left of our "gift tax exemption" at the time of our deaths becomes an "estate tax exemption." It is only after we use up our total exemptions, either during our lifetime or at our death, is that tax ever imposed.

And the tax is assessed on the fair market value of the transfer at the time that it occurs, whether during our lifetimes in the form of a gift, or at our death when our will or trust transfers the assets to our beneficiaries.

You should know that during our lifetime, most of the gifts that we make are not reportable, and hence, not taxable. So long as you don't gift more than the annual exclusion amount in any calendar year to anyone, then you generally won't have to file a federal gift tax return. But the annual exclusion amount includes all gifts that you make during the year, from that watch that you bought to the stock that you transferred. If the cumulative gifts to any one recipient exceed the annual exclusion amount, then you are supposed to report it.

In most circumstances, even when you report the gift you won't pay any gift tax. Under current 2014 law, each of us has a lifetime exemption of $5.34 million. When you make a "taxable gift" all that means is that you report it on a gift tax return, and the value of those gifts reduce your lifetime exemption amount. Once you have consumed your entire lifetime exemption amount, then you start paying gift tax. Under present law, one would have to make in excess of $5.34 million of lifetime taxable transfers before paying the first dollar of gift tax.

Getting back to the "how will they ever know" question, it is vitally important that you report the taxable gifts that you make. With today's recordkeeping and technology, the IRS has many tools at its disposal to pick up on transfers that were not reported. The IRS usually won't search for those transfers until after your death. But they can go back many years, looking at deed and property records, checking and credit card accounts. And since the issue usually does not come up until you die, you are no longer around to explain the transfer. The IRS also assesses what it believes to be the fair market value of the gift(s) when they find them on audit. Disputing their assessment can become very costly and time consuming.

Once the IRS finds an individual or an estate that has not reported prior transfers, things can get ugly in a hurry. Assume that when auditing an estate tax return, the IRS discovered an unreported property transfer from the deceased to his son back in 1998. The assessed value of the property was $500,000 at the time of the transfer on the property tax records. The IRS usually considers the tax assessments to be below fair market value. Assume further that using comparables the IRS considers the fair market value at the time of the transfer to have been $750,000 and not the lower assessed value. If the deceased had a taxable estate, the IRS would likely assess additional estate tax, interest and penalties. This could add up to $375,000 or more.

Once they uncover unreported transfers, then the IRS is likely to assume that there are others. And they start digging. They'll ask for checkbook ledgers, brokerage account histories and submit formal interrogatories for the executor to answer under oath. Whether there were or there weren't other transfers, the executors of the estate should then expect to incur some hefty attorneys' and accountants' fees answering the barrage of inquiries heading their way.

The bottom line is to report the transfers that you make. This keeps your estate clean and also allows your advisors the opportunity to proactively plan during your lifetime to reduce or eliminate taxes.

Because as far as the IRS is concerned, transfers that happen between you and your loved ones don't stay a secret forever.

Loans To Family Members

One recent Saturday synagogue chanted the Torah portion of Mishpatim, from the book of Exodus, which is the source for the injunction against charging interest to a fellow Jew: "When you lend money to my people, to the poor among you, do not act toward them as a creditor; exact no interest from them."

The idea behind this biblical instruction was to instill the notion that one should help his neighbor in need and create lasting impact without embarrassment through an interest free loan. Numerous Jewish organizations act to this day under the ancient biblical direction. One is known as the Hebrew Free Loan Society, which was originally established back in the 1890s to extend credit to Jewish immigrants who wanted to open businesses in their new homeland but couldn't get banks to extend credit. There is also another interest free loan organization that I personally benefited from thirty years ago while I was in college, which is now known as the Jewish Educational Loan Fund.

Since my parents had hit hard economic times, I put myself through college and law school. Minimum wage at the time was less than $3/hour (based on today's monetary values), so there was only so much money that I could earn while attending classes full time. The federal student loans that I secured at the time weren't enough to pay for all of my expenses, not to mention that the interest on those loans was accruing at the rate of 12% —a preferable interest rate at the time I was in school!

To bridge the gap that I found myself in without digging deeper into the proverbial hole, The Jewish Educational Loan Fund promised interest free loans to qualifying students, with generous payback terms. The amounts loaned were interest free but needed to be paid back within five years after graduation from full time studies.

I repaid all of my loans and have since contributed amounts to the Jewish Educational Loan Fund annually in an effort to help those who also needed non-traditional assistance to make it through college. But I don't tell this story to earn any kudos; instead, I use it to point out the reason for the biblical law. The law was written not necessarily to prohibit lending money at a reasonable interest rate, only that according to Jewish law, it is out of place to charge interest when it comes to family—and in the Jewish tradition, fellow Jews are all considered to be family.

Which brings me to this estate planning topic—loans to family members. You may be aware that under federal gift tax law (2014), you can make $14,000 of gifts to anyone without being charged a gift tax. That means that a married couple can give their child $28,000 of gifts annually without having to file a federal gift tax return.

But what happens when a child wants to purchase a first home and you want to gift that child something more—say $100,000? Or, what if you truly do want to loan a child some money to start a business? How do you do this and comply with the federal tax law?

Unlike biblical law, the federal tax law mandates that you charge your child interest for a loan at a rate known as the "Applicable Federal Rate" (AFR). The AFR changes monthly in proclamations issued by the IRS. There are different minimum interest rates—which are based on current interest rates—that one should charge their family member, depending upon the length of the loan in question, whether it is a short term (less than 3 years), medium term (3-9 years), or long term (greater than 9 years). You can easily find out what the current AFR rates are by Googling it.

If you don't collect the interest from the child it still should be reported as "imputed interest" taxable on your income tax return.

So in my example where you wanted to make a gift of $100,000 to your child but only had $28,000 of gift tax exclusion this year between you and your spouse, you could loan your child the additional $72,000 and charge an annual interest rate on a hypothetical five-year note at 1.12%. The child should pay you that interest annually. But there is nothing to prevent you from gifting them another $28,000 next year of which they can use to pay down the note—with recurring gifts until the note is paid in full.

You don't want to "forgive" the note, by the way. Forgiveness of debt would be considered taxable income to the debtor subject to the payment of income tax.

So if you are making larger gifts to family members or if you decide to loan family members amounts, it might make sense to visit with your estate planning attorney to ensure that it is structured properly within the tax law.

Libby's Delicatessen

Growing up in Indianapolis during the 1970s, my father and I would frequent Libby's Delicatessen in the City Market before attending Indiana Pacer basketball games downtown. It just so happened that the open-air counter restaurant was owned and operated by my Aunt Libby Fogle. The food was delicious, from the foot long kosher hot dogs to the pastrami on rye to her famous bar-b-que sandwiches, the latter of which I couldn't get enough.

An iconic landmark in its time, it wasn't uncommon to sit at the counter next to then Mayor (and future Senator) Richard Lugar or Governor Otis Bowen. Everyone was attracted to the restaurant, not only for the wonderful fare but also because of Libby's effervescent personality.

"HOW YA DOIN?!" She would shout at patrons through her broad smile from across the counters. "What can I getcha today?!" Libby was in constant motion, gesturing at her staff to quickly take care of her many customers, whether to take an order, slice the meat or refill the tall Coca-Cola emblazoned paper cups of soda.

She was a prototypical "glass is half full" lady. Libby found the proverbial silver lining around any cloud—a skill that I admire and try to emulate to this day. She died a few years ago, but I would suggest that if Libby were alive today she'd tell us that despite recent economic hardships, we live in extraordinary times, especially when we're speaking of planning opportunities with family businesses.

Libby's father established the deli counter back when she was a child, naming it after her. He built and worked at it for years, hiring his daughter as an apprentice before he passed the restaurant down to her. While successful in her father's day, it really hit its stride with Libby at the helm.

In this tough economy, it seems that many small business owners are reluctant to pass the torch down to the next generation. Sometimes it's because the owner fears losing control over the day-to-day operations of the business. Perhaps it's because the owner doesn't want to reduce the income he earns by sharing more of it with the next generation. Sometimes the current owners speak of a "generational gap," where there's a perception that the adult children are not up to the task of taking on more responsibility.

Current federal estate and gift tax law provides us a generous exemption to transfer business interests to the next generation. Depending upon the size of the business, estate planning specialists can usually recommend "leveraging" techniques, depending upon the clients' goals. Some families simply wish to make an outright gift transfer while others will need to structure it as a sale so that the retiring generation will have cash flow in retirement.

Nevertheless, the obstacle frequently encountered is the parent's fear of losing income and control. This concern can be ameliorated through consulting agreements, retention of voting interests, or by restructuring the form of legal ownership of the entity. Every business will have its own unique set of facts that good advisors can analyze to help the owners find the best solution.

Another commonly voiced obstacle to a transfer of ownership interests is the next generation's perceived lack of ambition. When this occurs, I often wonder whether the children know the bounty that might follow if they only work harder. If they have no idea how much the business truly generates, they may not fully see the opportunity before them. When the financial veil is lifted, even ever so slightly, the ambition and drive suddenly appear. The result is usually a dramatic shift from an employee attitude to that of an owner.

Yet another problem is deciding which managerial roles each person might play. Will one of the brothers be in charge of the others? What will the management team look like when Mom and Dad leave? There are various tools available, such as Kolbe profiles (www.kolbe.com) that can enlighten what each family member's propensities are and what kind of managerial flowchart presents the greatest opportunity for success.

If your adult children are working in your family business—and if you've thought about these issues—I'd suggest that you meet with your legal and tax team to determine whether now is a good time to start the process. After all, my ever-optimistic Aunt Libby would tell you that everything is going to turn out great.

This, despite a mishap her deli endured one afternoon when her then eleven-year-old nephew spilled his Coke all over Mayor Lugar, who couldn't have been more gracious. "Oh, I have a fresh suit hanging in my office, young man," he said to a very embarrassed and frightened me. "Don't sweat it!"

Gifting More With Less

Everyone loves receiving presents. Most of us get just as much satisfaction—if not more—when we give to our loved ones. An important estate planning strategy is to consistently use tax-free gifts not only to benefit those that you care about, but also to reduce the size of your taxable estate, so that upon your death, Uncle Sam doesn't become one of your primary beneficiaries.

Unfortunately, when we're talking about estate and gift tax planning, the law caps the amount that each one of us can gift tax free at $14,000 annually per individual, effective in 2014. This amount is called the "annual exclusion amount." I'm going to show you five different ways how you can give more than that $14,000 in value and remain under the annual exclusion amount.

1. **Gift Splitting.** Married couples can together give $28,000 to any individual and still fall under the annual exclusion amount. Sometimes, however, particularly in second marriage situations, the stepparent doesn't want to give his or her own funds to their stepchildren. They'd rather just give to their own children. Here, the biological parent can supply the total $28,000 amount, yet the gift will be treated as coming from both husband and wife if it is written from a joint account, or if the stepparent agrees to sign a Form 709 Federal Gift Tax Return to treat the gift as being "split" between them both.

2. **Buy Life Insurance.** A classic technique to "leverage" gifts is to buy life insurance and place it in an Irrevocable Life Insurance Trust (ILIT). Normally, premium payments won't qualify as gift tax free under the $14,000

annual exclusion amount because the beneficiaries aren't expected to enjoy the benefit of the gift until the policy pays after your death. This is called a "future interest" gift. In order for the gift to qualify as a "present interest" gift and therefore fall under the gift tax annual exclusion, ILITs contain "Crummey powers" that allow beneficiaries a window in which to withdraw their share of the premium contribution. Beneficiaries normally don't exercise their right of withdrawal, of course, because then the policy would lapse for failure to pay the premiums, and in most cases the death benefits lost far exceed the amount of premium contributions made.

3. **Pay for College Educational Expenses.** College expenses have been increasing at rates beyond normal inflation for many years now. Purchasing a prepaid college tuition plan for a loved one, or opening up a "529 Savings Plan" are two ways to leverage your gift giving. When your child or grandchild actually attends college, the amount of tuition and other college expenses that the plan pays for is likely to far exceed the amounts that you contributed to the plan. Moreover, you can "front load" a 529 plan with five years of contributions and not pay gift tax or use up your lifetime gift tax exclusion. Even better, the appreciation achieved within 529 Plans avoids capital gains and income taxes as long as the plan assets are used for qualifying educational expenses.

4. **Loan the Money Up Front.** When a child or grandchild purchases their first home, you may want to give more than the $14,000 threshold to assist with a down payment or similar needs. Here, it might make sense to loan the balance of what you want to give to your loved one, and

then give the $14,000 annually so that they can use that money to repay the note they owe you. By structuring the transaction this way, you avoid using some of your precious gift tax exemption while front-loading monies to your loved ones for major purchases. In order not to run afoul of IRS rules, the outstanding balance of the promissory note needs to bear interest at the "Applicable Federal Rate," which is published monthly. Currently, these rates are extremely nominal.

5. **Give Away Family Partnership Interests.** Rather than giving away $14,000 of cash, you might want to consider giving away interests in real estate or other income producing assets. Here, you would normally contribute the property to some sort of a family partnership and gift the partnership interests to your loved ones. Because these are private partnership interests and don't have a ready market, a valuation specialist can "discount" the interest from the value of its share of the underlying asset's true value.

There are a number of other leveraging techniques available to stretch the amount of gifts that you can make to your loved ones. A good estate planning attorney can direct you, based upon your goals and the types of assets that you own.

Diving In—Pooling Gifts For College Educational Expenses

My oldest daughter, Gabrielle, is a senior in high school, so now is the season for college applications. We've done the admissions tours at a variety of different colleges and universities. When friends ask me where she's applying, I tell them to look up a list of the most expensive colleges, and chances are if it's in the top 20, she's interested!

Now, for a guy who had to put himself through college and law school at a state university, it's a tough nut to crack when you see how much it costs these days. This brings to mind a question that I'm frequently asked, which is related to the best estate planning strategies when a grandparent would like to gift money for their grandchildren's education.

The most flexible strategy is to make gifts to irrevocable trusts. Since the trusts are irrevocable, the gifts will generally be excluded from the grandparent's estate for federal estate tax purposes. Trusts can be used for many different educational purposes, ranging from tuition to living expenses. Families can control the investments inside of the trusts and can control the trust distributions.

The question then becomes whether a large gift should be pooled into one trust for the benefit of all of the grandchildren, or whether separate shares should be created—one for each grandchild.

There are advantages and disadvantages to each strategy. The pooled fund approach enables the family to allocate resources according to relative need. If one grandchild's parents are affluent and don't need as much help as another's, funds can be allocated accordingly. Similarly, we never know which of the grand-children will even attend a college, or which ones might receive scholarships.

But the pooled approach isn't for everyone. Suppose you have grandchildren ranging in age from 2 to 16. If the older grandchildren attend expensive colleges, there's always the possibility that they consume all of the resources, leaving little for the younger ones—who may have an even greater need since higher educational expenses have tended to skyrocket over the general inflation rate. The converse can also hold true. If the family is stingy with the older grandchildren, then the oldest grandchildren might get the short end of the stick if there is ultimately too much in the pot when the younger ones come through.

Pooled educational trusts can also breed animosity within the family over the allocation of the resources, especially when one of your children may have several children of their own where another child has only one.

The alternative is to create a trust that has a separate share for each grandchild. The grandchild can only consume the amount in his or her share. This strategy is relatively easy to administer. The hard part comes in decisions related to how much should go into each grandchild's share? Should a three-year-old grandchild be funded with the same amount that a fifteen-year-old grandchild receives?

Besides, for trusts, there are a few different ways to contribute towards a grandchild's educational needs. A 529 Plan allows for the tax-free growth and withdrawals, provided that the money is used for qualified educational purposes. Grandparents can "front load" these plans with up to five years of tax free annual exclusion gifts, which under current law means that $70,000 can be contributed gift tax free, effective in 2014.

In addition to the annual exclusion gifts, one can make a tax-free gift for tuition regardless of the amount, as long as the gift is made directly to the educational institution. Assume that Johnny attends Brown University where the tuition is $54,000. Grandma can write a tuition check to Brown in full gift, tax-free.

Grandparents can also open Uniform Transfers to Minors accounts (commonly called UTMA accounts). Here, a custodian is named to hold the account for the minor, and upon attaining age 21 the minor has complete access to all of the money. But be careful not to open a Uniform Gift to Minors Act account (UGMA), since those accounts allow its beneficiary complete access to all of the monies at age 18. If restriction to access the account is important, then you may want to consider a trust instead of an UTMA account.

Whenever creating trusts or opening accounts for college education, you should also consider the effect that the account may have on the child's ability to receive financial aid. The financial aid applications do take into account resources available to the child, reducing possible benefits and/or need-based scholarships.

There are a lot of options out there. The facts and circumstances of each family often dictate which avenues offer the best alternatives. But even though current educational expenses will literally shock you, it's still an exciting time for the students, and nothing beats future earning potential than a college diploma.

Top Five Year End Gifting Rules

The end of the year—"'Tis the season where many like to make gifts to loved ones." There's a lot of confusion about the gift tax rules, so I thought that we could review a few of the more common ones together:

5. Gifts Aren't Usually Taxed as Income. Let's say that you make a cash gift to your daughter Suzie of $14,000. Does she have to declare that gift as taxable income on her Form 1040 income tax return? No, she doesn't. When we talk about "gift tax," we are referring to the transfer taxes—the estate and gift taxes. A transfer tax is a tax imposed on the donor—not the recipient—on the value of the gift. But beginning in 2014, there is also an annual exclusion of $14,000. This means that a donor can make a gift of $14,000 to anyone and it is not enough to require the filing of a gift tax return. Suppose a donor makes a gift of $100,000 to daughter Suzie. Now the donor has to file a gift tax return reporting the $100,000 transfer. Does the donor pay gift tax at this time? The answer is—it depends. If the donor has consumed his lifetime exemption (in 2014 that exemption is $5.34 million) then he does not actually pay gift tax. Instead, he has consumed a part of his lifetime (and death) exemption.

4. Paying Someone's Medical Expenses Doesn't Count as a Gift. In my example of making a gift to Suzie above, assume that your daughter Suzie has medical expenses of $20,000 that you would like to help her out with. You've already given her the $14,000, but she needs that for her necessities. Can you gift additional amounts to pay for her medical expenses without having to file a gift tax return consuming more of your exemption? Yes, you can, provided that you make the payment directly to the medical provider. If you were to give Suzie another $20,000 to pay her doctor bills, then you would have to file a gift tax return. If instead you made the payment directly to Suzie's doctors and hospitals, then the payment is considered gift tax-free.

3. Paying Someone's Educational Expenses Doesn't Count as a Gift. If Suzie has a $20,000 tuition bill, you are able to gift her $14,000 plus her tuition, provided that you pay the educational institution directly as you would have a doctor or hospital in the previous example.

2. Gifts Must Be Completed to Count. Suppose that you have some valuable artwork in your home. Knowing that you might have a taxable estate when you die, and that the valuable artwork is only going to only add to the tax liability, you decide to gift that artwork to your children. First, remember that if you make gifts above $14,000 in value, you are consuming your estate tax exemption anyway as you will have to file a gift tax return reporting the transfer. In any event, take those yellow sticky post-it notes to post on the back of each piece of art: "This painting now belongs to Junior." You leave the paintings on your wall. Under IRS rules you have not made a completed gift because you have not actually lost dominion and control over the asset. The painting must actually leave your residence to be considered a completed gift.

1. You Can't Sell Assets for $1 to Avoid Gift and Estate Tax. Some believe that they can outsmart the IRS by "selling" assets at an amount below fair market value to avoid the gift tax rules. Assume that Tom "sells" his rental house valued at $225,000 to his daughter, Suzie for $100. Here, Tom has made a taxable gift in the amount of $224,900, which is the difference of the fair market value of the property less the amount that Suzie actually paid for it. How do you determine the fair market value? Some assets—like stocks and bonds—have a ready market that is easily determined. Others—like real estate or family business interests—require you to engage the services of a qualified appraiser who can issue an appraisal report that must be attached to the gift tax return. I've seen instances where individuals instead obtained a Realtor's price estimate report to justify a transfer value. It's been my experience that the IRS doesn't consider Realtor's listing reports or price estimates to be a qualified report. When the IRS doesn't consider it to be a qualified report, then they (the IRS) are free to determine what they believe to be the accurate fair market value, usually resulting in the assessment of additional tax.

I hope that this helps you when you play Santa Claus this year. Merry Christmas and Happy Chanukah to all!

Year End Gift Giving—Avoid Gift Taxes

With the end of the year inevitably come questions about gifting and taxes. Most gifts to our loved ones are gift tax free, but you should know some basics before gifting anything of value to your children, grandchildren and other loved ones.

Under 2014 gift-tax laws, the most that you can give tax-free to any one person is $14,000 in any calendar year. This counts whether you give cash, a valuable painting, a car or any combination of items. A husband and wife together can give $28,000 worth of assets to any one person during a calendar year and count them as tax-free. If the assets aren't gifted from a joint account, you can still treat the gift as coming from both the husband and the wife as long as a Gift Tax Return Form 709 is timely filed, and the spouse elects to "split the gift" by checking a box on the return and signing it.

Gift splitting is more common in second marriage situations. An example might help assist in understanding this technique. Suppose that Robert is married to Doris, and that this is a second marriage. Robert has two sons from a prior marriage, Herb and Scott. Doris has two children from her prior marriage, Sophia and Rachel. Robert wishes to give each of his sons, Herb and Scott $28,000. Assume further that Robert and Doris maintain separate bank accounts.

So Robert transfers $28,000 each to Herb and to Scott. This would be a taxable gift exceeding the $14,000 per beneficiary rule unless Doris agrees to "split the gift" by signing a Gift Tax Return Form 709. Doris is not affected by splitting the gift, nor are her children affected. In this example, Robert is gifting money from Robert's separate bank account. Doris may therefore still give $14,000 each to her children and grandchildren. In fact, Doris can ask Robert to split the gifts to her children, Sophia and Rachel to give them $28,000 each as well and Doris can write those checks directly from her account.

In addition to gifts of money, many of my clients tell me that they intend to give other items, such as valuable paintings or jewelry. In order for a gift to be considered "tax free" and to remove it from the estate for federal estate tax purposes, the donor must actually transfer custody of the asset to the donee. Let's illustrate this by another example.

Suppose that Doris intends to give a valuable Monet painting to her daughter, Sophia. Doris tells Sophia that the painting is hers, but that Doris intends to keep the painting in Doris' living room until she dies. "After I die I want you to take the painting off the wall and put it in your home," Doris instructs Sophia.

Doris has not made a tax-free gift to Sophia. In fact, Doris has not made a gift at all. If Doris dies with the Monet still hung on her wall, then under the tax law the painting is included in Doris' estate for federal estate tax purposes. Clients often ask me how would the IRS know whether the painting was still hanging in Doris' home at the time of her death?

The answer lies in a number of places. The most likely clue of ownership might be uncovered when the IRS requests a copy of Doris' homeowner's insurance. The IRS would look to see whether at the time of Doris' death there was a rider on the homeowner's policy covering the Monet. If Doris truly transferred the Monet to her daughter, Sophia, then there would be no reason for Doris to continue to insure it.

Some folks think that they are clever by "selling" something of value as opposed to gifting it. Suppose Fred "sold" a piece of property to his daughter, Melanie for $10,000, when, in fact, the fair market value of the property at the time of the transfer was $110,000. Here, despite the fact that Fred "sold" it, the IRS would consider the transaction to be a $100,000 gift (calculated as a transfer of $110,000 of property for $10,000).

If you have any particular questions about gifting that may be affected by the tax laws, discuss them with your estate planning attorney prior to making the transfer.

Chapter Ten

Probate & Trust Administration

Selecting The Right Trustee

Everyone who has a revocable living trust has named a trustee of their trust. Typically you name yourself, which means that you have total control over all of the trust assets. Your trust will also name someone or some institution to administer it when you die, and ultimately make distribution of the trust assets to your loved ones named in the document.

But what happens if you get sick and are unable to manage your own affairs? If a certificate of deposit comes due and needs to be rolled over, who is going to make that decision for you? Who decides how much of your trust assets should be budgeted for long-term care and whether your assets can support in home nursing care? Who's going to make decisions regarding the sale of a property? Continuing lifetime gifts to support a child or grandchild?

All of these issues and more are addressed by your successor trustee. The trustee who acts in the event of your disability can be the same person or can be different than the trustee who administers your estate when you die. If you have different types of assets—a family business, for example—you might want to name a person as a separate trustee to run that in the event you are not able to, but you are still alive.

Let's say that you've named a bank or trust company to manage your investment assets. Those types of financial institutions are well equipped to decide what investments you should have and how to maximize the income that you will need for your care. Those same financial institutions, however, do not generally prefer to manage real estate investments or small businesses. There's nothing that prohibits you from naming different parties to manage the different types of assets that you may own.

Carefully consider the family members that you name to act for you in the event of your disability. Many prefer to name their spouse. But if your spouse has never managed assets before, or is failing physically or mentally herself (himself), then you might want to add a supporting co-trustee to act with your spouse, or consider bypassing your spouse altogether.

I've had several conversations with my clients about naming their children as a successor trustee or as a co-trustee. Often they'll want to name the eldest child, simply because he or she is the eldest, even if another child might be more adept at handling things. "I don't want to offend my eldest child," the refrain might go.

Here, I advise caution. Too much can go wrong if your legal and financial affairs aren't properly attended to. Consider naming the most responsible person for the job of successor trustee. And make no bones about it, acting as a successor trustee is a job. It is not an honor. It is rife with responsibilities and deadlines.

Finally, you should have a conversation with those that you have named as your successor trustee. Don't let them find out about it when the time actually arrives. They should be prepared to act, and should know basics—such as where you keep your financial statements and legal documents. They should know who your CPA is, who your lawyer is, and who your financial advisor is.

In the best of all worlds they've actually met your advisors and had a chance to talk to them, even if that talk is five minutes. Don't risk having a "transition in a time of crisis." The better prepared and knowledgeable those who you've named to fill important roles are, the easier it will be for everyone.

Including you.

What To Bring To Your Attorney When A Loved One Dies

It's always a difficult time when you lose a loved one. Usually one of the first places one visits will be the lawyer's office who drew the will or trust. The will or trust isn't usually read to a gathering of family "Hollywood style." Rather, the lawyer discusses the administrative steps that the personal representative (executor of a will) or trustee (of a trust) must take before distributions are made to the beneficiaries.

You don't want to wait too long before visiting with the attorney, since there are time deadlines, both legal and tax. With that said, visiting the attorney's office during the immediate days following the passing isn't usually helpful either, as the shock of the loss numbs senses. My suggestion is to wait a week or more, unless the parties are in town only for a few days and need to initiate the administrative process prior to heading home.

The question therefore arises as to what you need to bring to the attorney's office when a loved one dies. The following is a laundry list of items that will make that first meeting go more smoothly:

1. Original of the last will, revocable trust, and any codicils or amendments;

2. Certified copy of the death certificate;

3. Copies of most recent bank and brokerage statements;

4. Certificate of Deposit statements;

5. Savings bonds;

6. Copies of deeds to real property;

7. Copies of stock certificates;

8. Most recent Form 1040 Tax Return;

9. Federal Gift Tax Returns Form 709s previously filed;

10. Information related to any unreported taxable gifts;

11. Information regarding loans, notes, mortgages and indebted-ness;

12. Most recent credit card statements;

13. Amounts paid or forwarded for burial, clergy, service and reception;

14. Addresses and contact information of family members who may be beneficiaries as well as those serving as co-personal representative and/or trustee;

15. Names and contact information of financial advisors, insurance agents, CPAs, tax return preparers and other such professionals;

16. Copies of ownership interests in closely held businesses and any shareholders or partnership agreements that the deceased may have been a party to;

17. Prenuptial or postnuptial agreements, if any;

18. Copies of trusts and related account statements of which the deceased was a beneficiary at the time of his or her death;

19. Tangible personal property lists signed by the deceased that directed the distribution of such;

20. Automobile titles;

21. Information related to any safety deposit box leased;

22. Life insurance policies and statements including copies of the beneficiary forms; and

23. Annuity information, including gift annuities.

Each situation is different, so there may be items that I have not included on this list that are pertinent. Certainly, not everyone will have all of the suggested items and will almost always take time to marshal all of this information.

The more information that you can quickly provide your attorney, the better.

Probate Is A Public Process

It seems today that everyone is worried about privacy. Lifelock® is a new privacy company on the internet that offers a $1 million cash reward if their privacy systems don't work as advertised. When you want to secure your financial privacy in your estate plan, there are a number of things that you can do to protect yourself and your heirs.

The first is to use revocable trust planning as opposed to wills. Why is this? Because your will is subject to the probate process—which is a public. This fact surprises many. "You mean that anyone can march down to the court house after my death and take a look at my will?"

The answer to this question is, "yes."

The probate process, remember, is different from estate taxes and tax returns. Often the two are confused. Probate is the process under which your will is administered when you die. Before distributions are made to your beneficiaries, a court determines that the will submitted to the court is the true and correct last will.

Your personal representative (executor) is appointed and burdened with the responsibility to ensure that all of your creditors have been paid, and that your tax returns are properly filed. An inventory of your assets is filed, including the current fair market values. An accounting is filed with the court, along with a schedule of distribution. Parties have the ability to object. Upon meeting all of the legal requirements, distribution is finally made.

Because this is a court process, most of the filings and steps can be looked at by any person who walks in off the street. While your inventory and other sensitive matters are only supposed to be viewed by those parties who would have an "interest," the class of individuals who might have access may be broader than you care for.

Assume that you have a child whom you have written out of your will. They may have access to your will and to the inventory of your assets. Another example of a party that you don't want to have access to your documents would be a divorcing spouse of one of your beneficiaries. They may be able to have access to your probate file if they can prove that such access is material to their case.

I've had newspaper reporters call me about a client's private probate matters with knowledge that could have been copied from their probate file.

If your will, for example, contains clauses or restrictions on a beneficiary because he or she has special needs, or has had drug or alcohol problems that you don't want to enhance by leaving significant amounts of money, these facts might become public record upon your death in a probate file.

This public process is one main reason why revocable trusts are preferred to wills by most clients. While the trustee of your trust has many of the same responsibilities imposed upon the personal representative when clearing your estate, the trust is not filed with a court, and therefore is not a public document. When you have a revocable living trust you usually still have a will. These wills are referred to as "pour over wills." They usually do not contain very much information on who is entitled to what, when, where and how. The pour over will simply states that if there are any probate assets, those assets are to be distributed to the trustee of your trust for administration and distribution. This retains the privacy of your estate plan.

If you still are relying primarily on a will as the legal document to manage your estate, you may want to consider updating to a revocable living trust—for privacy reasons alone.

Do All Revocable Trusts Avoid Probate?

When you have a revocable trust, does that always mean that your estate will avoid the probate process when you die? You may be surprised to learn that the answer is "No."

Why is that? First, let's review what the probate process is. Many people think "probate" means "taxes." Probate is not a tax; it is actually a court process where your last will is admitted to court (authenticating that there are no other wills that supplant it), your personal representative is appointed to handle all estate matters (in some states this person is called your 'executor'), your creditors are cleared, taxes are paid, accountings are filed, and eventually the beneficiaries receive their inheritance.

While revocable living trusts are designed to avoid the probate process, you actually have to transfer your assets into the trust to make that so. Unfortunately, many people believe that they transferred their assets into their trust when they really haven't. I've found that a common misconception is that if you create a list of your assets and attach that list to your trust, then you have accomplished a transfer. That won't work.

The correct way to transfer your assets into your trust requires a change on the title to those same assets. Suppose that Ted Turner owns thousands of acres of ranch land in Montana that he wants to put into his revocable trust. He needs to sign a deed that transfers his Montana ranch to the trustee of the trust. Most of the time the person who creates the trust is also acts as his or her own trustee. So the deed in this example would likely be to: Ted Turner, Trustee for the Ted Turner Revocable Trust dated July 1, 2010 (assuming that is the day that Ted signed his revocable trust).

The same holds true with Ted's certificate of deposits, bank accounts and brokerage accounts. Ted needs to complete forms with his financial institutions that change the name on the account to Ted Turner, Trustee for the Ted Turner Trust. If he or his lawyer does not go through this exercise, then Ted hasn't transferred his assets into his trust, and those same assets will therefore have to go through the probate process on Ted's death.

Your wealth needn't rise to the level of Ted Turner's, by the way, to benefit from a revocable trust. If your net worth exceeds $250,000 then you should take the time to consider whether a revocable trust is right for you. This depends largely not only on the value of your net worth, but on the types of assets that you own and the facts of your individual and family situation.

Many people worry that once they transfer their assets into their revocable living trust, then they'll lose control over those assets. This simply isn't true. Since by definition the grantor of a revocable living trust can amend or revoke the trust at any time, he or she controls the trust and the trust assets as long as they are alive and competent. Generally speaking, the grantor of a revocable living trust can consume, sell and transfer any asset at any time without restriction.

It is not uncommon for people who have revocable living trusts to die with assets outside of the trust, requiring a probate. This isn't the end of the world. When you have a revocable living trust, your will becomes something known as a "pour over will." If you read the provisions of your pour over will carefully, you'll see that your will doesn't really say who is to get what from your estate.

Instead, you'll find that the will directs distribution of those probate assets into your revocable living trust. Your will acts as a "safety net," catching the assets that should have been transferred into your revocable living trust during your lifetime and transferring them at your passing into your trust.

This highlights another benefit to revocable trusts. Note that the pour over will doesn't say who gets what from your estate and how they get it. It simply says to transfer any probate assets into your trust for distribution in accordance with its terms. All wills are public documents since they have been filed with probate court. Anyone can go down to the courthouse and see your will after your death. In contrast, trusts are private documents. They are not filed publicly. So even if you have assets subject to probate at your death, if you have a trust, the general public will not be able to easily see who your beneficiaries are and what they are receiving. In today's world filled with scam artists, this is a rather important benefit to trusts.

There are certain assets that should not be transferred into your revocable living trust during your lifetime. If you were to try to transfer your IRA account into your trust, for example, you would likely have to recognize all of the taxable income inherent within the IRA. Since IRAs name a beneficiary, they do not go through the probate process at your death; and therefore, they do not transfer—and in fact, should not be transferred into your revocable living trust. Generally speaking, annuities also are not funded into revocable trusts for much the same reason.

If you are wondering whether the right assets have been properly transferred to your trust, you should visit with your estate planning attorney to review your current situation. Bring with you copies of your current deeds, brokerage, bank, financial statements and copies of any annuity, life insurance and IRA accounts along with their beneficiary designations.

Posthumous Gifts, Transfers And Payments

A few months after the death of her mother, "Janice" continued to manage her mother's trust as if she were still alive. "Mom used to give each of my kids $13,000 a year—which is tax free—so I thought I would continue that."

The problem is that once someone dies, the provisions that say who is to get what from the trust following the grantor's death is what should take place. Any gifts that the grantor used to make during her lifetime should no longer continue. To do otherwise invites a challenge by the rightful beneficiaries—and likely personal liability on the part of the person who is making the improper gifts.

Let's say, for example, that Mom's trust in this case is supposed to be divided equally between Janice and her sister, Karen. But Janice continues to make the $13,000 gifts ($14,000 since 2014) to her children that her mother would have made at Christmas. Since Janice is acting as the trustee, she could choose to treat those as gifts from herself to her children and charge them against her share alone. She certainly shouldn't reduce Karen's share by those gifts.

The same holds true when paying for travel expenses related to the last illness or funeral. If Janice pays money out of her mother's trust for her children to fly down to visit with their grandmother before her passing, or to later attend her funeral, these are not valid expenses of the administration. The only person whose travel expenses should rightfully be paid by the trust is any named trustee (Janice) or personal representative (executor) for the estate.

Another mistake that people commonly make after the grantor's death is when they continue to use the durable power of attorney. The word "durable" in the description of the power of attorney simply means that the power of attorney survives the grantor's incapacity. No durable power of attorney survives the grantor. When the grantor dies, so does her durable power of attorney. So if expenses need to be paid, or if checks need to be written, then those monies should be paid by the estate or trust by the personal representative and/or the trustee—not by the holder of the durable power of attorney.

When the estate doesn't have a whole lot of money and it is questionable whether the assets will even cover all of the deceased's bills and expenses, it is very important that the personal representative follow proper protocol before making any payments, or the personal representative might find themselves personally liable for improper payments.

I can explain this best by example. Suppose that Dad dies with $10,000 of credit card debt, $17,000 of medical expenses, and a mortgage in the amount of $120,000. His assets—other than the home— total in value of $50,000. Which bills, if any, should the personal representative pay?

That's actually a trickier question that you might imagine. Florida law provides that all known and reasonably ascertainable creditors should receive a notice of creditors during the estate administration. Assuming that they all properly file a claim against the estate, if the estate assets are insufficient to pay all of the claims, then Florida law prioritizes the claims as to which should be paid before others.

Secured claims, like the mortgage against the home, usually can't be discharged in an estate proceeding, while credit card debt may be. It all depends upon how the law prioritizes the claims. Moreover, other fees and expenses—such as those associated with probating the estate—usually have first priority. The reason for this is that estates with more creditors than assets would not be able to get representation if the legal fees and costs didn't have priority.

If the personal representative ignores the process and the legal priority, then she is likely to be personally liable for improper payments and may have to reimburse the estate from her own funds.

So, if you are managing someone's financial affairs during their lifetime or thereafter, it is always important to consult your estate attorney before making gifts or paying expenses. If you inadvertently make payments or transfers other than what the law allows, you could find yourself having to reimburse the estate from your own funds.

CRAIG R. HERSCH

What Is The Difference Between A Marital Trust And A Credit Shelter Trust?

"When I die," Larry began, "everything that I have goes over to Maureen, right?"

"Well, not exactly," I replied. "Remember you have a trust so that when you pass away your assets continue on in your trust for Maureen's benefit."

"Yes, it will be a Marital Trust," Larry stated.

"Well, not exactly," I continued. "To the extent that your estate is below the federal estate tax exemption amount, we first fill up the 'Family Trust,'—which is otherwise known as a 'Credit-Shelter' or 'Bypass Trust'—before we put anything into the Marital Trust."

"So Maureen isn't the owner of my trust when I die!?" Larry exclaimed. "I don't want my family to have the trust until after we both are gone!"

"Yes, Maureen is the primary beneficiary of the Family Trust for the rest of her life. You have even named her as your trustee. So she controls the trust and she is the primary beneficiary of the trust," I explained.

"So if I am the primary beneficiary of Larry's trust after he dies, why isn't it called a Marital Trust?" Maureen asked.

"That's the logical thing to call it!" I said. "But a Marital Trust is a legal term that refers to a trust that qualifies for the estate tax marital deduction. Even though it qualifies for the deduction, it is usually included in the surviving spouse's estate for federal estate tax purposes. In other words, the Marital Trust might only be a tax deferred trust as opposed to a tax exempt trust."

"So Marital Trust is still taxable? How can that be?" Larry asked.

"If I have a $7 million estate and die when the estate tax exemption available to me is $5.25 million, then the first $5.25 million goes into the 'Family' or 'Credit Shelter' Trust," I explained. "That Family Trust can be held for my wife for the rest of her life. It can double or even triple in value. Because it is tax exempt, since I applied my estate tax exemption amount against it, when she dies it is not taxed in her estate!"

"That's great. But what happens to the extra $1.75 million that I owned at my death?"

"That excess amount is funded into the 'Marital Trust.' As long as it meets with all of the marital deduction qualifications, it can be held for the rest of your wife's life, but when she dies it is included in her estate for estate tax purposes. If the total value of her estate plus the value of the Marital Trust is less than the federal estate tax exemption, then there won't be any estate tax due at her death."

"I think I understand it now," Larry said.

Maureen offered another good question. "But what happens if the income from these trusts isn't enough? Should I sell the assets in the 'Family Trust' or in the 'Marital Trust' first?"

"That's a good question," I said to Maureen. "It is usually wise to first consume the 'Marital Trust' assets or your own trust assets before Larry's 'Family Trust' assets are consumed. Remember that the 'Family Trust' can grow in value over the time between Larry's passing and yours—assuming that you survive him—and that the Family Trust will not be included in your estate for calculating the estate tax. On the other hand, the Marital Trust will be included in your estate. Consequently, if you deplete the Marital Trust first, then you will be consuming the assets that otherwise would be subject to tax."

"Yes, but the Family Trust assets got a step up in tax cost basis at my death," Larry pointed out. "So if she sells those assets and consumes them she has minimized her capital gains tax as opposed to selling appreciated assets in her own trust that have not received that step up in tax cost basis."

"True," I said. "The Marital Trust should also have received a step up in tax cost basis, so the capital gains taxes in that trust might be minimized, too. And since those assets will be part of Maureen's estate, maybe those are the smartest assets to consume, given all of the relative tax issues. It really is a case by case basis when you look at these things."

Larry and Maureen seemed satisfied with the discussion and appeared to understand the difference between the testamentary trusts that are embedded within their documents. Larry asked good questions relating to how the trusts worked and the best way to administer them in the future.

You should never be afraid to ask your attorney questions such as the ones posed by Larry and Maureen. They are important to know and understand and will have real potentially economic effect on you and your family.

Minimizing Risk In Estate Administrations

When a loved one passes away owning securities, there are steps that the personal representative and/or the trustee of the decedent's trust should immediately take to minimize investment risk during the estate administration. I'm now going to review these basic concepts.

Most folks own securities in some form or another. They may own stock in individual companies, such as Disney, Exxon or Proctor & Gamble. They may own mutual funds that own shares of stock in different companies. They may own some combination of individually held positions and mutual funds.

When a person dies owning shares of stock or stock mutual funds, it is often a good idea to sell the securities or some portion of them at the onset of the administration. This is due to several factors. First, the capital gains consequence that the decedent would have faced had he sold the securities during his lifetime usually is no longer a factor as of his passing. Second, he may have too many eggs in one proverbial basket. Finally, the administration of the estate, generally speaking, is a short-time horizon and in those situations it is usually wise to play it conservative, and stocks are by nature risky, especially in the short term.

Allow me to elaborate on those three points. First, the reason many of us don't sell stocks that we would otherwise sell and reinvest is because of the capital gains tax disincentive. If I bought shares in Eli Lilly Company, for example, and reinvested the dividends, over time the value of those shares has likely grown. If I sell the shares during my lifetime, I must pay a tax on the gain that I recognized when I sold the shares. The gain recognized is the difference between the sales price and my "tax cost basis" in the shares. The tax cost basis in my shares is generally the price that I paid for the shares plus the reinvested dividends on which I've paid income tax.

When I die, however, my estate receives a step up in tax cost basis equal to the date of death value. It no longer matters what I paid for my shares. That is irrelevant. The new basis for determining capital gain is the value of the shares as of the date of my death. My personal representative and trustee should request the date of death values from my broker or financial institution. If they sell the stocks or mutual funds at the new value, the capital gains are zero, and no tax is paid.

Second, it is not uncommon for decedent's estates to be heavily weighted in one or two holdings. Ask anyone who owned Enron stock during its collapse if they would have otherwise chosen to pay capital gains tax had they only known before the collapse what was about to happen. Too often individuals hold on to positions that they shouldn't because they are fearful of the tax consequences of selling. This is allowing the "tax tail to wag the dog" as I like to say. You should avoid making decisions based solely on tax reasons.

I have found that there are other reasons that families tend to hold onto positions that they otherwise shouldn't, and that is the emotional reasons. "Dad worked for that company for thirty five years and those are the shares that he broke his back for" is a refrain I've heard on more than one occasion.

Just as one shouldn't base decisions on tax consequences alone, one should not base investment decisions on emotion either. The goal of any investment strategy is to maximize the return on that investment. I'm sure that any parent would favor that goal over an emotional goal of holding onto shares of a certain company solely because that parent happened to work at that company for a number of years, or chose to buy the stock and hold it for a prolonged period.

Getting back to my point, many investors for one reason or another find their portfolios over weighted with just a few particular holdings. As we learned above, when those investors die their estates are no longer burdened with the capital gains tax consequences of the sale. The personal representative or trustee would be well advised to sit down with a competent investment advisor to determine which holdings would be best to sell to limit the investment risk during the course of the administration.

And that brings me to my final point. When you are serving as the personal representative of an estate or as the trustee of a trust, you are held to a fiduciary standard to invest and protect the money in a prudent and reasonable manner. While holding stocks for the long term is not outside the scope of reasonableness, it can be argued that holding a large share of equities during an estate administration is unreasonable.

This is due to the fact that an estate or trust administration is usually a short-term affair, meaning that it can take anywhere from six months to two years. In that short of a time horizon, a portfolio might have a hard time recovering from a severe dip in the stock market. Imagine if you were the trustee of a trust that consisted largely of securities just prior to the 2008 stock market collapse.

Imagine further that if the estate were to pay estate tax on the value of the date of death values and the estate were to drop suddenly in value. The estate would be paying taxes on an amount much higher than that the beneficiaries would receive.

There is, by the way, a six month alternate valuation date that might take care of this problem, but it isn't prudent to rely solely on that escape hatch.

If you should find yourself in the role as personal representative or trustee, it would be wise to bring up these issues with the estate attorney and with the investment advisor before too much time transpires.

Strategies for Dealing with Problem Trusts

What do you do if a trust becomes a problem, yet the trust itself is irrevocable and can't be changed? The trust might be irrevocable because it was originally established that way, or the grantor is deceased. Are there options? The answer to that question is "Yes!"

First, let's review what problems might exist in a trust. Common examples include a trust that has mandatory distributions to a beneficiary who doesn't have the maturity to handle the money; a change in family or financial circumstances; changes to the tax laws which render the trust obsolete or otherwise unworkable; too restrictive provisions imposed on the trustee and/or the beneficiaries; ambiguities that cause conflict between beneficiaries, and a desire to change a problem trustee.

There are actually a number of different strategies that may be employed when a problem trust is otherwise irrevocable. I'll briefly mention a few of those strategies here.

Change May Be Permitted by Trust Instrument Itself

Sometimes the answer lies buried in the trust instrument itself. If a beneficiary holds a "power of appointment" for example, he or she may be able to change the ultimate distribution of the assets at some point or another. Beneficiaries may also be able to remove a problem trustee. A thorough review of the trust instrument is always a good first step.

Decanting

When a trust's purpose remains good but its provisions obsolete for legal or tax reasons, sometimes decanting the assets from the old trust to a newly created trust is possible. Think of this as you would decant wine from its original bottle into a carafe—it's much the same concept. By breathing new air and provisions into the trust administration of its assets, the problems that exist today may be solved.

There are a number of statutory legal requirements that must be satisfied before decanting is possible. Unanimous approval of all "qualified beneficiaries" (as defined by Florida law) is usually necessary as well.

Judicial or Nonjudicial Modification

Where the trust instrument does not allow for the contemplated change, and if decanting is not an option, the parties may consider judicial modification. Here, the party that wants the change to the trust will file an action in Circuit Court asking a Judge to Order the change in the trust provisions. One has to allege that there is a valid purpose behind the modification, such as the trust is no longer consistent with the grantor's intended purposes. Here, one would argue that the purposes of the trust have already been fulfilled or have become illegal, impossible, wasteful or impractical to fulfill.

Another such argument is that due to unforeseen circumstances, compliance with the trust provisions would substantially impair or defeat a material purpose of the trust. Yet another is that a material purpose of the trust no longer exists. This may be seen in an educational trust, where all of the beneficiaries have already earned their diplomas.

Florida law also provides that a Judge can issue an Order changing a trust's terms where compliance with the terms are not in the best interest of the trust beneficiaries. Numerous cases involving trusts that require beneficiaries to marry within their religious faith, or attend a certain school to achieve a certain degree, or engage in similar specific behavior have been modified where the Court believed the provisions to be against public policy and not in the best interests of the beneficiary.

The Florida statutes also allow modifications to trusts where it is clear that there was a mistake made within their provisions, a scrivener's error, or a problem with the tax law subsequent to the signing of the trust. Most of these changes must be made by a Court through the judicial process. But Florida law also allows the trustee and all of the qualified beneficiaries to unanimously agree to change trust provisions without a Court Order—outside of the judicial process. This method is preferred as it saves time and money.

In order to do this, very specific factors must be present. The original date of the trust must be after January 1, 2001, the grantor must be deceased, the trust cannot have a charitable interest, and the trust cannot be subject to the pre-1997 rule against perpetuities governing how long the trust may stay in existence.

There are many legal and tax consequences associated with changing a problem trust, so consultation with a trust attorney is advised before acting. But all hope is not lost. If you are either administering or are a beneficiary of a problem trust, you may have viable options.

Trust Decanting

Previously, I wrote about a variety of ways to modify problem trusts. I mentioned one technique—"trust decanting"—as a viable option. Now I'll expand on what trust decanting is and how it works, as this is a little understood option that often isn't considered when it could be a solution that the family is looking for.

For those of us who have oenophile tendencies, you may know that decanting is the action of pouring wine from its bottle into a wide-based container. The idea is to separate the wine from its sediment and expose a large surface of the wine to oxygen, allowing it to express its desirable aromas.

Decanting also helps to soften some aromas which are overpowering or unpleasant. The same holds true when decanting a trust, which is the process of modifying an otherwise irrevocable trust to better reflect the maker's intent—to accommodate problems like scrivener's errors, changing the situs or governing law, modifying administrative provisions, to consolidate assets, take advantage of planning strategies, or dealing with changed circumstances after the trust became irrevocable.

When decanting, a new trust is drawn up and the contents (assets) of the old trust are then "poured into" the new trust. Florida law, ahead of many other states, offers a specific statute that allows decanting as long as proper notice is provided to all "qualified beneficiaries," which is a legal term also defined by statute, provided that the new trust does not impair the rights of any beneficiary or adversely affect the achievement of the purposes of the original trust.

Suppose, for example, that the beneficiaries of a trust want to change the way and method that trustees are removed, appointed or compensated. Here, a decanting from one trust to another with the new trustee provisions might achieve those goals. Or sometimes there might be two different trusts for each beneficiary—one created by their father and one created by their mother. Here, decanting from both trusts into a single trust could solve investment issues or even reduce the administrative expenses associated with carrying two different trusts that have substantially the same provisions for a beneficiary.

On the other hand, decanting may help solve issues involving pooled trusts, which are trusts that are created for several beneficiaries. If the beneficiaries are fighting over who is entitled to the assets, or if one beneficiary needs income and the other growth, or if distributions to any one beneficiary become an issue, decanting could allow for the pooled trusts to become separate shares for each beneficiary.

Another example is where there are two different trusts, one that is very liquid and one illiquid. It might make sense to combine the trusts, as the liquidity could assist with the carrying costs of the illiquid assets. Perhaps a trust is overly restrictive as to its investment strategies that have now become outdated. Here, a new trust that is more liberal in its investment options may be created, and the old trust could be decanted into it.

You may have a trust that was originally established in a state that imposes a state income tax and wish to move the trust situs to Florida, which has no state income tax. Here, decanting can help achieve that goal. Since the tax law continually evolves, an irrevocable trust that was once tax advantageous could become disadvantageous; therefore, decanting into a new trust could solve the problem.

Beneficiaries who encounter unexpected problems, such as creditor issues, divorce, having their own independent wealth, or even those with self-destructive behavior could benefit from decanting. Here the objective could be to make the trust terms more restrictive so that creditors and predators can't take the assets away from a beneficiary.

When creating revocable trusts that continue on for your beneficiaries, it may be a good idea to proactively provide for decanting powers so that an independent trustee (one who is also not a beneficiary—to eliminate bias or tax law problems associated with having certain powers over assets) can adjust the trust to future changes in circumstances. The options should be carefully considered, since an improperly drafted decanting power could backfire and cause more harm than it does good.

When including these decanting powers, moreover, you should discuss with your attorney your comfort level of allowing for such potential future modifications to your estate plan. Continuing trusts offer substantial benefits for your beneficiaries in the form of tax savings and creditor and divorce protection. With that said, I often counsel my clients that it's favorable to allow for flexibility in continuing trusts, since no one knows what the future brings. By specifically allowing for a decanting power, you can better ensure that your beneficiaries won't be caught by unexpected circumstances.

Dear Attorney: Why Didn't You Tell Me Sooner That Auntie Died—And Where's My Inheritance Check, Already?

You can't make this stuff up. I received a letter just this week that said, in essence "Why didn't you tell me sooner that my aunt died—and why haven't I received my inheritance check yet?"

I almost forwarded a reply that read, "Dear Nephew: You should be ashamed of yourself that you weren't close enough with your aunt (who lovingly included you in her will) to know of her demise, nevertheless, to send a demand for your inheritance when we are so early in the estate administration process."

But I didn't send it.

The nephew's letter points out a few things that I thought worthy of mention. When someone dies—even if there is a revocable living trust involved—the trustee of that trust has certain duties that he or she must perform before the assets of the estate are distributed to the beneficiaries. The trustee not only has a duty to the estate beneficiaries, but also to the decedent's creditors. So before making a final distribution, the trustee needs to make sure that all of the decedent's proper bills have been paid and that tax returns are all filed and approved.

Usually, the beneficiaries of the estate learn about the death through loved ones before the estate lawyer's office sends a notice of the administration. The beneficiaries are generally entitled to receive a copy of the will and/or trust as well as documents that would show who the trustee will be during the administrative process.

The trustee may need to sell assets. Perhaps there is a house or other properties that need to be sold. This obviously takes some time. Stocks or brokerage accounts may have to be liquidated to cash. Personal belongings need to be dealt with.

The whole process may take as little time as three months or it might take a few years. This depends upon the types of assets that the decedent owned, as well as the estate plan itself. Estates heavy in real estate and closely held business interests are going to take more time to administer than would an estate that has one brokerage account and a couple of certificates of deposit.

Estates that have irrevocable life insurance trusts, charitable trusts, grantor retained annuity trusts and private foundations will obviously take longer to administer than those that have a revocable living trust with straightforward distributions.

The value of the estate matters as well. Estates that are required to file a federal or state estate tax return will also take longer, since the tax return itself is filed nine months or more following the decedent's death (depending upon whether extensions are necessary). Where estate tax returns are required the trustee must get appraisals and date of death valuations on all of the assets. Professional appraisals take time.

Once the tax return is filed, it may take a year or longer before the IRS issues its tax clearance letter releasing the trustee from any further liability. And if there are any state death tax returns due, those offices usually don't issue their releases until after the federal government has issued its release.

Until the trustee is released, he or she really can't make a full and final distribution of the estate funds. Once he's made distribution, if the IRS comes back and says that more money is owed, the

CRAIG R. HERSCH

trustee is personally responsible to make that payment—even if it must come out of his own money.

So we hope that most estate beneficiaries understand that an estate administration is a process that can't be completed in just a few days. Part of this is setting expectations. The estate attorney will often communicate with the beneficiaries to advise what that estate administration timeline looks like. As an aside, if you go to my law firm's web site you'll find a free guide and video entitled "Legal Matters When a Loved One Dies" that offers useful information on the issues and timelines I'm addressing here.

Returning to the topic at hand, it's been my experience that the further degree of relation the beneficiary is from the decedent, the more likely it is that the beneficiary is going to be demanding. The nephew writing me that letter is a classic example. Children rarely make demands before the administrative process has run its course, mostly because they understand what their parents owned and what needs to happen. The children also tend to be more emotionally attached to the decedent and that will often make a difference.

But people sometimes act oddly. Another beneficiary once wrote my office a letter asking when the estate administration was going to be completed because he had just purchased a new car and needed the money to pay for it.

I wondered what he would have done had his relative not died!

What Happens To The Contents Of Your Safe Deposit Box?

Many people lease safe deposit boxes from banks. Some choose to keep legal papers in the box, such as their birth certificates, marriage license, wills and property deeds. Others keep valuables, such as diamond jewelry, expensive watches and gold coins. But do you know what happens to the contents of your safe deposit box in the event of your death?

You may be surprised to learn that there is a box on the Federal Estate Tax Return Form 706 that must be checked if the decedent leased a safe deposit box. The contents of the box must be inventoried and verified by a bank officer and reported on the return.

Some choose to have spouses or children as co-signors on the box. A number of interesting Florida statutes govern the rules that we must all follow with safe deposit boxes. I thought that I might highlight a few of those rules here.

Florida Statute §655.935 contains the rules surrounding the search procedure upon the death of a lessee of a safe deposit box. The deceased's personal representative, the spouse, parent or adult descendant may open and examine the contents of a safe deposit box in the presence of a bank officer. The bank officer must release the original will of the deceased, the deed to a burial plot, or any insurance policy, if found in the box.

The personal representative of the estate has the ability to remove the contents of a safe deposit box. An inventory of the safe deposit box is filed with the probate court and that inventory is signed, not only by the personal representative, but also by a bank officer.

In cases where the safe deposit box is leased by two or more persons, then Florida Statute §655.937 applies. This statute provides that either of lessees may, at any time, access and remove the contents of the box. If you've named another person on your safe deposit box, you should then be aware that this person may remove the contents after your passing.

If the other party removes contents that should have been distributed to someone else, the statute specifically releases the bank (lessor) from liability for the joint party's action. Therefore, it is important that you have confidence in the integrity of anyone you put jointly on your box.

The statute is somewhat ambiguous as to the inventory responsibilities of the joint lessee in the event of the death of a co-owner of the box. The law reads that after the death of one co-owner, the other co-owner *may* make a written inventory of the box. This implies the co-owner is under no legal requirement to open and inventory the box. As I stated earlier, however, in the event of an estate where an estate tax return is due, it is likely that the box must be inventoried for tax purposes.

Some believe that they can avoid claiming valuables on their federal estate tax return by placing them in a safe deposit box and putting a co-owner on the box. There may be several problems with this course of action. First, if the IRS suspects that there might be valuables not declared on the estate tax return, they may subpoena a copy of the deceased's homeowner's policy, looking for riders covering any such valuables.

Second, where the co-owner of the box takes the valuables for him or herself, the IRS may treat that as a taxable gift. And there's always the danger that the co-owner removes the valuables before the death of the other co-owner and does with them as he pleases.

The bottom line is that you should consult with your estate planning attorney when you have a safe deposit box that contains valuables.

Back-Up Your Noggin

Like many professional offices, ours has gone electronic and mostly paperless—at least as much as an attorneys' office can actually go paperless. So from time to time a client will ask me whether—and how—we back up our data and systems.

Thankfully, I can assure my clients that we have up-to-date, sophisticated off-site back-up systems. But then I ask them the same question. "How do you back up your data?"

I'm not asking, by the way, whether they have their computer data backed up. Instead my inquiry is directed at what's inside of their noggin.' By that I'm referring to the wealth of information that the client may have in their head, but that no one else knows, possibly not even their spouse.

What kind of data you ask? Think about all of the day-to-day decisions that you make regarding your legal, tax and financial matters.

What is your investment strategy? Where are the accounts? Which account is used to pay what bills? Are electronic banking accounts used? What are the usernames and passwords? When you need to pay big-ticket items, such as real estate taxes or for major repairs, what money do you tap?

When do you typically take your Required Minimum Distribution (RMD) from your IRA every year? Is it at the end of the year? Who calculates it? If there are multiple IRA and 401(k) accounts, is the RMD taken proportionately, or do you typically tap one of the accounts and leave the others intact?

Are there any financial dealings between you and your adult children? Are those arrangements written down? Where are they kept? Do they involve ledgers? Are those ledgers up to date? Who keeps them up to date?

Are there annual gifts being made for health or education? Are those expected to continue? Are there life insurance premiums due? Are those premiums paid to a life insurance trust that requires Crummey notices that must be sent to the trust beneficiaries? Who is responsible for that?

The list goes on and on. Because handling the finances of the house is so second nature to some, and because they have been doing so their entire adult lives, they don't think that any of this is extraordinary. They don't appreciate that someone coming in with no understanding of what they have done over the course of many years would have a difficult learning curve to understand what has transpired in the past, and what has to happen in the near term to keep things running smoothly.

And in most cases there is no back-up. All of this information is stored in the noggin, but if that noggin should have a traumatic event like a stroke, or worse, death, all of the loved ones who are affected by these daily decisions somehow have to reconstruct the data.

Believe me, it ain't easy.

So if any of this sounds familiar, what should you do? The first thing, of course, is to write down as much of the information as possible and keep it in a safe place. Secondly, instruct those around you about the most important legal, tax and financial matters you deal with on a daily, monthly or yearly basis. Then have your loved one participate with you in carrying out some of these tasks. That way, should your loved one be confronted with having to pick things up should you be unable to act, it all won't seem so foreign.

In other words, do your best to back up the data that sits between your ears. Then be sure to perform periodic back-ups, since the data tends to change over the course of the months and years.

About the Author

C raig R. Hersch is a Florida Bar Board Certified Wills, Trusts & Estates attorney who is also a Certified Public Accountant (CPA). His law practice is based in Fort Myers, Florida, where he manages an extensive client base consisting of wealthy retirees, individuals, families and business owners throughout the state. He has developed several unique estate planning processes, including *The Family Estate & Legacy Solution™* that you can find on his firm's website www.sbshlaw.com.

Craig has published professional articles in various trade journals, including *The Practical Tax Lawyer, The Florida Bar Journal* and *Estates & Trusts Magazine.* He prides himself, however, on his "down to earth" attitude and ability to communicate complex legal and tax solutions in language that his clients understand. Since 2004 he has written an estate planning column in Sanibel's *The Island Sun* weekly newspaper.

His firm's website features videos and webinars of Craig's client presentations, including *Florida Residency & Estate Planning, What Your Adult Children Need to Know About Your Estate Plan; The Perils of Joint Accounts; Legal Matters When a Loved One Dies;* and *Who Does What in Your Legal Documents if You Become Incapacitated.* These are all part of Hersch's trade-marked *Family Estate & Legacy Series™*.

His middle-class, no-nonsense background comes through in almost everything that Craig does. Because of financial difficulties his family experienced at the time, Craig worked part-time jobs and took out student loans to put himself through the accounting (BS 1986 MS 1987) and law programs (JD 1989) at the University of Florida.

After graduation, Craig's career began at Deloitte & Touche in their Atlanta and Tampa offices. Craig and his wife, Patti then discovered paradise in Southwest Florida, where they have resided since 1990. He joined his current law firm in 1992.

When not practicing law Craig enjoys adventure travel as well as competing in triathlons, including Ironman distance races. He can also be found cheering on his beloved Florida Gators on fall Saturdays and during basketball season.

Craig and Patti have three daughters, Gabrielle, Courtney and Madison, of whom they are very proud.